Creative Retreat Ideas

Sue Pickering is an Anglican priest, spiritual director, retreat facilitator and writer. She is the author of *Creative Ideas for Quiet Days* and *Spiritual Direction: A Practical Introduction*, also published by Canterbury Press.

Married with one son, she lives in New Zealand, is chaplain at an Anglican–Methodist Aged Care Village, and is a canon of the recently consecrated Taranaki Cathedral Church of St Mary, in New Plymouth.

Also by the same author and available from Canterbury Press:

Creative Ideas for Quiet Days: Resources and Liturgies for Retreats and Reflection

With CD Rom

'a veritable feast ... a treasury of ideas and encouragement'

Margaret Silf

Spiritual Direction: A Practical Introduction

'This is quite simply the book on spiritual direction we've been waiting on for years.'

Gordon Jeff

Creative Retreat Ideas

Resources for short, day and weekend retreats

Sue Pickering

CANTERBURY
PRESS

Norwich

First published in 2010 by the Canterbury Press Norwich
Editorial office
3rd Floor, Invicta House,
108–114 Golden Lane, London EC1Y 0TG, UK

Canterbury Press is an imprint of Hymns Ancient and Modern Ltd
(a registered charity)
13A Hellesdon Park Road,
Norwich, Norfolk NR6 5DR, UK

www.canterburypress.co.uk

British Library Cataloguing in Publication data

A catalogue record for this book is available
from the British Library

978 1 84825 021 5

Typeset by Regent Typesetting, London
Printed and bound in Great Britain by
CPI Group (UK) Ltd

Contents

Appendices

This book is dedicated to
the greater glory of God,
with thanksgiving to
Andrew Dunn and Margaret Dunn
for their lifelong commitment
to spiritual growth;
and in the memory of those
'older women' who have,
in times of struggle, learning
and celebration, helped me,
and countless others, discover
more of God's limitless grace.

Foreword

by the Very Revd Jamie Allen
(of the BBC series *A Country Parish*)

'I love silence.'

So said Sue Pickering, introducing herself gently to the group of which I was a part.

She does. But it goes deeper than that. Sue, in fact, *embodies* peaceful reflection, in contrast to the way some people embody busyness, frenetic activity or restlessness. It is because of this gift of *hers* that this book is, in turn, such a gift to *us*. Indeed, my response on my first reading of the book you are holding was ...

... quite simply a delicious peace, and a deeper knowledge of, and trust in, God's involvement in the detail of our lives. Read on, and you will be left yearning for quiet in the **words and noise** of today – not because these are necessarily negatives, but because they overlay something so beautiful tucked underneath.

It is not only an inner peace, though – for the book inspires the reader to know how to go about *sharing* that peace – pushing it *outwards*. For example, how to gather a group of teenagers to lay down mobile phones and rest in God's quietness – listening for the *'still small voice'*.

When we were filming the BBC TV series, *A Country Parish*, which featured a younger Revd Jamie Allen and family learning about life and ministry in a rural parish in South West England, we spent some time trying to capture moments of silence on film. As you might imagine, this was terrifying and uncharted territory for the film crew! But there was such a strength to those moments – strength that transcended conversation and drew the viewer from the white-noise into the sudden snap of attention – flickering wholly awake. We once filmed an extended time of prayer, in which a particular burden was brought before God. One of the crew was adamant that we should play music or use a voiceover at this uncomfortable point! Thankfully, we resisted, and suddenly the viewer's attention was quite powerfully drawn upwards to an awareness of *why* the prayer was actually happening, and what stillness it had birthed, through the Holy Spirit.

But, oh! What I would have given for a toolbox of ideas, better to guide people into learning that silence as a friend and a resource! This is what Sue Pickering has offered here. She has placed this Lamp on a Stand to the Glory of God. The lamp-stand includes a whole raft of resources for *you* to teach and guide others – beautifully honed, practically tested – yet excitingly fresh resources, benefiting from her long experience leading Retreats and Quiet Days. Every aspect of preparation is thought through and explained, so that you 'need not worry' (the very theme of one of the Weekend Retreats Sue leads us on).

Do not read this book if you are happy with a busy, nonstop Christian pilgrimage. Read it, and own it, if you too yearn to 'Love Silence'.

Introduction
'You give them something to eat!'

It was the mustard seed that did it. One of several parables about the nature of the kingdom of God, it was sitting patiently beside the 'pearl of great price', 'the yeast in the flour' and 'the treasure in the field', ready to turn my comfortable world upside down. Some years ago, after a busy week, I was staying at a friend's house in Wellington, New Zealand. Once she had gone to work, I settled down to a leisurely time of prayer and reflection, sitting in the sun with a coffee. I opened the lectionary to find the daily Gospel (a dangerous activity if you want to stay within your comfort zones) and before I knew it, I was caught up, as verses from another place and another time reached forward 2,000 years to touch and tickle my life:

> 'The kingdom of heaven is like a mustard seed that someone took and sowed in his field; it is the smallest of all the seeds, but when it has grown it is the greatest of shrubs and becomes a tree, so that the birds of the air come and make nests in its branches.' (Matthew 13.31–32)

Such a short reading and full of promise, but, that day, it was also provocative. God used, not my favourite kauri tree or a resplendent chestnut, but a tree I'd never seen, to launch me into a new awareness of what God was inviting me to be and do. Unsettled, I went out for a walk. I didn't have to go far before I was stopped in my tracks by the sight of a flight of tuis.[1] These shiny blue-black birds had often been significant on my faith journey – and now, here they were with their characteristic noisy melodic whistles and chuckles, flying in and around a large bottle-brush tree in full bloom, attracted to the sweet nourishment in the flowers. It seemed that God was showing me that my own 'mustard seed' faith had grown over the years and was large enough to provide encouragement and guidance for other people on their way to God.

But that wasn't the end of it. The next week I found myself discomforted by the parable of the servant who did not use the talents given to him because he was afraid of his master (Luke 19). And a couple of weeks later there was another familiar passage – the story of the feeding of the five thousand. In Mark's account of this miraculous provision for the crowds of followers, Jesus' disciples drew his attention to the late hour and the need for the people to disperse and find food in nearby villages. Jesus' initial reply challenged them: 'You give them something to eat' (Mark 6.37).

---

1 A tui is about the size of a large blackbird and was often referred to by early settlers in New Zealand as the 'Parson' bird, because of the tufts of white feathers at its throat.

Jesus' reply challenged me too. Was I going to procrastinate or accept the invitation to share with others what God had given me? It was quite clear that I was to stop *thinking* about it and start *writing* – so that is what I did all those years ago, and what I am still doing today.

There comes a time on the Christian journey when we are asked to move into the role of leader, or spiritual companion. Whether or not we think we are ready, others begin to come to us to talk about their lives and their struggles in the faith. For years I had relied on the support of older women, models of the Christian life far more disciplined and 'further along' the journey of faith than me. Now it seemed that God was inviting me to take the risk of 'being the older woman' for others.

Perhaps that time has come for you too.
Perhaps others are approaching you to ask for help with their spiritual lives.
Perhaps you want to explore contemplative spirituality with like-minded people?
Perhaps you've been asked to run a short retreat or Quiet Day.
Maybe you sense Jesus is inviting – or challenging – *you* to 'give "them" something to eat'.

There is a great need today for opportunities for soul-weary people to respond to Jesus' invitation to 'Come away to a deserted place all by yourselves and *rest* a while' (Mark 6.31a, *my italics*). This book is about helping you and others to *rest* and grow in God. You can use it:

- for your own spiritual growth
- if you are being drawn to contemplative spirituality: reflection, times of solitude, silent prayer
- if you are an experienced, but busy, minister or lay leader with little time to prepare a range of resources for retreat opportunities suitable for your people
- if you are less experienced, but sense that God is calling you to nurture those in your sphere of care, even if, to get started, you need to use materials others have prepared.

The disciples didn't initially nourish the crowd from their own resources, but brought to Jesus what was available to them at the time – the 'loaves and fishes' offered by a generous little boy:

'There is a boy here who has five barley loaves and two fish. But what are they among so many people?' Jesus said, 'Make the people sit down.'
Now there was a great deal of grass in that place, so they sat down, about five thousand in all. Then Jesus took the loaves, and when he had given thanks, he distributed them to those who were seated; so also the fish, as much as they wanted … from the fragments of the five barley loaves, left by those who had eaten, they filled twelve baskets. (John 6.9–13)

I wonder what it would have been like for that unnamed child as Andrew guided him forward; as Jesus, with a smile, took the bread and fish from him, gave thanks to God, and began to break open the elements of nourishment ... and continued breaking open ... breaking open ... breaking open ... until all were fed and filled. 'Awesome!' the child might have said if he'd been responding today! I bet he went home and told his family what had happened. He had been well fed in a literal sense; but also in another sense that he might not have been able to articulate – something in his spirit would have changed, for he had been close to Jesus and had seen with his own eyes how, in Jesus' hands, simple nourishment could become divine mystery.

This book is like that little boy's offering – spiritual food which you and God together can 'break open', and share with a range of people, for God's glory, and with great joy. It is arranged in five parts:

Part 1 introduces the *process* of facilitating retreats of varying lengths.
Part 2 provides 20 'Loaves and fishes' – spiritual formation resource sheets, which form the basic nourishment for retreatants[2] and can be used in a variety of ways to suit your context.
Parts 3, 4 and **5** describe in detail how the 'loaves and fishes' can be 'broken open' in a range of group retreat settings, helping retreatants move closer to Jesus.

- There are ten 'snacks' in Part 3, which are short in length – from 30 minutes to three hours – suitable for people new to retreats or those who cannot set aside more time. These short retreat times are also ideal for existing meetings in your parish or may be offered in a rest-home or prison, woven into a youth programme, introduced in a 'fresh expression' context, or made available to a community group wanting to explore spirituality.
- Next come five 'light meals' in Part 4 – Quiet Days lasting 6–8 hours. Full details of process and content are provided, as well as contemplative exercises to help retreatants go deeper with God.
- Finally there is the 'dinner' section in Part 5 – three overnight or weekend retreats in which the commitment, the effort and the journey combine with the darkness and stillness of the night-time to extend the retreatants' experience of listening to God and to their own inner longings for freedom and wholeness.

This book introduces some of the practices of the contemplative stream of Christian spirituality, described succinctly by Richard Foster as 'the call to prayer-filled living, to a life of loving attention to God through [which] we experience the divine rest that overcomes our alienation'. Foster encourages people to develop 'a holy habit of contemplative love that leads us forth in partnership with God into creative and redeeming work'.[3]

---

2 Retreatant in this context means anyone intentionally setting time apart to be with God.
3 Richard Foster, *Streams of Living Water: Celebrating the Great Traditions of Christian Faith*, London: HarperCollins, 1999, p. 58.

As we draw on the rich history of the contemplative stream of Christian tradition, we are in the company of Jesus whose earthly life and ministry was infused with prayer, and who modelled for us the dynamic relationship between contemplation and action:

- he was constantly attentive to God the Father
- he withdrew to places of solitude for reflection and deep spiritual infilling, and *then*
- the heart-to-heart connection with his Father refreshed, the quiet space within himself renewed, he returned to the bustle of life on the road, ready for the intensity of days spent healing, listening and teaching, as well as challenging injustice and religious legalism.

Contemplation is time spent resting in silent worship before God, when our ego's chatter is set aside and we make ourselves vulnerable to the work of the Holy Spirit. Not only does contemplation build our relationship with God and resource us for our work in the world, it also aids our discernment, helping us discover God's call on our lives, and giving us the confidence to step out in faith. In daily life, with all its ups and downs, we can choose 'to approach every encounter, every activity, every meeting from a *contemplative stance, trusting* God is already at work in people's lives, *listening* to the Holy Spirit, to others and to ourselves, *watching* for signs of God's grace, *paying attention to* everyday experience, and *exploring* our sense of God's presence and the shape of God's invitation to growth'.[4]

Our offering to others doesn't have to be spectacular or academically astute, but the best of which we are capable, given the limitations of our human frailty. Not only do we offer the 'loaves and fishes' from this resource book, but also those from our experience of life and faith and struggle and prayer, the raw materials with which God the Holy Spirit can do works that are beyond our understanding, in the lives of those whom we meet as we facilitate retreat times with God.

---

4 Sue Pickering, *Spiritual Direction – A Practical Introduction*, Norwich: Canterbury Press, 2008, p. 188 (slightly abridged).

The purchase of this book entitles you to download and copy from the Canterbury Press website, for non-profit use as required, such as distribution to retreatants, those pages in Parts 2–5 and the Appendices which carry this permission line:

While the spiritual formation sheets making up Part 2 each spread over two pages in this book, each spiritual formation sheet downloaded from the Canterbury Press website occupies a single page to make it easier to print off for use with retreatants.

Unless otherwise acknowledged, all poetry, and pictures with a title/location, are by Sue Pickering and are hitherto unpublished.

Supporting materials for this book, including handouts, pictures, appendices, and ideas for further reading can be downloaded from www.canterburypress.co.uk. Please search for 'Creative Retreat Ideas'.

Part 1
Getting started – a pattern for retreats, short or long

The preparation we put into anything we facilitate for others is vital. When we are meticulous in our own planning *and* open to the spontaneity of the Spirit, the retreat may be an inviting introduction to the riches of contemplative spirituality, and a new step on the journey towards intimacy with God.

We all have our own ways of preparing. I tend to start with a single stimulus – a line from a poem, a verse of Scripture, a piece of art work, a new discovery in my own spiritual journey, or a particular area of struggle that is still being worked on by the loving laser of the Spirit. From there I hold the theme in my mind in prayer and wait for the Holy Spirit to draw my attention to other elements that will fit/enhance the theme. This can be both an exhilarating exercise in trust and gritted teeth stuff!

Retreats based on contemplative spirituality offer opportunities for two kinds of prayer: kataphatic and apophatic. The kataphatic way to God uses senses and stories, imagery and music, pictures and external stimuli to aid our spiritual growth. I think it is safe to say that, for the majority of people, especially in the early stages of the Christian journey, the kataphatic way is more common. We certainly see Jesus pointing to the visible and external symbols in his own environment as aids to the spiritual growth of those who followed him. The stories of the seeds and the sower, the old and new wineskins, the lost sheep, the lost coin and the return of the prodigal, all enabled his listeners to connect with familiar parts of their experience and environment. From this starting point, they could begin to understand something about the kingdom of God present in their midst in the person of Jesus.

Apophatic prayer, however, is more about silence, receptivity, waiting, mystery and unknowing. Rather than prayer involving our voices or words, or using our minds to make connections or think things through, apophatic prayer is about 'letting go and letting God'.

This might be a common phrase among Christians, but it is uncommon in practice. Our spiritual lives are often effort-full: we talk about 'praying hard' for someone, we make sure we do 'good works', we read Scripture, attend services, workshops and cell groups, and we offer help to those in need. All of these are valuable for we are called to intercede, to learn from Jesus' example and to 'act justly, to love mercy and to walk humbly with our God' (Micah 6.8b, NIV). But sooner or later, if we don't step aside for times of solitude, reflection and resting in God, letting the Spirit renew our minds, refresh our bodies and reawaken our spirits, we risk becoming victims of

1

burnout or compassion fatigue, *and* we risk being sidetracked, lured into what may seem legitimate projects but which are not actually what God wants us to be doing.

Apophatic prayer helps us to *listen* to God's still, small voice and to *rest* in God's love. The Spirit works in us when we are open, available and willing to receive what God knows we need. Psalm 131.1–2 beautifully illustrates our attitude when in this form of prayer:

> O Lord, my heart is not lifted up, my eyes are not raised too high;
> I do not occupy myself with things too great and too marvellous for me.
> But I have calmed and quieted my soul, like a weaned child with its mother …

Instead of coming to God so we can *actively* suckle, *taking* the milk necessary for our early discipleship with Christ, now we come because we simply want to *be with* God, to climb up on God's knee if you like, to be nurtured by the closeness of God's being, our heartbeat in harmony with God's heartbeat, our fears and tension dissolving in the security of God's presence.

This chance to experience, however briefly, the love of God deeply at work within the resting soul, is what we offer those who will attend any of the retreats in this book. You may discover that those who are searching for 'something more' in their spiritual lives feel a sense of relief when they are put in touch with the Christian contemplative tradition and sink into the safe, warm silence where God dwells. The contemplative stream of the Christian faith is not widely known, yet after people attend a retreat at which silence, listening to God, and contemplative prayer practices have been offered, many say that 'it feels like coming home'. They have caught a glimpse of that 'something more' of God: they have found some water for their thirsty soul. That longing, which God plants in every human heart, can only be filled with God's fullness – something of that fullness touches people who willingly spend time with God on retreat. It is our joy to encourage retreatants in their desire for more of the God who loves them.

How does this sort of opportunity arise during a retreat time? Clearly we can't expect retreatants to move straight from rushing to get to the retreat on time into a deep silence with God. Figure 1, adapted from the work of Jane Vennard,[5] illustrates the process of gathering and introductory input, the slowing pace and then the deepening movement into silence where apophatic prayer may emerge as the retreatant moves from active reflection to resting in God.

Having had a time of silence and rest of this kind, people need to re-engage slowly with the world to which they will soon return, and so we have the gentle movement out of the silence, a chance to share a little, if they wish, before moving to a group-closing liturgy to honour what has been experienced and to offer a way forward as they go from the retreat venue back to their homes or workplaces.

---

5 Jane E. Vennard, *Be Still: Designing and Leading Contemplative Retreats*, Herndon VA: The Alban Institute, 2000.

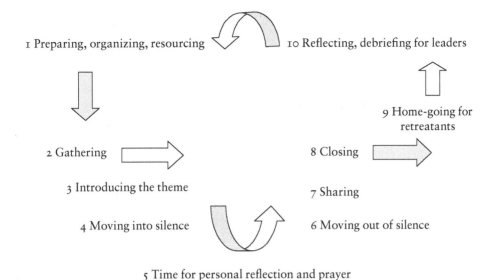

1 Preparing, organizing, resourcing   10 Reflecting, debriefing for leaders

9 Home-going for
retreatants

2 Gathering   8 Closing

3 Introducing the theme   7 Sharing

4 Moving into silence   6 Moving out of silence

5 Time for personal reflection and prayer

Figure 1

This pattern is as applicable to an hour's guided reflection as to a whole day or weekend retreat, but in the latter retreatants have an opportunity to stay in the place of silent prayer for longer. Some of the implications of this deepening prayer will be discussed in Part 5 when we look at longer retreat options.

Once you've familiarized yourself with the following descriptions of stages 1–10 in Figure 1, you can refer back to them whenever you want to.

1.1 Preparing, organizing and resourcing

Purpose:

- to ensure that we are in a 'good space' to offer a retreat time to others
- to have at the disposal of the Spirit a set of ideas, actions and resources to aid re-treatants' movement into silence, reflection and response to their God
- to provide an interesting, creative opportunity for others to share
- to introduce practices which, while possibly new to the retreatants, can enhance their spiritual formation
- to invite others to be part of this process through their prayer support and practical help.

In our often over-filled days, it can be tempting to cut corners somewhere in our preparation, but, when we give this first step in the process our full attention, we are doing our best for the retreatants and honouring our God, who is calling them to attend this opportunity.

☖ If you have already facilitated retreats for others, just take a few minutes to recall how you went about preparing. If you are just beginning to take on this responsibility, spend some time reflecting on how you intend to prepare, and what is important to you in terms of planning.

Retreatants won't be aware of how much goes on before the retreat is offered – the mixture of the personal, the prayerful and the practical as you make decisions and sift and sort and hope and pray.

Your gift to them is your willingness to put aside your own agendas and devote time to helping others on their journey of faith. God will honour all the effort that you put into this event, irrespective of how many attend. God will also honour the effort made by the retreatants, so no one need come away from even the shortest retreat, empty.

Personal preparation, support and experience:

- acknowledging that God is inviting you to run a contemplative retreat in some form
- responding to an invitation from the church leadership to provide a retreat time OR taking the step of offering such an opportunity to the church or community group of which you are a part
- drawing on your own experiences of being on retreats of different kinds – including silent ones
- drawing on your reading and exposure to Scripture, art, nature, music, worship styles, etc.
- drawing on your experience and capacity for stillness and trust in the Holy Spirit
- being willing to ask others for support and to share the responsibility with you at the event – you do not need to do this on your own
- accessing a supportive network who will uphold you and the retreatants in prayer
- making sure that your energy levels are not depleted before the event
- ensuring that you have some experience in managing group process: this may be formal or informal, but it is important that you are able to include the shy without embarrassing them, restrain the voluble without giving offence, shorten inappropriate input, and notice and respond to people's comfort/discomfort levels
- arranging supervision:[6] whatever the level of your experience in facilitating a group, talk with someone who understands group process and the benefit of supervision, before the event and then again after the event to 'debrief'.

---

6 'supervision' in this context means having a confidential conversation with someone whose task is, in an hour set apart for you, to help you acknowledge your strengths, identify limitations, affirm what went well and work out together how better to manage anything that caused you or the retreatants difficulty.

Prayerful preparation:

- praying for a theme/starting point so you have a focus
- praying for the right resources to become available
- praying with any central Scripture chosen for the retreat
- dealing with any anxiety or uncertainty by sharing with a trusted friend and with God, asking for what you need, especially if it is the first time you have led anything like this
- bringing the retreat and potential retreatants to God in your own prayer time
- being open for any further guidance of the Holy Spirit
- being ready and willing to set aside some of your carefully prepared material if it becomes clear that God wants to do something different, for example to emphasize one special part of the resources you have gathered.

Practical preparation:

- finding and booking a venue if you are not using an existing meeting time or place: in terms of suitability, you will need to check accessibility, toilets, heating, interruptions, cost, etc.
- looking through available resources, be alert and prayerful and be open to things from the natural environment, Scripture, other writings, such as poetry, prayers, short extracts relevant to theme, pictures, music and the internet
- gathering craft materials, such as clay, playdough, felt-tips, crayons, paper, scissors, glue, old magazines, other items depending on what contemplative activity you might be suggesting
- arranging some sort of advertising or promotion – pew-sheet, email list, local paper, fliers to other ministers and churches in the area if the event is open to other denominations, community newspaper, website, or blog-post
- copying of handouts – enough for each person to have a set
- considering any expenditure and cost to retreatants/reimbursement of your time/travel, etc.
- gathering the things you need for a central focus relevant to the theme, for opening and closing worship, art, icons, sculpture, candles, weaving, etc.
- elements for the Eucharist, etc. if being offered, holy oil for anointing if part of your tradition
- ensuring that you have what you need for the music, for example CD, iPod or MP3 player with speakers, batteries, extension cord, double plug – depending on where you are going to hold the event
- remembering to bring your own Bible and concordance
- buying/arranging for suitable refreshments, depending on the length of the retreat.

As a Girl Guide I was taught to 'be prepared!' and my personality type prefers to plan ahead. For some of you, however, this level of preparation may seem to be a bit 'over the top', and you may feel perfectly comfortable with less detail and more spontaneity. The ideas above are intended to support your retreat ministry not suffocate it, so take or leave any element that doesn't work for you!

1.2 Gathering

Purpose:

- to model the warmth and welcome of God
- to build a sense of community, even though the 'group life' may be brief
- to help retreatants focus on this opportunity to have quality time with God and to put aside (temporarily) other pressing issues
- to worship and pray together before entering the silence.

🕯 'Reflect on your own experience of the 'gathering' or 'starting' stage of a retreat or other similar event you've attended.

How did the 'gathering' help or hinder your capacity to settle gently and without undue delay into the event? If you had been in charge, what might you have done differently?

Creating a caring and safe environment:

Naturally we care about the well-being of the retreatants and want to provide a hospitable environment to help them develop their relationship with God. It is salutary to acknowledge, then, that every single thing we do as we facilitate these retreats has the potential *either* to enhance a retreatant's positive experience of God, of the spiritual life, of church, *or* to reinforce earlier negative perceptions. Unfortunately we cannot take for granted the sensitivity of our retreatants. I can still picture a group of Quiet Day retreatants, eyes closed and heads bowed, gathered for midday prayer many years ago. When I invited them to pray silently for the person seated next to them, one man put his hand on the shoulder of his neighbour and I saw her flinch at the unexpected and uninvited touch. It was a reminder for me to discuss safe practice with participants before each retreat begins and to agree upon such things as maintaining confidentiality, keeping the silence, respecting each other's space, and being free to 'pass' during discussions.

Nuts and bolts:

Some people appreciate knowing the shape of the retreat, what is expected of them, and practicalities of refreshments and break times, toilets and food. A brief timetable can be printed on the retreat programme (see Appendices); other matters can be dealt with by the facilitator, and time given to answering any queries *before* the opening worship.

Programme templates for the Quiet Days and weekend retreats are also provided in the Appendices.

Opening prayer and worship:

Unlike many more formal services and gatherings, the opening prayer and worship for retreat times is simple in the best sense of that word, and contemplative, that is, it incorporates silence and spaciousness to enhance reflection. As leaders we do not rush people through the words or readings but model the slowing down and quietness the retreatants need if they are to listen to God. Useful elements of any opening prayer and worship will include some or all of:

- a visually attractive or evocative centrepiece which connects with the theme
- instrumental music or chants
- a short Scripture reading and/or other text input relevant to the theme
- simple liturgical responses such as using a brief litany prepared for the retreat, or part of a psalm
- candle lighting or some other suitable ritual which involves several retreatants
- an opportunity to pray together as a way to build community
- offering the retreat time to God, praying that the Holy Spirit may work in each retreatant.

1.3 Offering input

Purpose:

- to provide material which retreatants may use to stimulate their reflection
- to encourage a focus on prayer and personal relationship with God
- to offer resources which retreatants may use once the retreat is over.

🕯 When you last attended a retreat or day of reflection, what did you notice about the input from the facilitator/retreat conductor? What did you find helpful? What did not work for you? What might you have done differently?

The input from the facilitator will be a combination of commentary to open up the theme, an introduction and description of spiritual and contemplative practices, and the provision of resources to encourage retreatants in their own reflection. In short retreats there will be only one input time, but for longer retreats there may be several as we shall see later. The input can be sourced from the facilitator's own experience, from Scripture (perhaps using a translation or paraphrase which will give a fresh presentation of the text), from poetry, imagery, art, natural items, music, etc. The opening input 'slot', while often a short *talk* on the theme, may take a number of other forms, all of which will be referred to in this book:

- a facilitated group discussion, with key comments recorded on a whiteboard
- a short exercise for the group to 'warm' them up to the theme
- a visual presentation – involving objects or items associated with the theme
- a brief introductory talk, followed by time for questions/comments
- a short role play to enhance a key point
- a conversation with a co-facilitator – such as sharing experience of something relevant to the theme
- an opportunity to listen to a particular piece of music and to respond to that music as they wish
- a guided meditation
- an introduction to a relevant painting, pictures or other artistic stimulus
- an exercise involving movement, for example walking, stretching, gentle body awareness.

The input should be offered in ways that are accessible for all those present – this means having a range of resources pitched at different levels of conceptual complexity, and some opportunity for people to clarify any queries before they go into their time of personal reflection. Usually there will be reflection sheets or prompts available for retreatants to work with – these will reinforce the key themes of the retreat and suggest ways of *personalizing* them. For example, if the theme is 'celebration', the reflection material would invite retreatants to identify something in their own lives they wished to celebrate and, with the help of the Holy Spirit, to create a thanksgiving ritual or prayer. This moves the 'input' from being purely an intellectual exercise to being something anchored in the retreatants' experience, something 'real' to engage both head and heart.

1.4 Moving into silence

Purpose:

- to provide a space in which people can pay attention to their own interior life and the still, small voice of God
- to reconnect people with a key spiritual practice, missing from most church services/Christian gatherings and from society at large
- to help extroverts discover that they can actually 'fast from speaking'
- to follow Jesus' practice of seeking silence and solitude for prayer (for example Luke 6.12).

People who seek time apart with God will inevitably have different experiences of silence; it can be helpful for those who are new to this journey to reflect, even briefly, on what silence means to them. It can also be helpful to 're-present' the concept of silence in a positive light, for example silence might be described as 'fasting from talking – so we can focus on God', or even 'taking a rest from having to interact with others'.

Extroverted retreatants may be nervous about the amount of time they will be expected to be quiet. A real but often unspoken concern for extroverts is that if they take the time to listen to their inner world there might be nothing much going on. It is really helpful for them if, as facilitators, we encourage them to trust that God is waiting for them in the silence, so that it need not be threatening and will not be empty. We can also make it clear that if they need to talk they can come and talk to us, rather than interrupt others.

1.5 Reflecting and responding – going deeper in prayer

Purpose:

- to encourage retreatants to *think* about their own spiritual life and daily journey
- to encourage honest one-to-one communication between the retreatant and God
- to try a variety of spiritual practices so they can find what works for them
- to develop their capacity to slow down, to stop, and wonder with God
- to help them indentify what they want to ask God for in petition – for themselves, and, particularly in the longer day or weekend retreats,
- to provide a context in which kataphatic prayer may shift to apophatic prayer.

What space do you give to reflecting on your spiritual life/on life in general?
How do you describe prayer? What aspects of prayer do you treasure?
How has your prayer practice/understanding changed over the years?

Because life for many people is so full, chances to stop and reflect are diminishing. Although retreatants may be given an hour (or considerably longer) to spend with God, some may struggle with the length of 'empty' time, so it is important as retreat facilitators that we keep alert for those who seem distracted, uncertain or anxious. Alongside this culturally shaped unfamiliarity with reflection, we must place human wilfulness – our tendency to dodge spending time with God. Somehow, although we know we need it, we put it off as long as possible! Adult resistance may be deep-seated, born of fear and an unhelpful image of God. If we can help people understand that resistance is a common part of the spiritual journey, retreatants can begin to acknowledge their own reluctance, and can then be encouraged to talk directly to God about that resistance.

Above all, the time for reflection in silence is an opportunity for retreatants to listen prayerfully. God meets us in the *present* moment, and we encourage retreatants to share with God the truth of their *current* reality with all its ups and downs as honestly as they can. It seems obvious that if we believe God loves us, we should have the confidence to share our hurts, triumphs and wonderings with God. But time and time again, as I hear people's struggles with all sorts of life events, when I ask them how they are praying about these difficulties, the response is 'Well, I haven't actually brought that to prayer.' What stops people sharing with God what is important to them? There are a number of possibilities:

- they have little experience of sharing their innermost thoughts and feelings with *anyone*, let alone with God
- they don't think that God will be interested in the details of their lives
- they are ashamed and want to hide from God – yet they long for God or they wouldn't be on retreat
- they are habitually self-reliant and don't ask anyone for anything, and that includes God
- they may have difficulty noticing their feelings and putting words around them
- deep down, they don't trust God to act in their best interest.

While retreat times cannot 'fix' the pain so many people carry, they can begin to reveal a God who:

- responds when we draw near (James 4.8a)
- is interested in the details of our lives (Matthew 6.25–33; Acts 9.10–19)
- wants to heal our shame and sense of alienation (Matthew 11.28–30; Ephesians 2.13–22)
- welcomes our dependence (1 Peter 5.7)
- longs for us to open ourselves to God's all-encompassing love, because God already knows us to our core (Psalms 51,139, etc.)
- assures us of good intentions towards us (Matthew 7.7–11).

Most retreatants will be very familiar with intercessory prayer and may have been actively praying in this way for years. BUT – while they are attending a retreat, the focus is on building their own relationship with God, strengthening their foundation in Christ, empowering them for service. This deepening relationship can only happen if retreatants are encouraged to share honestly with God what is going on in their hearts and lives, and, at some point, that sharing will include asking God for the grace or wisdom they need for a particular situation or problem. Once retreatants have managed to share their truth with God, they are more likely to feel free enough to sit with God in the silence, to be open to God's loving touch and encouragement, and perhaps even to experience some of the deep rest available to them in apophatic prayer.

1.6 Moving out of silence

Purpose:

- to make the transition between personal time with God and reconnection with their community
- to gather the retreatants together so they can move into the closing stages of retreat
- to acknowledge that for most of us, much of life is lived in the midst of noise.

🕯 What has helped you make the transition from personal, silent reflection to being part of a group again, when you've been in a retreat setting?

As you will probably know from your own experience, an encounter with God can leave you feeling a little 'spaced out', reluctant to leave that graced awareness of God's personal touch. For some retreatants, the time of silent prayer and reflection will have been profound, and so the return to company or conversation can seem abrasive. Even if a retreatant feels that 'nothing has happened' in a deep sense, the time just 'to be' will have been significant, and its coming to a conclusion may bring a tinge of regret, especially for those for whom such times are rare.

In shorter retreats, one gentle way of helping people move out of the silence is to have a chant playing softly in the background as retreatants gather for the closing stages of the retreat time. The music and the words can provide a transitional focus as people gather and begin to think about the rhythms of their daily routines once more.

When retreatants have basked in the slower pace and quietness of a longer silent retreat, there is often an understandable reluctance to return to normal conversation and the speed with which much social discourse is conducted. Where there has been sustained silence over a weekend for example, the movement back to conversation may be gradual and may take place within the context of a meal or a liturgy, or both. Sensitive facilitation is required to enable this transition.

1.7 Sharing

Purpose:

- to provide a context in which those who need to speak in order to deepen their experience, can do so
- to build confidence in retreatants as their words encourage others
- in some contexts, to build community and deeper levels of trust.

🕯 When you want to explore your thoughts and feelings about something, how do you normally go about doing that? To what extent do you need others for this process to work well for you? What helps you to feel comfortable enough to share aloud in a group?

When I first began offering retreats, I was very conscious of the rarity of silence in most people's lives, and so I was careful to protect the silence for the retreatants as much as possible. This is fine for those of us who, as introverts, do most of our processing internally. Lately, however, I have found that for more extroverted people, it is important to provide some 'talking time' so they have a chance to clarify what they are thinking and feeling, as they speak. Ideally this could be accomplished if the retreatants went for a walk and talked aloud to God, but, if taking a retreat of any length is a really new experience, it can be better initially to make this sharing a part of the retreat format.

There are various ways of doing this, for example, by offering individual spiritual direction appointments during a Quiet Day. In shorter retreats, this can be done by scheduling – midway between the opening and closing – a chance for those who need to talk, to do so. It is made clear that this is *optional*, done in pairs or threes depending on numbers, *brief* (perhaps 15 minutes), and *focused* on what is happening for each retreatant, rather than general conversation. Before the closing liturgy, once everyone has returned to the gathering space, the facilitator can simply invite retreatants to turn to their neighbour and, for a few minutes, share a little of their experience during the retreat time.

1.8 Closing

Purpose:

- to offer the gift of the sacrament of the Eucharist and/or anointing if appropriate to the group
- to consolidate some of the personal learnings during the retreat
- to bring together the gifts of the retreat
- to prepare the retreatants to continue their spiritual journeys in their own contexts.

🕯 Reflect on your own experience of the 'closing' or 'ending' stage of a retreat or other spiritual event you've attended. How did the 'closing' help or hinder your capacity to honour the day gently and begin to re-engage with your family/work etc.? What might you have done differently?

The closing ritual or liturgy is offered as a way of acknowledging what God has been doing in the retreatants' lives, and of giving space for people gradually to disengage from the group and the place as they prepare for 're-entry' into everyday routines.

The longer the retreat, the more important the closing becomes – rather than being rushed and rambling, we can gently bring together the themes and discoveries of the time given to God in silence and reflection. It follows then, that during the closing ritual we pay attention both to individual wonder *and* the cessation of the group life. We shall focus on the closing of longer retreats in Part 5. For now, the elements of the closing liturgy will simply be named; how these elements are brought together and what emphasis is placed on each one will vary according to the nature of the retreat time.

Gathering	Recollecting	Music	Listening
Sharing symbols	Reflecting	Silence	Eucharist
Thanksgiving	Encouraging	Anointing	Sending forth

1.9 Home-going – on with the journey

Purpose:

- to encourage retreatants to continue to practice those spiritual disciplines which they have experienced during the retreat
- to help retreatants focus on what God may have revealed to them during the retreat so that the momentum is not lost
- to take with them some tangible reminder of the gifts of the retreat
- to link them with other retreat opportunities/providers of events in their area.

If you can, think back to the close of a retreat experience – the home-going. What comes to mind? What questions or worries did you have? How did you feel?

When we return from a retreat, it's not uncommon to struggle to find someone with whom it is safe to share some of the discoveries and wonder of a new awareness of God or a deep sense of healing. We might even find that, after a few days, the retreat experience takes on an 'other worldly' quality, as if it had little connection with the raw reality of the daily grind. That is why, before the retreatants go home, it can be very helpful to offer them a sheet on which are listed opportunities for ongoing spiritual growth. With a little homework first, we can offer them:

- names and contact details of spiritual directors for intentional one-to-one spiritual growth work
- details of any contemplative prayer groups
- information about local or regional retreat houses and their programmes
- timing and location of any contemplative services such as those using Taizé or Iona-sourced material

- contact details for anyone running Bible *prayer* and study groups
- the date and details of the next retreat or prayer focus we are offering.

We can also invite those who've been on the retreat to leave their email addresses or other contact information so that we can send them details of anything else which we think they might be interested in, for example visiting speakers on themes around prayer and spiritual growth.

1.10 Reviewing and debriefing for leaders

Purpose:

- to identify anything that was clearly helpful or unhelpful to those present
- to review the balance and effectiveness of different elements of the retreat time
- to modify the retreat structure, content or process if necessary
- to gain confidence when things have gone well and to receive support if things haven't gone well.

In many work situations, debriefing after an event is routine. Leaders are encouraged to reflect on their attitudes and behaviours, and on the outcomes achieved or goals missed.

What is your experience of debriefing conversations or meetings? What did you find valuable? What process was used to ensure that learnings from both 'good' and 'bad' outcomes were possible?

As retreat facilitators, we can also benefit from sitting down with someone – preferably our supervisor – to discuss our sense of what worked and what didn't. It is particularly important to debrief if something has not gone well so that mistakes are not repeated, future preparation is adequate, skill deficits are named and rectified, and dented confidence rebuilt with the support and wisdom of a competent supervisor.

If we have worked with a co-facilitator, it also pays to meet *together* with a supervisor when debriefing. This enables each of us to hear the other, while a supervisor notes any issues that emerge which might compromise the working relationship or affect the way retreats might be run in the future.

Part 2
Loaves and fishes – spiritual formation resource sheets

In the Leader's preparation section of each description of a short retreat, you will find spiritual formation resource sheets relevant to that retreat. These 'Loaves and Fishes' will be referred to as 'L&F resource sheets' and numbered for ease of identification and use. Each resource sheet contains:

- a description of a spiritual formation practice and how it may be used
- Scripture passages for prayer and meditation to expand the resource's meaning
- an extension exercise and suggestions to help people use the particular spiritual practice
- a reading resource or website to explore.

The resource sheets can:

- provide a reference point, and information for you to use, as you introduce a new spiritual formation practice
- be copied and given out to retreatants who are new to contemplative spirituality
- provide options for you – once you are familiar with them all, you can use any of them in any retreat, depending on your theme and how you decide to present it.

Each of the retreats described in Parts 3, 4 and 5 will make use of some of these resource sheets so, over time, those who attend your retreats can build up a 'toolkit' of spiritual practices to help them grow in their relationship with God. You are free to use *any* of the resource sheets for *any* retreat depending on who will be attending and their familiarity with contemplative spirituality.

While the spiritual formation sheets making up Part 2 each spread over two pages in this book, each spiritual formation sheet downloaded from the Canterbury Press website occupies a single page to make it easier to print off for use with retreatants.

L&F 2.1 Attitudes and expectations – waking up to God

Is your cup half empty or half full? A simple question, but the answer can illustrate a life attitude of optimism or pessimism, a tendency to look on the bright or the broken side of life. Often this life attitude simmers below the surface, unexamined. It is 'unconscious' or 'asleep' and as long as it remains so, it can exercise power over us, subtly controlling our expectations, until such time as we 'wake up', notice what's going on and examine the attitude before choosing to modify, accept or reject it.

The parable of the prodigal son rightly concentrates on the gift of unconditional love, modelling for us the Fatherhood of God, but there is a telling clause in the narrative which is pivotal to our understanding of 'waking up':

> He would gladly have filled himself with the pods that the pigs were eating; and no one gave him anything. But *when he came to himself* he said, 'How many of my father's hired hands have bread enough and to spare, but here I am dying of hunger! I will get up and go to my father ... (Luke 15.16–18, *my italics*)

Before the son can receive the father's love, he has to 'wake up' to his own reality, his own need of care, his longing to return 'home', even though his motives are mixed. He takes the first steps of 'metanoia' – conversion, a turning back towards wholeness. The father's delighted welcome and the celebration the 'prodigal' had not expected, enable him to 'wake up' to the realization of how much he is loved

You are reading this because you have responded to an invitation to come closer to God. Who sent the invitation? God did, but not by letter, text or email! Only you and God know your life circumstances and what you need at this point, but you can be assured that God is delighted that you have chosen to set time aside to listen and be with God today. If you have an attitude of hopeful expectation, paying attention to whatever touches your heart, catches your imagination, or makes you think, anything, anywhere, anytime can form part of the way God will communicate with you. Whatever you expect from God, be assured that even a 'little' given to you with love, will be more than you can imagine.

🕯 What is your attitude towards God? What do you expect of/from God? *Whatever your response*, share it with God as honestly as you would with a trusted friend. Once you've finished, ask God for the grace you need to 'wake up' to God's love for you.

📖 *Scripture for prayer and meditation:*

> For I am convinced that neither death, nor life, nor angels, nor rulers, nor things present, nor things to come, nor powers, nor height, nor depth, nor anything else in all creation, will be able to separate us from the love of God in Christ Jesus our Lord. (Romans 8.38–39)

OR

> Do not fear, for I have redeemed you; I have called you by name, you are mine ... you are precious in my sight, and honoured, and I love you. (Isaiah 43.1b, 4a)

Extension exercise and reading:

- ⚜ Spend some time each day noticing your attitudes and expectations of yourself, of others and of God. Talk to God about what you discover. Then ask God for the grace you need to change those attitudes and expectations which are destructive of growth or relationship, and to consolidate those attitudes and expectations which develop in you the fruit of the Spirit: love, joy, peace, patience, kindness, generosity ... (see Galatians 5.22–23)

- ⚜ Read Fr Anthony de Mello, *Awareness*, London: Fount, 1990 (still in print and readily available).

OR

> Watch de Mello on http://www.youtube.com/watch?v=4Y3Q7H2urto.

L&F 2.2 Being honest with God and with yourself

Many of us struggle to share what is going on within us with *anyone*, let alone with God. Years of shaping by significant adults interact with our own personality, abilities and circumstances to influence not only *how* we process the thoughts and feelings that tumble through our days and nights, but *what* we are prepared to 'put out there' as we risk speaking our deepest truth to others. While we may discuss everyday matters and share some personal thoughts and ideas, even opinions, with family, colleagues or friends, we may be reluctant to let others hear how we *really* feel about something. Nor do we often speak of deep 'heart' stuff, the critical matters of meaning and purpose, forgiveness and redemption, the things of the spiritual life. Wondering whom we can trust, we may hide from other people, and from God, the very things that matter most to us, the very core of who we are, and what we truly value.

Growing with, and in, God, means facing our tendency to put up barriers to hide the truth of who we are from God, from ourselves, and from others. Sometimes those barriers are made up of unacknowledged pain from our past, or feelings of shame or guilt; sometimes our barriers are put up as a defence in response to being betrayed or let down by people we should have been able to trust. But – *we do not have to defend ourselves against God*, because God always wants our highest good, and draws us towards fullness of life. Whatever has caused our reticence or shyness before God, if we truly want to get closer to God, we need to be honest and 'tell it like it is'. Two practices can help us:

Firstly we can learn to recognize our feelings, share them with God, and express them to others without being hurtful. A simple four-part model, drawn from the work of Fran Ferder,[7] remains helpful:

1 *Noticing:* paying attention to our physiological responses, as many feelings express themselves through a change in our bodies, such as blushing, sweaty palms, 'butterflies' in the stomach.
2 *Naming:* putting a label on the feeling to bring it 'out in the open'. Although this might seem straightforward, many people struggle to put their feelings into words.
3 *Owning:* acknowledging the feeling. We do not pretend it doesn't, or shouldn't, exist. Emotions are neutral in themselves: they simply 'are'. In order for us to learn from them, we have to accept their reality in our lives, unpleasant or embarrassing or surprisingly joyful they may be.

---

7 Summarized from Fran Ferder, *Words Made Flesh*, Notre Dame, Indiana: Ave Maria Press, 1986, pp. 49–66.

4 *Responding:* expressing what we want to say or do. Feelings shed light on our inner world of thoughts and motivations, so once we recognize what a feeling is, and where in us it comes from, we are freer to choose responses which will be fair, compassionate and wise.

Secondly we can pray with the Psalms. These vibrant examples of honest-to-God communication help us to increase our emotional vocabulary. They are:

- *Direct:* addressing God openly.
- *Personal:* they contain details of the writer's life, current situation and longings.
- *Communal:* speaking of a people's displacement or thanksgiving, putting life in a wider context.
- *Revealing:* there is no attempt to hide feelings or censor them before God.
- *Confident when asking for help:* petitions are made in the context of relationship with God.

Just as honest and caring communication between human beings builds relationship, so our willingness to pray about what is going on, deep in our being, helps build our relationship with God.

📖 *Scripture for prayer and meditation:*

> O LORD, you have searched me and known me ... You search out my path and my lying down, and are acquainted with all my ways. (Psalm 139.1, 3)

Extension exercise and reading:

✳ Jesus was both fully human and fully divine. Read the Gospel of Matthew slowly, and list all the feelings Jesus felt. Then think back over your life – when have you felt similar feelings?
Talk to God or Jesus about what you have discovered.

L&F 2.3 Beginnings – breath prayer

A spiritual practice which can help us stay connected and open to God is a 'breath prayer'. Put simply, this is the rhythmical repetition of a small portion of spiritual text as we rest, or as we walk, swim, run, cycle, row or otherwise move through our day. You can repeat the words aloud, even sing them to your own tune if you prefer, or you can let the words run kindly through your mind as you travel, or wait or engage in some repetitive activity. How to choose what to use? If you already do a regular morning Bible reading, you can use a phrase or verse that catches your attention, and simply revisit it regularly throughout the day. A phrase from another spiritual reading, or a line from a hymn or song, can also be used, as long as it means something to you about you and your God.

Breath prayers from Scripture could include for example:

'My Lord and my God.'
(Thomas's words to Christ after the resurrection, John 20.28)

'Peace I leave with you, my peace I give to you.'
(Jesus with his disciples, John 14.27a)

'I am the bread of life.' (John 6.48)

Perhaps the most ancient breath prayer is the Jesus Prayer, which uses all or part of the following form:

Lord Jesus Christ, Son of God, have mercy on me, a sinner.

Emerging from St Catherine's Monastery at Mt Sinai in the seventh century, this prayer is a powerful invocation of the Name and Presence of our Lord. It draws us into stillness and deepens the spiritual life of the pray-er in ways that transcend our understanding:

- said when we wake in the night, it can lead us gently back into sleep
- said when we are in shock, it can anchor us
- said when we are ill and weak, it can offer us strength
- said when we are confused or uncertain, it can clarify our vision
- said when we are lonely or isolated, it can warm our hearts and bring us hope.

More than anything, this ancient breath prayer is prompted by the Spirit in order to deepen our relationship with the triune God. Over time this prayer will begin to pray itself within us so that we will indeed be 'praying without ceasing', as Paul encouraged the new disciples 2,000 years ago (1 Thessalonians 5.17).

📖 *Scripture for prayer and meditation:*

Jesus said to them again, 'Peace be with you. As the Father has sent me, so I send you.' When he had said this, he breathed on them and said to them, 'Receive the Holy Spirit.' (John 20. 21–22)

OR

Let everything that breathes praise the LORD! Praise the LORD! (Psalm 150.6)

Extension exercise and reading:

⁂ In your prayer time, talk to God about your desire to pray the Jesus prayer. Then begin, perhaps before you go to sleep at night, or when you are sitting quietly and can bring reverence and purity of intention to the saying of this beautiful and compelling prayer.

⁂ Read St Ignaty Brianchaninov, *On Practicing the Jesus Prayer*, Orthodox Christian Information Centre, http://www.orthodoxinfo.com/praxis/ignaty_jesus.aspx.

L&F 2.4 Beginnings – practising the presence of God

No matter how full our days may be, there are naturally occurring short spaces as, for example, we wait for the kettle to boil, stand in a queue, or mute the television during the ad-breaks. Instead of filling these moments with the concerns of daily living, we can use these spaces to turn our thoughts towards our God, to 'tune in' to the One in whom 'we live and move and have our being' (Acts 17.28).

In the seventeenth century, a French lay brother called Lawrence left behind a series of letters which give us a glimpse of someone *in love with God*. Whether at work in the kitchen or sandal-making, or in formal times of prayer, he 'practised the presence of God' by repeatedly turning his mind to God, in love, all through the day. Not only did this simple practice deepen Brother Lawrence's own connection with God, but it also enabled him to be a vehicle of God's grace to those around him. There was no division between 'sacred' and 'secular', between leisure and work, for he did *everything, for the love of God*.

If we believe that our very being is made in the image of God, then it follows that, as soon as we take a moment to turn our focus towards the centre of our soul, to make that 'interior glance' Brother Lawrence described, we can be re-minded of God's presence there within us. We do not have to 'come into God's presence' as if we are outside in the darkness, waiting in uncertainty like a nervous servant hoping to be allowed to come into the same room as his master. Instead, as God's beloved children, we have simply to change focus for a moment and, with love as our intention, turn our minds to God, who is already there in our heart, to Jesus who befriends us, and to the Spirit who is ready to guide, console, instruct, support and encourage us.

Every time we turn towards God in this way, we are 'practising the presence of God', welcoming God into the middle of our lives, into our difficulties and our dreams. As we do this more and more often during the day, we build up the holy habit of awareness of God at the centre of our lives, part of all that we are and do, inspiring and supporting us as we reach out to others. Instead of thinking God is far away and disinterested, we recognize that God is close at hand, nearer than our own breathing. With this awareness, our love for God, for our neighbour and for ourselves steadily grows.

📖 *Scripture for prayer and meditation:*

> The LORD went in front of them in a pillar of cloud by day, to lead them along the way, and a pillar of fire by night, to give them light, so that they might travel by day and by night. Neither the pillar of cloud by day nor the pillar of fire by night left its place in front of the people. (Exodus 13.21–22)

OR

> Jesus said, 'Remember, I am with you always, to the end of the age.' (Matthew 28.20b)

Extension exercise and reading:

⁂ To start *'practising the presence of God'*, set aside ten minutes when you won't be interrupted, for example when you are doing the ironing, or sitting with a coffee, writing an essay, or weeding the garden – whatever you are doing, ask for the guidance of the Holy Spirit and then, simply and gently, go through the next ten minutes, lovingly turning towards God as many times as you remember. (Don't worry about being distracted.)

⁂ Read Brother Lawrence (trans. John J. Delaney), *Practising the Presence of God*, New York: Doubleday, 1977. This Christian classic is widely available in new editions.

L&F 2.5 Caring for Creation

We are made in the image of God and are invited to be co-creators, partners with God in an ongoing movement towards freedom for people and wholeness for the planet. It follows then that human communities, and particularly Christian people, should be good stewards of the earth's resources. Rather than being 'so heavenly-minded, we're no earthly use', we are called, at the very least, to be prudent and dedicated caretakers of the corner of God's vineyard in which we find ourselves.

The Creation – God's 'Second Book' – not only declares to us the wonder of God (Psalm 19) but, if we work in harmony with Creation and with each other, can support and sustain humanity. Although we may feel overwhelmed by the environmental changes we see around us or in the media; although it is clear that human beings have systematically and greedily stripped the earth of its resources; although it might be tempting to shrug our shoulders and say it's all too hard and one person can't make a difference, the truth of the matter is that we *can* make a difference by starting out in a small way in our own part of the earth and joining like-minded others to form a community of caring.

🕯 Who has made a difference to your appreciation of the natural world?

We've probably never met Rachel Carson, Jacques Cousteau, David Bellamy, Jane Goodall or David Attenborough, but over decades their books, research and TV programmes may well have influenced our attitude towards our world and its creatures. There are countless others whose names rarely reach the public eye: women and men who decide, for example, to camp out on a windy headland to protect albatross eggs from vandals, or to clean up a messy stream and plant bushes and trees nearby, or those who talk their family into recycling waste, or who set up a community vegetable garden and share with new generations their experience and passion for nature and the environment.

Two people who 'started small' are Peter Harris, an Anglican priest and his wife Miranda who, over the last two decades, have been instrumental in the founding and development of A Rocha, described on its website as a 'Christian nature conservation organisation … whose projects are frequently cross-cultural in character, and share a community emphasis, with a focus on science and research, practical conservation and environmental education … in eighteen countries.' The network they have helped to create is making a difference, resurrecting hope, in the communities where A Rocha is working.

The world is alive with God if we have eyes to see it. As we wake up spiritually and grow in awareness, so our compassion increases, and this in turn produces in us a deep sense of connection with all the created world. We cannot stand idle, and ignore the earth 'groaning in labour pains ...' (Romans 8.22).

God will guide us if we are willing to be co-creators, rather than rampant consumers.

📖 *Scripture for prayer and meditation:*

The Creation story in Genesis 1 and 2, in The Message Bible paraphrase to get a fresh perspective on this familiar material.

OR

Romans 8.18–25.

Extension exercise and reading:

✤ Read Peter Harris, *Kingfisher's Fire*, Oxford: Monarch, 2008.
OR visit the website of A Rocha http://www.arocha.org/int-en/index.html.

✤ Pray about how *you* might make a difference – start small and who knows where the Spirit might lead? ☺

L&F 2.6 Drawing or doodling as prayer – creating a sacred space or mandala

The 'mandala', a Sanskrit word loosely translated as 'circle', provides a focus for spiritual contemplation. This sacred space may be seen in a range of forms, whether a centuries-old stained glass rose window, the top of a Celtic cross, a labyrinth, a mosaic floor pattern in a cathedral, or the more ephemeral sand mandalas made by today's Tibetan monks.

Hildegard of Bingen was an eleventh-century Benedictine abbess, theologian, artist, healer and musician. We don't know if she knew the term 'mandala', but she certainly created sacred circular drawings with a central focus to help her to express her appreciation of the seasons and the spiritual truth of the divinity at the centre of the created order.

As a Christian spiritual practice, this form of reflection can illuminate any aspect of our life, with the help of the Holy Spirit. Some possible starting points could be:

- representing in symbolic form an illness or disability with which we are struggling
- sketching a familiar symbol from our faith such as a cross, a rose, bread, wine, light, water
- naming a close family member who is in our heart
- using colours to write a verse from Scripture which has special meaning for us
- drawing a shape that represents our life stage or emotional state.

As we spend time with this type of drawing, letting our thoughts and hands be guided by God's Spirit, we can add to the sacred space – colours, names, verses of Scripture or poetry or song/hymn lyrics, other shapes, questions, diagrams, anything which seems fitting. What often happens is that, as we do this, something we hadn't realized before is revealed; we can take this discovery to prayer or share it with another trusted person. A mandala can be a safe and valuable tool when working our way through grief; when trying to discern a way forward; and in times of transition.

📖 *Scripture for reflection using the mandala as an aid:*

In the beginning was the Word. (John 1.1)

OR

Your word is a lamp to my feet and a light to my path. (Psalm 119.105)

Extension exercise:

✤ Draw your own mandala, choosing any one of the starting points suggested above or something else if it is more fitting. Don't hurry, but let the central portion of the space fill gradually as you reflect on the theme you have chosen and make appropriate colour choices. Be alert for the Spirit's guidance.

✤ Draw your own Celtic cross – on the long shaft of the cross depict your own spiritual journey, the formative events and people who have shaped your life. The cross and circle at the top represent 'victory, wholeness, the transforming power of Christ in all creation',[8] themes central to Celtic spirituality.
How does your life reveal or illustrate those themes?
What else would you like to include at the top of your Celtic cross?

✤ Go for a walk and be alert to beautiful circular shapes in nature, such as the centre of a sunflower, the rings of an old tree …

---

8 Ray Simpson, *Exploring Celtic Spirituality*, Suffolk: Kevin Mayhew, 2004, p. 131.

L&F 2.7 Examen – a simple review of the day

Unlike keeping a diary, which may later prove of benefit to family genealogists, reviewing the day as a Christian practice is designed to help us to recognize patterns or themes in our behaviour and responses, and to identify those things that energize us, or which cause us, little by little, to shrivel inside. One review practice, the Examen, can help anyone who is serious about spiritual growth.

Traditionally the Examen has two parts:

1 The Examination of Conscience in which we make a moral inventory,[9] thinking back over the events we've experienced or the encounters we've had with people. Doing this each day is ideal, but even a weekly Examen of Conscience will build in you the fruits of the Spirit. As we do this exercise, we invite God to highlight any self-deception, show us our faults, and help us acknowledge areas of faithfully sound decision-making or conversation.

2 The Examination of Consciousness in which we pay attention to those things which have touched our awareness, moved us or caused us to stop and think about our lives and motivation. This practice also involves noticing our thoughts and our feelings, and what brings us closer to God or takes us further away from God.

The actual process of doing the Examen is flexible, lending itself to adaptation for a range of ages and personal circumstances. It involves:

- Safeguarding 10–15 minutes each evening when you are unlikely to be interrupted or fall asleep.
- Having at hand a journal and, if doing this by yourself, your Bible; otherwise have a family or group 'prayer log' in which answers to prayer can be recorded.
- Symbolically acknowledging the presence of the Spirit to guide and support us – you can do this by lighting a candle or using a religious picture, cross or something from the Creation as a focus.
- Asking for the guidance of the Holy Spirit and thanking God for God's care for us.
- Taking two minutes to sit in silence, gently allowing our attention to focus on the day we've had.

---

9 Richard Foster, *Prayer: Finding the Heart's True Home*, London: Hodder & Stoughton, 1992, pp. 27–8.

- Asking one or two pairs of questions (as suggested by the Linns, see reference below). These questions are decided upon beforehand and are put in language suitable for those present. They are designed to give space for both elements of the Examen to be considered – where we fall short of God's standards, and where we recognize God drawing us, or helping us, to see where our true self can best find expression. For example:

  What helped me feel close to God today? What made me feel far away from God today? How have I given love today? How have I received love today? Where have I struggled today? Where have I felt fully myself without striving today?
- When all have had their turn, invite each person to ask God for the grace they need for themselves and for someone whose needs have come to mind during the Examen. These prayers can be summarized in the family or group log if you want to.
- Give thanks for the time together and for the guidance of the Spirit, and then commit those present to the care and love of God and a quiet night's sleep.

The spiritual benefits will emerge only if the Examen is practised regularly over time. Then the process can assist us in our discernment, vocational choices, personal relationships, and lifestyle priorities – in short, it is a useful tool both for noticing trends in our responses to a wide range of situations met in everyday life, and in paying attention to God's unfolding invitation to growth and service.

📖 *Scripture for referencing and for prayer:*

Psalm 51, especially vv 6–7, 10; Psalm 139, especially vv 23–24, Matthew 7.3–5

Extension exercise and reading:

✳ Read Matthew Linn, Sheila Fabricant Linn and Dennis Linn, *Sleeping with Bread, Holding what gives you life*, New York: Paulist Press, 1995.

L&F 2.8 Exploring our image of God

Jesus asked his impetuous disciple Peter, 'Who do you say that I am?' (Mark 8.29), and sooner or later, that same question will be asked of us. Our image of God will be shaped by our upbringing, our storehouse of Scripture or stories from our faith tradition, our experiences of the power of our caregivers and teachers, the doctrines and customs of a particular faith community, our individual and corporate religious/spiritual experiences, representations of God/Jesus in the media, arts or literature, and whether we have suffered abuse or trauma. Each person's image of God is complex and unique.

🕯 Imagine Jesus asking you, 'Who do you say that I am?' How would you respond?

Our answer to this question is affected not only by our formative experiences but also by major life events such as birth, migration, grief and death which have particular power to shape or challenge how we look at God. If, for example, we hold dear an image of God as protector of all little children, what happens to that image when a much-wanted baby dies accidentally, a toddler disappears, or a natural disaster costs the lives of the innocent? It is at this very point that people's faith comes under scrutiny – and rightly so. If our faith is to have the tough integrity which can respond to suffering without platitudes; if we want to be able to trust the loving care of God in the midst of tragedy, we have to have the courage to look at our image of God.

🕯 What is your current understanding of where God is when 'bad things happen to good people'?

Years ago Viktor Frankl, a Jewish psychiatrist and author of *Man's Search for Meaning*,[10] witnessed children being hanged in a concentration camp. Someone near him muttered, 'Where is God now?' and, from another prisoner, Frankl heard the words, 'He is there, hanging on the gibbet.' Somehow that prisoner had come to see the vulnerability of a God who chose the way of powerlessness and pain, experiencing what it can mean to be fully human. Jesus shows us that love in his life and death, a love that risks undefended openness to life with all its beauty as well as its suffering, a love that remains with us now, through thick and thin, as the Comforter, the Holy Spirit.

---

10 Viktor Frankl, *Man's Search for Meaning*, first published in 1946 under the title *Ein Psychologe erlebt das Konzentrationslager*. Translated into English in 1959. Still in print.

📖 *Scripture for prayer and reflection:*

John 14.15–16, 25–27 (the promise of the Holy Spirit).

OR

Mark 8.27–30 (the question about Jesus' identity).

Extension exercise and reading:

✤ Divide an A4 sheet of paper into the number of decades you have lived. In each space write a few words or sketch a symbol that represents who God was for you at that time of your life.

　　Pay particular attention to any big changes from one decade to the next, and reflect on what might have triggered that shift in how you see God. Take the time to talk to God about what you have noticed.

✤ Is there any incongruence between the God you say you believe in, and the way you actually live out your life?

✤ Read some of the prayer material that comes from David Adam (Lindisfarne), for example *The Edge of Glory*, SPCK/Triangle: London, 1985, and see how these prayers, which are influenced by Celtic Christianity, include the Trinity in a very down-to-earth way.

　　Then, write a prayer of your own for an everyday event, patterned on what you have read.

L&F 2.9 Keeping a spiritual journal, and writing as prayer

Putting pen to paper may have unhappy associations for some, particularly those who have struggled at school or who found writing essays difficult. It's important to acknowledge these earlier experiences so they don't put you off using a spiritual journal as a whole new way of connecting with God.

⸙ What is your history of writing, doing assignments or keeping a diary?
How do you feel about keeping a journal as a tool for spiritual growth?
If you already keep a spiritual journal, what have been the benefits or difficulties?

A spiritual journal is a highly personal record of our own journey with God. It is not concerned with spelling, grammar or punctuation; nor does it have to fit into anyone else's ideas of length, content or style. A journal may contain some comments about life events, but its focus is really on where God might be found in those events, what God might be doing in our life; stories of grace will sit alongside stories of struggle in prayer or relationships. For some people, a journal might be a series of written reflections on Scripture verses, song lyrics or poetry that have touched our hearts; for others it might be a compilation of pictures, doodled diagrams with a few words here and there, or collages copied and reduced in size so they fit. Whatever shape the journal takes, whether a simple, spiral-bound notebook, a scrapbook bulging with special bits and pieces, or a series of reflections in a protected computer file, one thing is paramount: that the journal holds the story of our walk with God in the valleys and on the hilltops of life, and, just as importantly, along the paths of daily routine with their inevitable potholes, curves and cul-de-sacs.

Why is keeping a spiritual journal such an important aid to spiritual growth? First, a journal provides us with a safe place in which to vent feelings, to write our own psalms and poetry without any fear of critical eyes, to speak to God as we write, and to listen to God as we reflect. Second, we know from our reading of Scripture that it is easy for human beings to forget the grace of God towards them and to 'follow other gods' (Deuteronomy 6.14). The Israelites, who had been awed by God's acts in liberating them from Egypt, soon forgot both God's power and provision. We are no different. We may think that we won't forget the ways God touches us, but, unless we consciously reflect and record those moments of grace, we risk them slipping beneath the surface of our awareness. Keeping a spiritual journal helps us savour God's activity in our lives, helps us learn more about our own functioning and foibles, and, in times of struggle or despair, helps us remember God's faithfulness, reminding us that God is with us, whatever we are experiencing.

📖 *Scripture for referencing and for prayer:*

When God finished speaking with Moses on Mount Sinai, he gave him the tablets of the covenant, tablets of stone, written with the finger of God. (Exodu 31.18)

Extension exercise and suggested reading:

⚗ Choose a favourite, short passage of Scripture or other spiritual reading, song or hymn. Spend 10–15 minutes reading it slowly, and then begin to record some of your thoughts and feelings. Try different ways of making your thoughts and feelings visible on the page. For example:

- make a diagram or do some doodling that fits with what you are discovering
- write out the short passage or key words using coloured crayons or felt tips
- find a picture or symbol that connects with what you have been reading
- make up your own psalm of praise, lament or thanksgiving.

☺☺ If it would help, talk over what you have discovered with a trusted friend or spiritual director.

⚗ Read: Jane Goodall with Phillip Berman, *Reason for Hope – A Spiritual Journey*, Melbourne: Warner Books, 1999.
Pope John XXIII, *Journal of a Soul*, New York: Image Books, 1980 (or other versions). Or
Mother Teresa, *Come, Be My Light*, Brian Kolodiejchuk (ed.), New York: Double-day Religious, 2007.

L&F 2.10 Learning to lament

particularly the loss of innocents as in Dunblane and Beslan
come together to share their outrage and grief. They may
provide a context in which the mystery of suffering and the
of 'why' can be articulated through liturgies that might,
holding place in the midst of overwhelming despair and
about corporate liturgical life in the wake of Dunblane, Paul
Bradbury says, 'We have lost a critical ability in our language of faith expression to
articulate anything of integrity and truth in the context of suffering and tragedy.'[11]

Lament as a spiritual practice has all but disappeared from Christian liturgy and
personal prayer, yet it remains available to us if we would only turn to the Scriptures
and recognize the robust nature of the covenant relationship which the Hebrew
people had with God. Here we will find lament – the 'crying out' of the people
– and the 'saving response' of God woven through the Old Testament, and explicitly
explored in the book of Lamentations. But it is in the Psalms that we best see how to
share honestly our pain and confusion, our disappointment or real anger with God.
Jesus faced his pain at Gethsemane and, when no other words could adequately
express his anguish on the cross, cried out, using the words of Psalm 22, 'My God,
my God, why have you forsaken me?'

✦ Being authentic in our life and in our faith, includes reclaiming the practice of
lament. Because Jesus chose to convey the truth of his felt experience of God's
absence, we can trust that God – in Jesus – knows the depths of human misery, no
matter how raw or unsavoury that reality might be. Bradbury writes, 'biblical lament
provides a form that ensures the pain can be managed, it can be laid out, re-examined
and contained in such a way that the possibility of healing emerges ... all within the
context of a relationship with God [thus] the lament is not a formless cry of despair
but an expression of faith'.[12] He helpfully offers a pattern for lament which can be
used in an existing liturgy, or as a separate focus, to enable people to express their
own sense of disorientation or to cry out in solidarity with others and, in doing so,
to access the indefinable and real shift from plea to praise:

---

11 Paul Bradbury, *Sowing in Tears: How to Lament in a Church of Praise*, Cambridge: Grove,
2007, p. 3.
12 Ibid, pp. 8–9.

Opening hymn/song	Addressing God.
Teaching on lament	This aspect will lessen as a group/person becomes familiar with lament.
Space for lament	Complaint (details the difficulties and pain of the situation).
	Petition (speaks requests, couched in bold, direct language).
	Motivation (gives reasons for God to act – God's character, justice, etc.).
Silence	Space for a movement from pain to emerging hope.
Praise	Assurance of being heard (trusting the relationship we have with God).
Vow of commitment	We promise to keep our part of the covenant.
Doxology	A reassertion of our relationship with a God who hears and responds. [13]

📖 *Scripture for referencing and for prayer:*

Psalms 13, 22, 44 and 88; and the book of Lamentations.

Extension exercise and reading:

⚜ Take note of the use (or lack of use) of the Psalms in services you attend. Talk to God and to others in your church about how this might be changed – gracefully!

⚜ Read Paul Bradbury, *Sowing in Tears: How to Lament in a Church of Praise,* Cambridge: Grove, 2007. Or
Walter Brueggemann, *The Message of the Psalms,* Minneapolis: Augsberg, 1984.

---

13 Ibid, p. 21 with added notes from pp. 22, 24–5.

L&F 2.11 Making – personal creativity

Mention the word 'creativity' and people respond – 'Oh no, not me, I can't ...' Somehow the word 'creativity' has become synonymous with fine art, or exemplary public performance, rather than saying something about who we are in God. Creativity is not simply *a gift* from our Creator, it is *at the core of who we are meant to be*, as bearers of God's image in our community. God's creative energy *is* at work in artists, but also in the author of a recipe book on a hundred ways to cook mince, or in the mum on a tight budget making a fancy-dress costume for her child, or the grandfather making gifts for grandchildren as birthdays come around.

🕯 How does creativity move in and through your life? Where are you the most creative?

We can be creative in the midst of daily life by the way we manage resources, build up relationships, solve problems, find a path through difficult circumstances, or commit ourselves to working alongside others. We can invite God to inspire our ideas as we express our creativity through interior design, gardening, and a whole host of crafts such as quilting, woodturning, etc. But we can also be creative *in our spiritual life* for we are invited to bring the fullness of who we are into our relationship with God. To do this, we can begin by trying some simple creative activities to help us deepen our sense of who God is, and who we are in God. For example:

Collage: in its simplest form, collage is a contemplative activity which involves pasting pictures, words, letters or colours cut out from old magazines on to a sheet of paper in response to our reflection on such topics as: where we are on our journey of faith, what we are struggling with, a favourite Scripture verse, a crossroads in our lives, or something relevant to a particular retreat theme or focus. What often happens is that this activity provides an avenue for the Spirit of God to touch us as we take the time to sit with ideas, colours, shapes and images and arrange them on the page.

Spiritual journey in a shoebox: this exercise also involves gathering pictures, etc. from old magazines or cards, or our own drawings, but this time there is a different focus. The visible outside of the shoebox represents those parts of our lives that others see and the things in the outer world which give us joy, hope, love and a sense of connection. The interior of the shoebox represents those parts of our lives that we keep to ourselves, hidden from most people and maybe even from God. We can use the cut out shapes, etc. to cover the outside and the inside, but we can also place in the box items to help express something of our interior life: what we're quietly hoping for or nervous about; the habits we want to eradicate, or the love we desperately long to find. It's not hard to see how, if we invite God to be part of this process, we will discover more of who we are and will gradually be able to let the Holy Spirit of God soothe the sensitive places in our lives, to bring light and peace.

Making prayer beads: these can be a simple tool to focus prayer and develop interior stillness. Often such aids are available at cathedral shops or via the internet, but making a set is not difficult. The King Of Peace Episcopal Church website, http://www.kingofpeace.org/prayerbeads.htm, not only gives clear instructions on how to make prayer beads, but also gives suggestions on how to use these beads as an aid to contemplative prayer. We can use any combination of our favourite prayers such as The Lord's Prayer, the Jesus Prayer, a simple 'thank you God for ...', or a more complex, 'Holy God, true and trustworthy, hold [name] this loved one in your heart.' We start at the cross and gradually pray our way around the beads, until we return to the cross and our closing prayer. One of the key benefits of using prayer beads is that it slows us down and helps us to pay total attention with mind, body and spirit as we focus on those who need our prayers.

Extension exercise and reading:

✤ Try making your own prayer beads, or read Sybil McBeth, *Praying in Color,* Orleans MA: Paraclete Press, 2007, a book which explores colour and contemplation.

L&F 2.12 Making – communal creativity

In 2009, television covered the funeral of Sir Howard Morrison, a Maori New Zealander who had entertained Kiwis and many other people around the world for over 50 years. What was especially moving was the deeply communal nature of the *tangi* (mourning ritual). Those who loved him – scores of close family and *whanau* (extended family) gathered in Rotorua, lived together on the *marae* (gathering place), and welcomed and fed over 8,000 people – Maori and non-Maori – who came to pay their respects. For five days people shared their creativity with songs, storytelling and music in both grief and celebration. The poor and the powerful, the old and the young waited, laughed, cried and ate together – and all were held in *aroha*, the deepest respect and love.

☖ Reflect on your own experience of being in community – where, when, why and how?

We are all meant to live as part of a rich and loving community rather than in the desperate, enforced isolation that many people, especially the elderly or the mentally unwell, endure today. When family and friends are far away, when people are sidelined socially, or when immigrants seek a new start, the church surely has an opportunity and a responsibility to model loving community – to be a place of welcome, fun, sharing and laughter, as well as a place of spiritual nurture for the whole of life. Even for people passing through our churches and our neighbourhoods, the chance to be part of something in a creative way provides a powerful sense of connection; for example visitors to Ely Cathedral are invited to add a prayer thread to a symbolic eel net already carrying pieces of coloured wool to represent all the people who have prayed in that ancient place. On the other side of the world, visitors to Wellington Cathedral are encouraged to add their unique stitches to an embroidery depicting a labyrinth, symbol of journey.

A simple way to begin to build community is to make something together. Corporate creativity has a special quality to it because it enables us to be both learners and teachers, both givers and receivers. It helps the weak to be strengthened, and those on the edges to be included, as a project is brought to completion. This 'making something together' can be on a large scale, such as building a new home over a few weeks as Habitat for Humanity manages in a number of places around the world (see www.habitat.org). Frequently, though, communal creativity occurs on a smaller scale – quilting circles, gardening makeover groups, catering or fund-raising teams – often with the common aim of helping others, of making a difference. Jesus promised that 'where two or three are gathered in my name, I am there among them' (Matthew 18:20).

Where a small number of faithful people humbly gather to listen to the Spirit, God will show us how to respond to a need in our community or sphere of influence. A creative way forward can emerge from our combined wisdom, experience and connections, which God can use to help those on the margins.

When we welcome God into the centre of our shared activity, however modest it may be, when we honour God as Creator of a new depth of community, we become co-creators with our God, as well as with each other. This adventure may be filled with trial and error, but it will also be filled with the laughter and love of God for us all.

📖 *Scripture for prayer and meditation:*

Luke 5.1–11 – the calling of the disciples.
1 Corinthians 12.12–26 – Paul's teaching on the Body of Christ.

Extension exercise:

⁂ Explore what part communal creativity plays in the life of your church, and in the wider community.

⁂ Consider starting a community vegetable garden. Gather the good gardeners you know and pray together about how this initiative might find expression in your neighbourhood.

L&F 2.13 Moving – meditative walking

Meditative walking may be counter-cultural – at odds with the normal rush and bustle of modern life – but it does connect us with the pace of Jesus and his disciples as they walked the hills and towns of Palestine, listening, talking, asking questions, wondering and watching. Just as they did, we can walk and reflect, and draw closer to the One who was human *and* God with them, God with us.

Meditative walking is distinctive because it is clearly S-L-O-W. There is no sense of pushing ourselves to our bodies' limits or trying to record a 'personal best'. The slower pace allows us to be open to the wonder of the environment around us, and alert to God reaching out to us through the diversity of rural or city life. In addition, meditative walking has these features:

- it is purposeful, focusing on our relationship with God, rather than on other people, the time or our stamina; our intention is simply to be with God and to let God's Spirit move within us
- our minds are not playing with a multiplicity of ideas and possibilities or regrets; but are instead focused on something that keeps us connected to God – a word of Scripture, a prayer, a hymn or melody, or even a troubling personal issue if it needs prayer
- the rhythm of our walking and our breathing synchronize with the rhythm of the words we are mulling over with the Spirit's guidance: an example of integration of body, mind and spirit
- we do not walk alone, we walk with Jesus, as an invisible companion beside us, within us
- it can be a personal, even solitary, activity done anywhere, any time, such as walking a labyrinth, or
- it can be done in a group as part of a meditative walking retreat in which silence is maintained while walking, and reflection and group prayer take place at the prayer-posts along the way
- it can be adapted for those with mobility issues, for example people can use a mobility scooter or walking frame or stick if needed.

An ancient spiritual practice being reclaimed today is the walking of a labyrinth, a continuous pathway such as the one illustrated below, based on the labyrinth at Chartres Cathedral, which many people walked in the Middle Ages when they were unable to journey to Jerusalem. Nowadays the labyrinth helps us to reflect on our lives, our inner landscape, and our journey with God. Walking with a receptive mind, we can discover our feelings in response to the direction of the pathway and its proximity to the *centre*, and what that symbolizes for us. Unlike a maze, Christian labyrinths have no dead ends, and so we cannot get lost. The pathway steadily leads us towards the centre where time can be taken for prayer and reflection before retracing our steps. Labyrinths are accessible for people who cannot walk long distances and can be made in all sorts of materials – set in a stone pavement, mowed in grass, laid out on large pieces of fabric, chalked onto a floor, or even printed on an A4 piece of paper, so we can use a single finger to trace the pattern.

📖 *Scripture for referencing and for prayer:*

Luke 24.13–35 'The walk to Emmaus', or John 1.35–39 'Come and see'.

Extension exercise and reading:

⁂ Pilgrims still walk to places like Holy Island, Lindisfarne (see http://www.northerncross.co.uk/ for information about annual Easter pilgrimages); or to Santiago de Compostela in northern Spain where St James is buried (see http://www.santiago-compostela.net/ for information about the Camino (road) to Santiago de Compostela, accommodation, etc.).

⁂ Read the story of someone's modern pilgrimage, such as:
Joyce Rupp, *Walk in a Relaxed Manner: Life Lessons from the Camino*, Maryknoll, NY: Orbis, 2005.
Paul Hawker, *Soul Quest: A Spiritual Odyssey through 40 Days and 40 Nights of Mountain Solitude*, Kelowna, Canada: Wood Lake, 2007.

⁂ To find out about the labyrinth at Norwich Cathedral, and ways to walk it. Visit:
http://www.cathedral.org.uk/visitorinfo/the-labyrinth--the-labyrinth.aspx.

L&F 2.14 Moving – including your body in your prayer

We think nothing of using our mind as we reflect on the needs of those for whom we intercede; we may use our imagination as we pray with Scripture, entering into the reality of the Gospels. How often, though, do we invite our bodies not only to participate in our prayer, but also to enrich our life with God.

Scripture reminds us that our bodies are a temple of the Holy Spirit (1 Corinthians 6.19). By actively involving our body in our prayer, we are practising bringing the whole self before God.

Sometimes we may not have *the words* to give shape to the complexity of how we may be feeling; expressing ourselves *physically* provides a safe and private emotional outlet, and helps us to be honest with our loving God. What would it be like if, as we were reading a Scripture passage that talked of struggle, we locked our hands and *pulled*, one against the other? Or, if we were praying about a loss, wringing our hands in grief or shaking our fists in the air, to express our rage? Or, as we read a psalm of praise, we begin to dance, letting our bodies give fuller expression to our love and gratitude.

How do you respond to the idea of letting your body participate in your prayer?

There are two other situations when consciously involving our bodies in prayer is helpful:

- If we are ageing and our movement or speech is limited, we can still use our hands – even one hand and what remains of our mobility – to praise and honour God, and to express our pleas for strength and grace.
- For those who find it very hard to sit still for prayer, it can be a relief to go for a power walk with God, striding out to the rhythm of a favourite song or hymn; or, whether we swim lengths at the local pool or methodically knead dough for baking, we can let a breath prayer from Scripture or song, flow through our minds.

We are made for loving connection with God our Creator. Letting our bodies participate in this love nourishes us and helps us feel the reality of that connection more intimately.

Ancient hymn for prayer and walking meditation:

God be in my head,
  And in my understanding;
God be in my eyes,
  And in my looking;
God be in my mouth,
  And in my speaking;
God be in my heart,
  And in my thinking;
God be at my end,
  And at my departing.
(Pynson's Horae, 1574)

Extension exercises:

✤ Move with music – choose something that fits your mood such as a melody that takes you to a point of thanksgiving, a jig to get you energized, a sensuous tango to express your passion, or a lament that helps you communicate your pain.

✤ Change your posture – sit, or stand, with arms stretched high or wide; lie prostrate on the floor, or curl up as a child might. Let your words, thoughts and posture harmonize as you pray.

✤ If you're brave, look at yourself in a mirror unclothed. Take a long, loving look at your physical reality. Gently let your hands trace the patterns of your form from top to toe – or as much as you can reach! Talk to God about any aspect of your body's well-being which needs attention, then take a warm shower, imagining yourself blessed by God's love.

L&F 2.15 Music – singing and playing our way to God

Music has the capacity to transport us to places we cannot reach in any other way, the ability to touch our emotions, to soothe or excite us. While we may have our favourites, shaped by our culture and age and preferences, over the millennia the songs of the faithful have served to bring people to a sense of connection with God. In a media-full contemporary world, music remains an integral part of our spiritual formation, as lyrics, melodies and different styles speak to us about the mysteries of God and our life in Christ.

🕯 How has music been part of your faith journey?

Musical appreciation is subjective; what might move one person, may not appeal to another. But the paradox is that sometimes the very style of music we least enjoy proves to be exactly what the Spirit of God uses to draw our attention!

See if any of the following have been instrumental in moving you closer to God:

Psalms – sung in King David's time and no reason to think that Jesus wouldn't have sung these – part of his life growing up and in adulthood.

Hymns – we have the capacity to retain hymns even into old age, even in minds affected by dementia.

Scripture in song – a recognized way of helping Scripture texts stay in our minds.

Gospel music – spirituals sung by slaves to lift them beyond the pain of the present into the hoped for future of a better life 'across the Jordan' – other combinations of indigenous music and Christian beliefs such as in Ladysmith Black Mambazo.

Organ Music – can often connect us with something of the majesty, awe and wonder of God.

Boys' choirs – whether traditional King's College, Cambridge, or the contemporary sound of Libera.

Requiem Mass – legacy of stirring music that lifts the spirit and expresses the depths of grief.

Gregorian and Taizé chants – gaining in popularity – sung in a range of languages; for most listeners the lyrics are secondary to the mood created by the repetition of the melody, which holds us in a prayerful place.

Rock band renditions of praise and worship songs – appealing to younger generations – Hillsong for example – or the songs of writers such as Graham Kendrick.

Celtic influence – music from Iona and Lindisfarne, shaped by the landscape and Celtic Christianity.

📖 *Scripture for referencing and for prayer:*

Make a joyful noise to the LORD, all the earth.
Worship the LORD with gladness;
come into his presence with singing. (Psalm 100.1–2)

OR

For there our captors asked us for songs,
and our tormentors asked for mirth, saying,
'Sing us one of the songs of Zion!'
How could we sing the LORD's song in a foreign land? (Psalm 137.3–4)

Extension exercises and reading:

⚜ Look back through the list above and find an artist or style which is not familiar but whose music is accessible, for example on CD or as a video-clip on YouTube.
OR download the music from 'Pray-as-you-go', a Jesuit website to help folk deepen their walk with God using Ignatian prayer with Scripture (see www. pray-as-you-go.org).

⚜ Listen to some of Hildegard of Bingen's music, for example: *11,000 Virgins: Feast of St Ursula*, CD recorded by Anonymous Four, Harmonia Mundi, # HMU 907200; *Heavenly Revelations*, CD recorded by Naxos, 8.550998. Released 1995, now available for purchase/download at www.naxos.com.

L&F 2.16 Praying with Scripture 1
Sacred reading/*lectio divina*

Lectio divina, or sacred reading, is a simple and ancient way of praying with Scripture. Through slow reading aloud of a small piece of Scripture, the process unfolds naturally, leading from a rational consideration of how these verses might connect with our current life, to a personal response in prayer and a gentle resting in the love of God – the beginnings of contemplation. *Lectio divina* emerged in the early history of the Church, finding its way into European monasticism through Cassian and St Benedict. Now it is being reclaimed by Christians throughout the world as another way of opening ourselves to the grace and growth available to us in Christ. The four elements of this rich practice are:

1 *Lectio*: *very* slow reading, preferably aloud, savouring the words as if they were a delicious morsel on our tongue, letting the 'honey' of God's word, drip gently into our soul.
2 *Meditatio*: from which we get the word 'meditation' – letting our mind engage with the words, making connections with our life and concerns, seeing what thoughts arise as we look at these words from all angles, alert for the richness of a new insight or the soothing of a familiar restatement of God's faithfulness.
3 *Oratio*: making our response to God with our *voice* – talking or singing or shouting; with our *bodies* through posture and movement; with our *hearts* as we let ourselves love God. The key is to be as honest as we can be in our 'conversation' with God.
4 *Contemplatio*: from which we get the word 'contemplation' – sitting in silence, resting in God, not striving to do anything or make anything 'spiritual' happen, just trusting that, in the depths of our being, God is at work, bringing healing and refreshment.

While the four elements of *lectio divina* are described as if the sequence were linear, in practice it is much more of a circle, so don't worry if you seem to be going back and forth a bit, particularly between *meditatio* and *oratio*, before sinking into the unconditional embrace of God in *contemplatio*. The most important thing is that we do actually spend some time in this final place of stillness. It can be really tempting to rush off as soon as we have done our reading, thinking and praying, but the richness is lost if we don't wait with God for a while, letting ourselves slow down long enough for the words and thoughts and prayers to take root in our innermost selves, where God welcomes them and us.

A final word on this practice – *lectio divina* nourishes us so we can, in turn, be there for others in loving service. Once we know ourselves renewed by God, once we have been close to God for the quiet time of *contemplatio*, we may like to explore a fifth element, *actio,* as a way of linking contemplation with action. We ask God to help us act in a way that enables the personal spiritual gifts of the text, to be expressed in our everyday world. Acting for justice, peace-making, may take place on a small, personal scale, in our community, or even globally: the Spirit will guide us, if we are willing.

What is your experience of praying with Scripture in this way?

Scripture for referencing and for prayer:

2 Timothy 3.16, and Ephesians 6.17.
Jesus says, 'I am the bread of life.' (John 6.35)
... it is well for the heart to be strengthened by grace ... (Hebrews 13.9b)

Extension exercise and reading:

Pray using a devotional Bible with contemporary text, arranged in a *lectio divina* format for daily use. Such a Bible is *The Message//REMIX Solo: An Uncommon Devotional*, Eugene Peterson, Jan Johnson, J.R. Briggs, and Katie Peckham, Colorado Springs, CO: Navpress, 2007.

L&F 2.17 Praying with Scripture 2
Imaginative prayer, entering a Gospel story as if you were there, then, or as if Jesus were here, now

Imaginative prayer helps us to enter more fully into the passage of Scripture we are reading, by using our mind's ability to form pictures or inner impressions and to 'play with' a range of ideas and possibilities.

We may be used to reading Scripture to learn more about Jesus and the story of God's relationship with people throughout history, but praying with the Scriptures using our imagination may be a new experience and, for some Christians, one that may feel a bit uncomfortable, even risky. However, if we are serious about getting closer to God, we can be assured that God will sanctify our imagination, using it as a powerful tool to help us grow closer to God and learn more about ourselves.

What is your history of using your imagination?
How has your imagination been part of your Christian journey to date?
Talk to God about your hopes or fears before reading on.

Prayerfully placing ourselves in a Gospel scene is a spiritual practice commonly associated with St Ignatius of Loyola, founder of the Jesuits. The process is simple and easy to do on our own:

- Choose a Gospel passage in which someone is meeting Jesus. Offer to God any concerns you may have about using your imagination. Ask the Holy Spirit to guide and protect you.
- Read through the passage two or three times until it is familiar.
- Using all your senses, let the Gospel passage gently unfold in your awareness – imagine you are in first-century Palestine, so you can see the people, hear the voices, taste ..., smell ..., touch ....
- Then put yourself into the Gospel passage – perhaps as an observer, or some-one helping another; perhaps near the action, even talking to Jesus. Let the story unfold, let the dialogue take shape, simply be present without striving to make anything happen.
- At the end of the prayer period, remain in silence with eyes closed for a couple of minutes.
- Spend some time reflecting on what has taken place. You may want to make a note in your journal and share something of what has happened – or not happened – with someone you trust.

Not everyone finds this easy, so do not worry if it does not seem to 'work' for you – some people, for example, are more likely to get an inner awareness of some sort, rather than 'see' places or people in clear detail. Whether or not you see or feel anything, God is touching your spirit, and will work good purposes out in your life.

📖 *Scripture for referencing and for prayer:*

Any Gospel passages in which Jesus interacts with people, for example the woman with the haemorrhage (Mark 5.25–34), or the call of the first disciples (Matthew 4.18–22).

Extension exercise and reading:

✤ A very powerful variation of using your imagination as you pray with Scripture is associated with St Augustine. In this practice, instead of imagining ourselves back in Jesus' time, we bring the Gospel passage *forward* to our own time and visualize a setting familiar to us today. For example, if you are praying with the annunciation to Mary (Luke 1.26–38) you might imagine this taking place in your kitchen or garden; the story of the lost coin (Luke 15.8–10) might be about a lost child or something else you hold close to your heart! Imagine meeting Jesus in your favourite cafe, instead of on a dusty far away road: this might well give your relationship with him a new sense of immediacy and intimacy.

✤ Explore *The Spiritual Exercises* of St Ignatius of Loyola. His material is widely available, but a very readable and helpful starting point is Margaret Silf, *Landmarks*, London: Darton, Longman and Todd, 1998, reprinted several times.

L&F 2.18 Praying using an art work as a starting point

'Rychard Dale Carpeder Made Thies Windovs by the Grac of God'

This ancient inscription above the complex leadlight windows in Little Moreton Hall in Congleton, Cheshire, UK (built in 1559), is a moving testimony to the creative partnership between human beings and God, and reminds us that, for generations, artists from all disciplines have consciously used their creative gifts, not just for their own glory, but to the glory of God. Just as cathedral stained-glass stories of their faith enabled people in the Middle Ages to find their way to God, so, in gathering places and galleries across the world today, countless examples of art provide us with access to the mysteries of God. Whether or not these works are overtly 'religious', if we take the time to look we can see signs of the Spirit illuminating artists' paintings or photographs with colour, light and shadow; their sculptures, bridges and buildings with form, strength and balance; their weavings or collages with patterns and surprises.

What work of art – old or modern – has touched your heart? Notice your feelings and thoughts as you recall your encounter with this example of human/divine creative partnership.

Our response to visual art of any type can be fleeting *or* lasting. Many of us have visited art galleries and been so overwhelmed by the sheer quantity of art displayed that we've left with a series of hazy images in our muddled brains! But occasionally, perhaps, we've been drawn to one painting and, however briefly, been taken into the scene before us, deeper into the painter's heart and hopefulness, deeper into our humanity and even into the nature of God's love. That is what happened to Henri Nouwen, author of many books on spiritual growth. In the hours he spent with Rembrandt's *The Return of the Prodigal Son* at The Hermitage in St Petersburg, Nouwen made space for the painting to reach into his soul. In subsequent reflection, he grappled with the different parts of himself which the painting revealed:

> I was prepared to accept that not only the younger son, but also the elder son would reveal to me an important aspect of my spiritual journey ... It was only gradually, ... painfully that I came to realize that my spiritual journey would never be complete as long as the father remained an outsider ... Rembrandt, who

showed me the Father in utmost vulnerability, made me come to the awareness that my final vocation is indeed to become like the Father and to live out his divine compassion in my daily life.[14]

We too can be nourished by all sorts of visual arts if we take the time to stop and look – really look – at a work of art to which we are drawn. One way of doing this is to use a process similar to that of *lectio divina*:

- We first take our time with the art work, 'reading' it slowly, spending time with its detail as we gaze at it with an open heart and mind.
- We let the art work spark off connections with our own circumstances, seeing what it might have to say about our relationship with ourselves, with others, with God.
- We respond to what the art work has shown us, talking to God about what we have discovered.
- We sit in silence with the art work, resting in God and being open for the cycle of reflection to begin again if the Spirit so moves.

 Take a visit to a city art gallery and sit with a painting on a biblical or religious theme. If you live too far away, visit a gallery via the internet! For example http://www.nationalgallery.org.uk.

Then pray with the scripture passage to which the painting relates and journal your response.

Extension exercise and reading:

 Read Fr Henri Nouwen, *The Return of the Prodigal*, New York: Doubleday, 1994.

 Watch Sr Wendy Beckett in conversation with Bill Moyers, especially Part 5, available on http://www.youtube.com/watch?v=cjFVRXjrjAE.

---

14 Henri Nouwen, *The Return of the Prodigal*, New York: Doubleday 1994, pp. 120–1.

L&F 2.19 Silence and solitude

Most of us live in a noisy world, 'surround-sound' no longer an advertising gimmick, but the harsh reality of contemporary life. Even a loud ticking clock can intrude into the space we want to hold open for God's goodness. Solitude too can be elusive – the television, internet chat rooms and social networking can fill our minds and mimic connection with people we may never meet. Paradoxically, even a life of good deeds can keep us too busy to be aware of God. Although we may long for silence and solitude, for most of us it does not come easily. When the noise around us stops, we may wonder, quite literally, what to do. We may find the silence evokes early feelings of disapproval, or rejection, even memories of punishment, which can catch the breath and revive difficult experiences from the past. In our culture, solitude is often equated with loneliness or loss – the empty chair and solitary meals when a loved one has died; the daily diminution of having no one to talk to when something has delighted or touched us.

🕯 What is your experience of silence or solitude – in your growing up, life today, prayer practice?

Why are silence and solitude so important to spiritual growth? In essence because they encourage us to come out of hiding so we may pay attention to God. As Elijah found when he escaped to the desert, silence and solitude enabled him to listen for the 'still, small voice' of God (1 Kings 19).

Instead of filling the space between God and us with a worry of words, we clear that space so God can reach out to us with the tenderness of a loving mother. Instead of having to keep up with those around us, or protect our position, we can just 'be' ourselves. By doing so, we engage in a different form of worship: we let go of our word-filled ego defences and, instead, choose to 'fast from words', accepting our poverty of heart, making room for God to work deeply in our spirit and psyche.

The call to solitude and interior silence, to quieting ourselves before God, can be hard at first. The slingshot wanderings of our busy minds initially intrude when we try to listen deeply to God. We can manage these distractions by:

- minimizing external interruptions (even if this means turning off the phone)
- having pen and paper handy so that anything 'important' which surfaces can be noted briefly
- keeping our eyes on a visual focus (for example a cross or icon) if we get distracted when our eyes close
- relaxing our body and slowing our breathing
- repeating a sacred word or phrase to which we can return whenever our mind wanders.

Silence and solitude increase our availability to God. We may not feel God's presence. We may even think that we are 'getting nothing done'. But the fact that we are 'turning up' to be with God is a gift of our heart to God's heart; a sign of our desire for our spirit to be informed and inflamed by God's spirit; an offering of who we are to all that God is, so we may be an expression of divine Love.

Keeping company with God is not a waste of time; it is contemplative prayer – simple and strong.

📖 *Scripture for referencing and for prayer:*

> I wait for the LORD, my soul waits, and in his word I hope;
> my soul waits for the Lord more than those who watch for the morning,
> more than those who watch for the morning. (Psalm 130.5–6)

OR

> Jesus rising early and going to a deserted place to pray. (Mark 1.35)

Exercise extension and reading:

※ Read Jim Borst, *Coming to God in the Stillness* (revised, illustrated edition), Stowmarket UK: Kevin Mayhew, 2004.

L&F 2.20 Using everyday symbols to aid spiritual growth

Christianity is packed with symbols: the cross, bread and wine to connect us to the Messiah who was to come in Christ; shield, foundation, stronghold to speak of God's strength; tongues of fire to represent the presence of Spirit; a potter and the clay to help us appreciate the firm, yet tender, touch with which God forms our lives and character. For some of us, these powerful symbols convey rich meaning shaped by the teaching and tradition of the Church and by our own experience.

🕯 Bring to mind your favourite faith symbols. How has your understanding or appreciation of these changed over the years?

In John 3.1–21, we read the story of Nicodemus who was told by Jesus that he must be 'born again'. We see a puzzled Nicodemus struggling to move away from a familiar, literal level of understanding. Meaning can be mined at different levels: literal, symbolic, spiritual, personal and communal. Any one of these may be helpful, but if, through prayer and reflection, we become aware of several levels of meaning, our spiritual journey can be enriched. Nicodemus had to make that leap in understanding before he could receive in himself the possibility of a new life in Jesus Christ and a new freedom to be moved by the mysterious perfection of the Spirit of God.

One of the most exciting things about our spiritual walk is that God not only uses Scripture or the natural world to make a connection with us through symbols, but encourages us to pay close attention to ordinary things as well. When something in the everyday world draws our attention, we can stop and contemplate it, letting it become a platform for a movement from a literal understanding of what we are seeing to a symbolic, spiritual, personal and communal understanding.

Take for example the ordinary mobile phone. At a literal level it is a means of communication between friends and family, but symbolically it might represent our availability, our fear of isolation, our own sense of importance, our need to be kept 'in the loop' socially, parents' longing to keep children safe from harm, and so on. If we take this a step further and wonder about the 'spiritual' level, we might recognize that we pay more attention to our friends than to God who is waiting for us to 'ring or text home'. Personal and communal meanings will also emerge as we ask ourselves questions like 'How does the way I use my phone affect my key relationships?'

A literal mobile phone is commonplace, but if we work with it as a symbol it can improve our communication in a deeper way – with ourselves and with our God! If we are open to the ordinary becoming extraordinary through the grace of God and the guidance of the Spirit, our whole lives can be transformed as we deepen our understanding of who God is calling us to be.

Scripture for prayer and reflection:

Nicodemus in John 3.1–21, and the parable of the sower and the seed in Luke 8.4–8, 11–15.

Extension exercises and reading:

✤ Go out into a garden or park and look closely at a *rose bush*. Spend some time with this rose bush and notice what thoughts come to you. Ask God to help you see what it might have to say to you about your life and circumstances.

✤ Now do the same thing, but this time go and look at a *door*. Any door will do. Again, spend time looking closely at this door with your mind attentive to any thoughts that arise and your body aware of any physical changes which might signal a stirring of emotion. When you are ready, make some notes about the different levels of meaning you've noticed: literal, symbolic, spiritual, personal and communal.

✤ Working with the symbols in our dreams can also help our spiritual growth. For a thorough treatment of dreams and dreamwork methods, read Louis M. Savary, Patricia H. Berne and Strephon Kaplan Williams, *Dreams and Spiritual Growth: A Judeo-Christian Approach to Dreamwork*, New York: Paulist Press, 1984.

Part 3
'Snacks'– short retreat times with a range of themes

We know that it is unwise to fill our stomachs with junk food; similarly it is spiritually unhealthy to fill our minds with 'what does not satisfy', as the prophet Isaiah writes:

> Ho, everyone who thirsts, come to the waters;
> and you that have no money, come, buy and eat!
> Come, buy wine and milk
> without money and without price.
> Why do you spend your money for that which is not bread,
> and your labour for that which does not satisfy?
> Listen carefully to me, and eat what is good,
> and delight yourselves in rich food. (Isaiah 55.1–2)

The invitation is clear: for each and every person to take deeply into ourselves the priceless riches of grace that God holds out to us in Jesus Christ. Like a child learning to eat solid food, we need to begin this adventure into the depths and heights of God gently, starting with short retreat times and then, as we get used to silence, solitude and waiting upon God, we can more confidently put more time at God's disposal. If we develop even the simplest set of spiritual practices, and incorporate them into our daily routines, this will build up in us that trust in Jesus, that openness to the prompting of the Holy Spirit, which will form solid ground on which to stand, whenever we have to face life's challenges.

'You give them something to eat' was the challenging response of Jesus when his disciples pointed out to him that the crowds were getting hungry and evening was approaching. As you set about the task of using these resources to introduce people to the nourishment inherent in contemplative spirituality, it's helpful to 'start small', helping them gradually build up a quality of stillness and attentiveness which can help them become attuned to the presence of God in the midst of life.

Even though these 'snack' retreats are short, varying from an hour to three hours in length, they still require solid, prayerful preparation, so each is arranged in the following sections:

- an indication of who this particular 'snack' would suit or how it might be introduced
- the leader's preparation, which you will notice is quite detailed because it is designed for those with little experience of leading retreats. If you already have a

lot of experience, much of this preparation will be second nature to you and won't take long at all.

- a description of a prayer focus to begin the retreat
- some details of the gathering time – particularly if there is anything that needs special attention
- an opening prayer
- leader's input
- group exercise leading into silent personal reflection
- concluding comments
- closing prayer
- reflection sheet for retreatants to use and/or to take home with their other 'loaves and fishes' (L&F resource sheets).

Once you're familiar with all the resource sheets, you can use them in any combination in other retreats you may facilitate. Just as competent cooks can 'stretch' ingredients if extra people suddenly 'turn up', so you can turn 'snacks' into 'a packed lunch' or a 'light meal' by introducing a new spiritual practice, adding time for prayer with Scripture, or offering a guided meditation.

The main thing to remember is that these 'snacks' are to be ENJOYED by everyone, including YOU!

Snack 3.1 God is both present and gift

Suitable for any group – as a stand-alone 20–30 minute exercise or as part of a longer gathering.

Leader's preparation:

- read L&F resource sheet '2.4 Beginnings – practising the presence of God'
- cut out pictures of everyday activities and put one in an envelope for each retreatant, for example walking the dog, vacuuming, fixing a drain, watching TV, running a race, shopping, etc.
- make three large notices (see under *Focus* below) and get a suitable plain cloth for your central focal point
- have enough copies of the resource sheet L&F 2.4 and the reflection sheet for each person
- ideally, read Brother Lawrence's *Practising the Presence of God.*

Focus:

Place a cloth on the floor or low table in the centre of the gathering space. On it put the three large colourful notices (and a lit candle if you wish):

PAST   PRESENT   FUTURE

Gathering:

Welcome those present and ensure everyone is comfortable, knows each other's first name, has pen and paper handy, knows what the topic is for this retreat time, and when the session is due to finish. Make sure that all realize that part of the time – ten minutes – will be spent in silence – but that there will be time for brief, optional sharing before they leave or move on to other elements of the meeting.

Give each person a sealed envelope in which is a picture of a simple activity. Ask them not to open it!

Opening prayer:

We begin with some silence so our busy minds can settle into God's peace.

Allow at least a full minute's silence before turning over the PAST and FUTURE signs, leaving only the PRESENT sign visible – give people a few moments to reflect on this action and then pray:

God of the present moment, giver of mind and memory,
teach us to turn our attention towards you, with love, in all that we do.

Invite participants to open their envelopes and, in turn, to hold up the picture, describe it briefly and then place it on the central cloth.

May we be re-minded of your ongoing loving presence
in the midst of the routines of our lives.
Help us to become more aware that you are with us always.
Through Jesus Christ. Amen.

Leader's input:

When we fall in love, we think about the beloved all the time, sometimes distracted and daydreaming! Although the beloved one may be far away, all we want to do is imagine the person and, by doing so, bring the reality of his or her presence to us in a tangible way.

We can do the same with God. Although we might have to start by consciously and intentionally bringing God to mind from time to time during our day, as this holy habit grows we will find ourselves naturally turning to God more and more, enhancing our awareness of God's presence with us always, whether or not we can *feel* that.

✣ *As a way of helping the retreatants to get in touch with their own sense of God's presence in the day, ask them to note their responses to the first set of questions on the reflection sheet:*

Where do you think God is –
  when you are praying?
  when you are at church in a worship service, etc.?

We might know in our heads that the 'right answer' is that God is present in all of the above situations, but the truth for many of us is that it doesn't seem that way. We are often so caught up in the emotional or intellectual or survival demands of the moment that we either don't notice or forget to include the One who made us and knows us profoundly. Much of life today is lived at a frenetic pace, but if we are attentive to the Spirit's leading, if we truly want to turn to God, then even in the midst of our busy lives we can practise what Brother Lawrence called the 'interior glance'. It takes only a second to bring God to mind in love as we move through our day, *whatever we are doing.*

We don't have to invite God to be present, for God is already present in and among us as we bear God's image in the world. God is already present in and through the creation, in all acts of love and movements towards the good and the just, towards peace and wholeness.

Group exercise:

✤ We are going to begin *'practising the presence of God'* now, intentionally turning our minds towards God, acknowledging God's presence here with us. You may want to get up and walk around outside, or you may prefer just to sit quietly. Whichever you choose, just gently and lovingly turn your thoughts to God, or to Jesus if you prefer, for the next ten minutes. Don't struggle or strive and don't be hard on yourself if you get distracted. Simply turn back to God, peacefully, making an 'interior glance' in God's direction.

☺☺ *When a full ten minutes has passed (don't be tempted to shorten it!), provide for the group:*

- a few minutes of personal reflection time
- a few minutes to talk a little about this exercise with one other person
- a chance for the whole group to raise any questions or comment about the experience.

Concluding comments:

Although this may seem an odd thing to be doing at first, if we persevere and begin to do more and more of our daily tasks aware of God's presence and 'for the love of God', somehow our attitudes soften, we slow down, we approach the work we do for others with a new awareness of the worth of each person and the value of the contribution we each can make to the lives of those around us. No task is menial: whether we are making the children's lunches, doing a spreadsheet on the laptop, washing the car, writing a sermon, listening to a friend. As Mother Teresa taught:

> To show great love for God and our neighbour we need not do great things. It is how much love we put in the doing that makes our offering Something Beautiful for God.[15]

Closing prayer:

Help us O Guiding Spirit to turn our minds towards God more and more each day.
Help us O Loving Jesus to turn our hearts towards God in everything we do,
so that we may go through each day lovingly, and grace-fully. Amen.

---

15 Mother Teresa of Calcutta, *A Gift for God*, London: Collins, 1975, p. 77.

God is both present and gift – reflection sheet

Where do you think God is – when you are praying? when you are at church in a worship service? when you have a performance review at work? while you are walking slowly round the supermarket with an ageing neighbour? when you pick the children up from day-care, and you're all tired and grumpy? when you've just received bad news?	Spend some time with God, just thinking back over the last week or two. Ask the Holy Spirit to bring to mind a time when you were particularly aware of God's presence, such as a felt sense of the peace or love of God, or when something 'fell into place' or your prayers were answered, or you felt a new sense of connection to someone you'd struggled with, or a new door opened to you … What was the gift in that present moment?
Jean Vanier, founder of l'Arche communities for people with disabilities, says: 'God loves us today … God does not live in the past or in the future but in the "now" of the present moment. God sees me in my present reality, as I am in each present moment.' *Befriending the Stranger,* London: Darton, Longman and Todd, 2005, p. 32.	## Alpha and Omega We know that Jesus Christ is the same yesterday and today and forever. *Hebrews 13.8* Why do you think it is important to recognize that God wants to communicate with us in the midst of our present life?

God is both present and gift – spend some time reflecting on this play on words.

You may like to do some drawing or write a poem or prayer of your own.

Snack 3.2 Breathing with the Spirit

Suitable for any group – as a stand-alone 30–45-minute exercise or as part of a longer gathering.

Leader's preparation:

- pray with the post-resurrection appearance of Jesus to his disciples: John 20.19–22
- read L&F resource sheets '2.3 Beginnings – breath prayer' and '2.20 Using every-day symbols to aid spiritual growth'
- gather several balloons, some small hand-mirrors, an asthma inhaler or nebulizer, bubble-making items and any pictures you can find that represent some aspect of breath or breathing, for example inflated hot-air balloons, blowing out a candle, people blowing bubbles in the air (enlarge pictures to A4 size).

Focus:

A circular cloth – in the centre put a series of boxes, of different sizes, on which are placed the mirrors. The pictures are spaced evenly around the boxes. (If you wish, use several small tea-light candles too.)

Gathering:

Welcome, as in 'Snack 3.1'. Check that no one has any problems with asthma or other respiratory conditions.

Opening prayer:

Invite those present to spend a few minutes in silence, just being aware of their breathing and letting their respiration rate slow as they settle from the busyness of the day.

O God, giver of breath and life, inspire us now as we spend this time together.
May your Holy Spirit move among and within us,
drawing us gently towards your Welcome,
which is eternal. Amen.

Leader's input and discussion questions:

We all know that breath is essential to life, but it may come as a surprise to realize that the word 'spirituality' is derived from the Latin word *'spirare'* to breathe. Our spirituality is at the centre of who we are, and today we are going to focus on *'breath*

a spiritual practice that can help us deepen our connection with God, wher-
⌣ are, and at any time we choose.

Mirrors are interesting things *(ask people to pick up the small mirrors)* – we can
see ourselves in them of course – and in the way of human nature we often criticize
our appearance – but mirrors had another use before the days of hospitalization
and respirators. *(Ask if anyone knows what that use was.)* Mirrors were held to the
nostrils of a person thought to have died to check if they were still alive.

*Ask those with the mirrors to breathe on them and to show the others the misting
of their breath on the mirror.*

Mirrors – and really cold weather – enable us to *see* our breath – we are clearly
physically alive. But how do we know we are alive spiritually? What can be seen of
our life with God?

*Answers may include fruits of the Spirit, love for neighbour, capacity to transcend
tragedy, solid prayer life, self acceptance ...*

For some people *breathing* is a struggle. For others the *spiritual life* is a struggle.
But it's not meant to be like that. Look at the pictures – what can they tell us/what
do they symbolize about life with the Spirit of God?

*Hot-air balloons – silence and mystery – fun and risk – moves at the bidding of the
wind/spirit/'ruach' in Hebrew*
    *Blowing out a candle – celebration of life, endings and beginnings, gathering of
community, growth*
    Blowing bubbles – forgiveness and cleansing, joy and fun, fragility and beauty

I wonder what it was like when Jesus 'breathed on his disciples'?

Read the passage from John 20.19–22.

In some cultures the blending of breath is a profound act of connection, symbol-
izing a sharing of the very essence of life itself. In New Zealand, Maori culture has
in its tradition of welcome, the practice of the *hongi*, not a 'rubbing of noses' as
often described, but an act of intimacy and trust as well as a sign of goodwill and
the hope of friendship. Breath is shared, noses are pressed, foreheads often touch
each other, hands are clasped and our common humanity is acknowledged. In this
present moment two people are profoundly connected.

The L&F resource sheet '2.3 Beginnings – breath prayer' introduces a practice
that helps maintain this sort of connection between us and God anywhere, at any
time, especially when we are going about routine chores or parts of our day.

Refer to the key elements of the '2.3 Beginnings – breath prayer' resource.

As a starting point with breath prayer, we can use Jesus' greeting to his disciples, 'Peace be with you' – imagine Jesus saying that to you …

Group exercise:

✤ Before trying to weave the breath prayer into an activity, spend a few minutes first, letting your own breathing pattern* and the prayer you've chosen, find their own natural connection. Then add your chosen prayer and let the words melt into the rhythm of your breathing for the next few minutes. Once you feel comfortable with the blend of words and breathing, get up and spend a few minutes in your chosen activity, letting yourself enjoy the sensation of breathing your prayer as you jog or walk or peel the potatoes!
(*If you have asthma or any other respiratory condition which makes your breathing potentially problematic, *only* use breath prayer when you are well and your condition stable.)

Concluding comments:

It may feel a bit strange or contrived when you first begin, but as you practise this spiritual discipline, you will be able to incorporate it more naturally into your day, whether you are walking the dog or doing the photocopying at work!
If we work in harmony with the Spirit, listening and obeying, accepting our fragility and our beauty, we are embarking on a journey which will blend our lives uniquely with God's life.

Closing prayer:

God you are closer than our breathing,
woven into every cell,
lighting all our being.
As we open ourselves to your Spirit,
may we welcome your Breath of Life,
flowing in and through us.
May your peace and wisdom inform our actions and warm our inner life.
May others come to see in us something of your boundless love.
We pray this in the name of Jesus Christ, our Lord.
Amen.

Breathing with the Spirit – reflection sheet

Consider this photo[16] of the singer Russell Watson participating in a *hongi* in New Zealand several years ago.

What is your response?
How might you feel about being invited to share the 'breath of life' with someone in this way?

Spend some time reflecting on what grace or gift you need from God. Then take a balloon, write on it your petition, inflate it, and prayerfully, hopefully, release it to the wind and to the Spirit's action in your life.

If you are carrying any guilt or want to talk to God about anything that you regret, spend some time doing that now.

Then, take some of the bubble mixture and go outside and let your breath gently send the bubbles heavenward.

As you watch the bubbles float and eventually disappear, let the Holy Spirit of God touch you deeply, assuring you of God's love and giving you inner peace.

Using imaginative prayer (see 'L&F resource sheet 2.17') read John 20.19–22 slowly several times until you feel familiar with the story.

Then, using your imagination, begin to get a sense of what the scene was like, the sights and sounds, the smells around you …

Picture yourself as one of the disciples gathered there when Jesus makes his sudden appearance …

What happens for you as Jesus says, 'Peace be with you'?

What happens as Jesus turns towards each disciple, to breathe on them …

What happens as Jesus turns towards you?

---

16 Picture by Mark Dwyer, *Taranaki Daily News*. Reproduced permission of Fairfax Media © 2009 Fairfax New Zealand Limited.

Reproduced by permission   © Sue Pickering 2010

Snack 3.3 How's the day been – *really?*

In this 'snack' retreat we're going to introduce a simplified practice of the Examen suitable for a family, including young children. However, as a stand-alone 15–30-minute exercise or as a closing ritual, this practice lends itself to any group you are working with, such as the elderly, a mixed-age house group, teens or a group of ordinands. Details of a more comprehensive approach for adults are given in L&F resource sheet 2.7. A reflection sheet is also provided for people to take home. Or you can incorporate some of the suggestions as part of the discussion, if time permits.

Leader's preparation:

- read L&F resource sheet '2.7 Examen – a simple review of the day'
- ideally, spend some weeks yourself doing the Examen on a regular basis (daily or weekly), adapting it to your context and getting a 'feel' for the rhythm and benefits
- gather some objects to represent a range of end-of-the-day family routines, such as toothpaste and toothbrush, a story book, a teddy bear, a lamp or night-light, a blanket, a Bible, a CD or MP3 player, a glass of water; and a large picture of a *night* scene – choose one that relates to a rural or city evening, depending on your situation
- select some music with a 'close of day' theme, for example Secret Garden's 'Nocturne' (*Songs from a Secret Garden*, Polygram, 1996, 528 230-2) or Taizé's 'Within our darkest night' (*O Lord Hear My Prayer: The Songs of Taizé*, Kingsway, 1994, KMCD 736)
- print off on card in a large font a Scripture verse relevant to the 'close of day' theme, for example Psalm 139.12b:
  the night is as bright as the day, for darkness is as light to you.

Focus:

Place two small square or rectangular cloths on the floor – on one, set up the elements associated with the bedtime routine; on the other, the night-scene picture and the Scripture verse in large font.

Gathering:

As for earlier 'snacks'.

Opening prayer:

Allow time for people to get settled and then play the music you have chosen.

God you are with us every moment of every day.
As we spend time together now, help us to discover
new ways of seeing your daily care and
your invitation for us to grow in Christ. Amen.

Leader's input:

We all have our day's end routines, some associated with the evening meal, others associated with the time just before sleep.

Spend a few minutes discussing the retreatants 'night-time' routines – keep it low key and fun, not too serious!

Today we are going to explore a spiritual 'night-time' routine that has been part of Christianity for centuries.

Share a little detail from resource sheet 2.7.

Over the next 15–30 minutes we're going to look at how we might incorporate this into our family life as a way of helping both children and parents to think about the good and not-so-good parts of their day, and to talk to God about it. Once you have been through this modified examen yourself, you will be able to lead it yourselves with your families.

Group exercise:

Lead a discussion based on the following questions.

⚜ Do you currently practise any sort of review of the day – such as keeping a diary, making a mental note of what was good and bad about the day before you go to bed, etc.?
   If 'yes', is this practice linked to your prayer life, or are they separate?
   If 'no', what gets in the way of your doing something like a daily review?

The leader guides the group through a simple review of the day for a family (adult/s and children in this particular example), which begins with a story on page 70

How's the day been – *really?* – reflection sheet

Pray with the following Scripture, asking the Holy Spirit to guide your reflection.

You were taught to put away your former way of life, your old self, corrupt and deluded by its lusts, and to be renewed in the spirit of your minds, and to clothe yourselves with the new self, created according to the likeness of God in true righteousness and holiness.
So then, putting away falsehood, let us all speak the truth to our neighbours, for we are members of one another. Be angry but do not sin; do not let the sun go down on your anger …
Ephesians 4.22–26

How does this passage apply to your current life and relationships?

Make some notes in your journal about what God has shown you. Talk to God about anything that is worrying you or for which you want to give God thanks.

Take an imaginary walk with Jesus. Sit somewhere you won't be disturbed and take a few deep breaths. Invite the Holy Spirit to be with you, read through the description, and then begin.

It is night-time after a busy day.

You are tired, Jesus is tired.

You are somewhere out of doors. It is one of your favourite places and Jesus knows it well.

The weather is fine, not cold, it is a balmy night. No one else is around but you can see the lights of some houses – your own home included – not far away.

You walk up a small hill, find a dry spot and sit down.

For a while you sit in silence, looking at the stars. What do you want to say to Jesus?

What does he want to say to you?

When you are both ready, get up and walk in companionable silence back to your home.

What are your 'good night' words to Jesus?

And his to you?

Spend a little time considering your end-of-day routines.

What do you need to do to protect some 'God and me' time before you go to bed?

Talk to God about your desire to begin a review of the day, and listen for the inspiration of the Spirit to help you get started.

Guidelines for a simple review of the day for a family

Share the following story.

> During the bombing raids of WWII, thousands of children were orphaned and left to starve. The fortunate ones were rescued and placed in refugee camps, where they received food and good care. But many of these children could not sleep at night, fearing waking up to find themselves once again homeless and without food. Finally someone hit upon the idea of giving each child a piece of bread to hold at bedtime. Holding their bread, these children could finally sleep in peace. All through the night the bread reminded them, 'Today I ate and I will eat again tomorrow.'[17]

Like these children, we can benefit from holding our 'daily bread' while we sleep. The insights of a few minutes' nightly reflection can nourish us and help strengthen us for the next day and all the days ahead. The key idea is to look back over the day to see what has happened and how we have felt about those events. It is not difficult to explain that sometimes there will be things that we did well or feel really happy about; but sometimes there will be things that cause us sadness, tears or a sense of failure or disappointment. Even these, however, can become 'gifts' if we look at them long enough to see beyond the outer wrapping to the learning inside, the seed of new understanding of a situation or of ourselves.

❈ *Have ready one or two simple pairs of questions to provide a framework for the family-time. These questions explore the hard/helpful events of the day or the joyful/worrying times, etc.*
Light a candle as a signal that you are all going to be thinking about what the day has been like.
Say a short prayer – this can be rotated around the family once all are familiar with it or family members can say their own prayer – something simple, such as:

Thank you God that we can think about today together.
May the Holy Spirit be with us as we share what has been good today and
   what has been difficult.
Bless us we pray, in Jesus' name. Amen.

Take a few minutes (use a silent egg-timer ⧗) so that you all get used to sitting in silence together for up to three or four minutes. Begin with a shorter time and build up if necessary.

---

17 Dennis Linn, Sheila Fabricant Linn and Matthew Linn, *Sleeping with Bread*, New Jersey: Paulist Press, 1995, p. 1.

One by one share your answers to the pair of questions that your family has decided to use, for example:

What have I enjoyed today?   What have I not enjoyed today?
Who has helped me today?   Who have I helped today?

(Remember these can be altered to suit the ages of those present and areas of concern.)

When you have all had a turn, each person is encouraged to ask Jesus for the grace they need. For example:

Dear Jesus, I struggle to ask for help in my maths class – help me to have the courage to put my hand up and ask, next time I don't understand something. Amen.

OR

O Jesus, I am nervous about the report I have to present to the Board tomorrow. Please give me clarity of thinking, and the words I need to respond to their questions. Amen.

Concluding comments:

Some suggestions about implementing this spiritual practice: in the week before you hope to begin, ask some of your friends to pray for you as a family that this practice will build communication and faith. Introduce this practice at a time in the week when family members are not stressed. Before you begin, make sure that everyone agrees to a few 'ground rules' – no interruptions, no put-downs, no mobile phones, no analysis or problem-solving, and no leaving the table until everyone has had a turn.

Closing prayer:

Thank you O God for all we have shared tonight. Bless us as we sleep. Amen.

Snack 3.4 Learning to lament

Suitable for a mature group of people whose lives have had their ups and downs, but it can also be used as a way of introducing LAMENT as a spiritual practice to the ministry team/gathered lay readers/or even as a special service for a larger group.

Leader's preparation:

- read L&F resource sheets '2.10 Learning to lament' and '2.9 Keeping a spiritual journal and writing as prayer'
- read Paul Bradbury, *Sowing in Tears: How to Lament in a Church of Praise*, Cambridge: Grove, 2007
- familiarize yourself with psalms which demonstrate the movement from honest lament to petition to praise within the context of covenanted relationship with God, for example Psalms 13 and 44
- do some personal reflection on your experience of the church providing a safe place in which people who have had a relationship with God, however tenuous, can express their 'disorientation' and be supported as they move towards 'reorientation'
- because this can be a painful topic, but also because it's a bit more complicated than other short retreats, make sure you have someone else to share the leadership, and access to good supervision to help you with the planning and the review
- depending on what prayer places (stations) you want to offer, gather a range of objects, dark and lighter fabrics, deep purple and white candles, pictures, newspaper clippings of recent natural disasters, an empty eggshell, a picture of a baby in utero, broken natural items like shells, branches, etc., which can give a focus for people to reflect and make their own lament
- at each station, provide writing and drawing materials, a box of tissues and a waste-basket, clay or playdough (with wipes), a bowl of water (and paper towels), and a sand tray with one lighted candle and other small candles ready for retreatants to light as part of their prayer, copies of the suggested prayer pattern (see reflection sheet) and the key verses if you want to use them
- give each retreatant a list of stations so they can decide which to visit, and a copy of Psalm 13
- for the closing, have available copies of the prayer and several small phials of anointing oil.

Focus:

Set up 'stations', preferably in the church itself, choosing from the following:

1 *Personal relationship breakdown* – separation, divorce, estrangement, etc.
   Key verses: Psalm 18.6, 16–19; Psalm 51.1–12
2 *Death*
   Key verses: Psalm 23.1–4
3 *Hidden loss* – infertility, loss of a faculty or function such as deafness, redundancy, dreams
   Key verses: Psalm 40.11–17
4 *Serious illness, ageing*
   Key verses: Psalm 22.9–21
5 *Injustice* – personal, local or global
   Key verses: Psalm 26.1–6
6 *A recent significant natural disaster*
   Key verses: Psalm 69.1–3, 13–16

Gathering and opening prayer:

Play an appropriate chant, such as Libera Free, EMI, CD 7243 5 57823 2 8, 2004, *Track 10 'Lament' or Track 12 'Be still my soul'.*

You are welcome to this place – a sacred place made holy with the prayers of the saints, the tears shed and the laughter shared. Let us pray:

O God who walks with us, seen or unseen, through all of life's valleys and shadows, help us now to reflect on the hard places in our lives. Help us to face some of the pain, so that we may place our lost loved ones, our lost hopes, our fears and our failures into your merciful hands. May we be released from the heaviness of sadness, of guilt, of disappointment or shame, and begin to live lightly again. Through Jesus, 'a man of sorrows and acquainted with grief'. Amen.

Leader's input:

Both lamenting and celebrating are integral parts of human life. We celebrate great feats of courage or endurance; we have funerals to grieve the dead and lost. We parochially shout for joy when England wins the Ashes and, globally, mourn the passing of Princess Diana and, more recently, Michael Jackson.

As Christians we enjoy beautiful corporate celebrations at major feasts and festivals, but these events usually *far outnumber the times of liturgical lament.* Only Good Friday, All Souls Day and national Remembrance Days find their way into the Church's calendar, days when the Church stops and we mourn together, binding our hearts to our Lord in his agony, and remembering those who have suffered pain and loss in previous years.

On a personal level, we often recoil from talking about losses on any scale; many losses are hidden from other people: infertility, impotence, failing faculties, dreams dashed, or relationships buried in the silence of indifference. Circumstances may require us to get on with life and it seems easier not to think about the awfulness of a death or accident or the effects of a natural disaster. However, if we do not take the time to deal with our pain, when the next loss occurs its effect is often intensified, as old grief is scythed open and salt rubbed into its rawness. Lamenting, in the biblical record, was part of the way people stayed connected with God – no matter what happened, they told God how they felt – disillusioned, abandoned, puzzled, they may have been – but silent, never! The Psalms, the 'Prayer book of the Church', included the whole range of human emotion and provided a vehicle to express the longing of the human soul for dynamic connection with God in the midst of daily struggle or tragedy. This was life-giving for the Hebrew people then, and for us today. Though we may enter the desert of disorientation, when our world falls apart, yet we can still keep talking to – or shouting at – God. We can be REAL in our words and feelings shared, instead of putting on a brave face.

Several stations are set up around the church – take your time in discerning where to begin, and then be guided by the Spirit as you begin to reflect and pour out some of your pain to God in the privacy of the written word or in the colours or clay used to express your loss or confusion.

Before we begin this process, let us say together Psalm 13, which begins,

How long, O LORD? Will you forget me forever?
How long will you hide your face from me?
How long must I bear pain in my soul,
and have sorrow in my heart all the day long?

Give everyone a copy of Psalm 13, say the psalm together, and then allow five minutes for reflection before people move to their chosen stations.

You may want to have some Taizé chants playing quietly in the background. When you need to gather again, turn the music up.

Closing time of prayer

Silence

We give you thanks and praise O God,
that you have heard our lament;
we are your children, we depend on your love,
we trust that you hear us always,
even when it seems you are far away.

We give you thanks and praise, O God,
for you have not left us alone in our sorrow,
unconsoled in our pain,
but, in your compassion, have held us and
brought us the promise of hope and of healing.

We claim this promise.
We will go on talking and crying
and sharing our truth with you,
no matter how hard it may be.
For in this raw and gritty reality
lies the strength of our bond with you –
God who comes alongside us
to walk the road of suffering
moment by painful moment,
to bring us to new life
hour by patient hour,
until we are all we can be,
true to your image and joy.
Amen.

With soft music playing in the background anoint each other, saying:

May God continue in you the healing begun today.
Through Jesus Christ
Amen.

We go now in peace to love and serve the Lord.
Amen.

Personal prayer pattern –
for a time of lament – reflection sheet

Spend time quietly settling into this prayer space.

When you are ready, begin to focus on the items in front of you –
notice what touches you, what you are drawn to, or what you pull away from.

Take your time.

Make your complaint to God, naming the loss you are lamenting, and
detailing the pain that you are bringing.
Use the materials available to help you express your feelings and your
thoughts as honestly as you can as you lament before God.

Take your time.

Make your petition to God, asking for what you need. Be direct and bold.
Tell God why you have the confidence to approach God with your pain, for
example because of God's faithfulness in the past or because of what you
know of God's character, mercy and grace.

Wait upon God in silence.
Be alert for any inner shift and the gentle emergence of
even a tiny hint of hope.

When you are ready to leave this station,
light a candle as a sign of movement towards healing.

Snack 3.5 Breakfast with Jesus?

Suitable for a Saturday or weekday morning for business people using a timetable such as this.*

6.30 am	Gather for introduction, prayer and brief sharing of ways of praying with Scripture
7.00 am	Breakfast
7.30 am	Use imaginative prayer with a Scripture passage, move into reflection and silence
8.15 am	Gather, brief sharing in pairs, closing prayer
8.30 am	End of 'Quiet Breakfast' – on with the day ...

The starting time can be varied if people in your group need to be at work earlier or later.

Leader's preparation:

- read L&F resource sheets '2.16 Praying with Scripture 1 – sacred reading/*lectio divina*'; and '2.19 Silence and solitude'
- pray with the Gospel passage John 21.1–12a NRSV
- so you can concentrate on facilitating the retreat, ensure that a helper at the chosen venue has:
  a) got a simple breakfast organized – cereal, fruit and toast, etc., nothing elaborate, and
  b) can be part of the brief 'breakfast' role play
- have enough copies of the L&F resource sheets and the reflection sheet ready for participants
- have an assortment of items commonly found on a breakfast table, including a morning paper. If you can, record a portion of a breakfast TV show ready to play back through a laptop computer ... it doesn't have to be high quality or very long, just enough to get the 'flavour' of the busy morning routine many experience.

Focus:

Arrange a breakfast table – with the morning paper half opened on one side of the table. Place the laptop computer on another table nearby, and start playing the recorded breakfast channel at a volume that is loud enough for you to have to raise your voice to get everyone's attention.

Gathering:

After attending to all the practicalities, once people are settled, you and your helper do a mini role play of a noisy rushed breakfast situation, such as one of you trying to read the paper, eat toast and drink coffee, while the other tries to listen to the TV, make lunch and find something ...

Just do whatever works best – and end with both of you grabbing bags, coats, etc. and hurrying out of the room. Wait half a minute, and then come back in, turn off the recorded TV channel, and sit down.

Opening prayer:

Allow at least a 30-second silence before praying:

Loving God, you are present with us every hour of every day, in our rushed lives and in our moments of stillness. Thank you for bringing us here to share breakfast with each other and with you. May we listen as your Spirit guides us; may we be open to your words of love and encouragement; may we know ourselves to be precious in your sight this day.
In Christ's name we pray. Amen.

Leader's input 1:

Breakfasts can be times of mild chaos as our little role play illustrated. There's not much time to listen to each other or to 'be present' to what we are doing. Instead our minds are all over the place, and we rely on the familiarity of the morning routine to get us out of the door and on our way.

This 'Quiet Breakfast' opportunity provides a bit more than physical nourishment and soundbytes of information or conversation. Yes, there will be time to talk over cereal and toast, but there will also be time to rest and reflect in the presence of our God.

Drawing on the L&F resource sheets, cover the following points succinctly so breakfast can happen at 7 am:

(About silence:)

- lack of silence in modern living
- some of our personal history with silence can put us off – talk to God about that if need be
- silence can be a different form of worship in which we 'fast from words' and give room for God to work deeply in our spirit.

(About praying with Scripture:)

- not a new thing but very old – savouring a very small portion of Scripture or a Gospel story
- *Lectio divina* – sacred reading – hear the passage read slowly several times, listen for a word or phrase that stands out for you, chew that over, talk to God about it and then rest in God – this order may vary, the retreatants may move in and out of 'meditating on the passage' and 'talking to God about it' a few times, before coming to a place of stillness before God, resting in God
- reassure retreatants that there is no need to strive when praying with Scripture; just trust that the Spirit will work in their lives if given room.

End your input by reading John 21.1–12a aloud once reasonably slowly, and give Jesus' invitation: 'Come and have breakfast' (v.12a). Offer a blessing for the food and fellowship and let them know that the second session starts at 7.30 am.

Leader input 2:

Give time when the group gathers for closing – 8.15 am – remind them about the gift of silence to each other, and silence as an act of worship; distribute the reflection sheet so people won't be disturbed at the end of the third reading of the passage. Pray:

Loving God we bring this time of praying with Scripture to you. Help us to trust your love and your Spirit at work in our deepest selves. May we be open to a fresh awareness of your provision for us and your delight in us. Amen.

Summarize John 21.1–6 and then continue:

The passage John 21.7–12a is going to be read through slowly *three* times – as a word or phrase catches your attention, simply 'tune out' my voice and begin your meditation. When the third reading is finished, move gently into personal reflection in silence. You can either engage with the word or phrase that has touched you, or with something from the reflection sheet if you are drawn there instead.

Some music will be put on to signal that it is time to return to the group for our closing.

Read John 21.7–12a aloud slowly three times ...

During the period of silent reflection, wander around the group as unobtrusively as you can, so you are available should anyone be struggling with silence or want some clarification, etc. When it is time, put on the music; something from a classical compilation or instrumental versions of chants by Taizé or Margaret Rizza would be ideal.

☺☺ *Once everyone is back together, offer the retreatants time to talk about their prayer experience with another person – five minutes each should be adequate.*

Concluding comments:

What we have done today honours God. We have chosen to begin our day listening to the Word of God coming to us, not only through Scripture, but through our own prayerful reflection and our willingness to be open to God's touch. We have taken the time to listen deeply with the 'ears of our hearts'. In doing so, we acknowledge that sustained and focused listening to God will bring changes at our very core; changes that will help us to be more loving – towards God, towards others, and towards ourselves.

Closing prayer:

Stand and sing the Grace together if that is your practice, or say a blessing, or simply close with the following short prayer.

We give thanks to you O God for what you have begun in us this morning. We trust that your Spirit will continue to deepen our compassion for others and our desire for you.
May we go in peace to love and serve you this day.
Amen.

Breakfast with Jesus? – reflection sheet

How do you start off your day?

Is there room/time for Jesus at the beginning of your day?

How might you protect some time
– even five minutes –
so you and your Lord can enjoy
the start of the day together?

Bring to mind a memory of a
happy breakfast.
Spend some time imagining it in detail:
who was there, where it took place,
what you ate and did ...

Talk to God about your fear or your desire
to 'have breakfast' with Jesus;
remember to listen for God's reply,
now or in the days ahead.

What was it that made it such a happy
time?

Talk to God about what you have
recalled or discovered.

If you go to an early service on a Sunday, why not invite somebody home to share
breakfast with you?

Meditation on John 21.9–12.

What would it be like to invite
Jesus to 'come and have breakfast'
with you at your place.

a beach
the smell
of flames
and fish
the wonder of His presence
His body warm and strong
His eyes clear and caring
alive
alive
alive
for
you
for
me

Let yourself imagine this very thing ...

Notice what you are thinking and
what you are feeling as you let yourself
see Jesus in your own home, in your
kitchen perhaps
or sitting outdoors.

What would you want to talk about?
What questions might you ask?

What does Jesus want to say to you?

Snack 3.6 Entering the story – praying with Scripture using the imagination

Suitable either for an established group with a lot of experience reading and studying the Scriptures but little or no history of imaginative engagement with the Scriptures, or a relatively new group who are open to learning prayerful ways of encountering the biblical text.

Leader's preparation:

- read L&F resource sheets '2.9 Keeping a spiritual journal and writing as prayer', and '2.17 Praying with Scripture 2 – imaginative prayer' and have enough copies for each person to take home
- if you're not the group's normal leader, it might be wise to talk to the person who is so he or she is aware and supportive of what you are going to be doing. You can also see the venue and check that people will be able to work on their own for 30 minutes in a reasonably private space, AND that they will be bringing their Bibles with them
- we'll use the story of blind Bartimaeus now *(Mark 10.46–52)* but, if the group has recently studied this passage, you can prayerfully select any passage of Scripture in which Jesus meets with another person and issues an invitation, heals, challenges or restores to community
- find a whiteboard and markers, or a large piece of paper and felt-tips for a brainstorming exercise
- gather the items for the focus as described below
- think through your own attitude to using the imagination in prayer, and be prepared to address any concerns the retreatants might have about using the imagination
- visit the website http://ignatianspirituality.com/ignatian-prayer/the-spiritual-exercises/pray-with-your-imagination to get more details of this type of prayer if you wish
- pray imaginatively with the blind Bartimaeus story yourself.

Focus:

On a low table put the Bible commentary and other reference books used for Bible study and, alongside them, arrange a notebook or journal, crayons, coloured pencils, paper, a pair of spectacles and a magnifying glass.

Gathering and opening prayer:

Will follow the normal pattern for the group.

Leader's input (approx. 15–20 minutes):

Many of us are familiar with ways of studying the Scriptures – perhaps we've used tools like these study guides and commentaries, almanacs and Bible atlases. *Pause for a little discussion if people want to share their experience.* Sifting and sorting information, making a comparison between the context of these stories and our contemporary context, perhaps even getting to grips with the more complex issues of translation sources or modern scholarship, are all good ways of using our rational capacity to help our understanding of Scripture and God's covenantal relationship with God's chosen people.

The Old Testament is full of stories about the Hebrew people, their faith and frailty, their journey towards the promised land and the prophetic voices pointing to the coming of the Messiah, our Lord Jesus Christ. The New Testament too may have moved or challenged us, as we read of the self-giving love of Jesus and the confidence of the disciples, once the resurrection life of the Holy Spirit began to course through their minds and hearts. The stories of so many ordinary people are our stories too, for human nature has not changed over the millennia; nor has God's faithfulness and desire for us.

Today we are going to be very intentional about using another aspect of our mind – our imagination – to help us pray with a Scripture passage, instead of studying it in the usual way. Let's begin by taking a few minutes to think about the following questions, before we brainstorm some ideas.

✼ What does the word 'imagination' mean to you? How does it fit into your spiritual life?

Give about five minutes to this as an individual exercise and then ask for feedback, which you write on the whiteboard or large piece of paper so others can see clearly what is being said and discussed. Feedback may well include the following:

- can't see any link between the imagination and the spiritual life
- have been taught in Christian circles that the imagination is not to be trusted
- was told off as a child – 'it's only in your imagination' so it doesn't count or matter because it's not true
- worry about getting carried away by what is being imagined, moving into the realm of fantasy not reality.

We each have our own imagination 'history'. Some of us will have had parents or teachers who acknowledged our imaginary friends and praised the stories we wrote full of talking animals or flying people; others of us may have had such flights of fancy drilled out of us and have become a bit wary of anything we can't understand or prove or touch. Yet the imagination is something we actually use all the time, perhaps without realizing:

- we imagine what we are going to cook for dinner
- we daydream about a holiday or new relationship
- we think up games or stories for our children
- *invite other examples.*

The imagination is active in our daily lives but may not be so active in our prayer life and that is a tragedy because the imagination can be a valuable vehicle of God's grace. Like our mind, body and emotions, our imagination is a way of connecting with God, a faculty that Jesus certainly employed as he invited his listeners into scenes familiar to their daily lives. Those gathered to hear Jesus in first-century Palestine would have had no trouble using their imagination to visualize the context of the stories of the lost sheep, the lost coin and the prodigal son (Luke 15). As we listen to Scripture, *we too* can find ourselves imagining the key characters or actions – the stilling of the storm; Peter walking on the water, sinking and being rescued by Jesus; the raising to life of the widow's son ... the list is endless.

Two millennia later, these stories and others like them can still provide us with the starting points for exploring major human themes such as panic and fear, loss and celebration. We've got two ways into these stories: the first one, the more familiar way, is to study the text, look up what other people think about the stories, consult books about the history and lifestyles of those living in that time and place; and we can check out our findings with a mentor or study guide or in our discussions in a group like this one. The second way into the stories is to use our imagination, not simply to visualize the scene as the listeners did in Jesus' day, but to *enter* the story ourselves, to let ourselves become part of what is taking place, weaving the details of our own experience into the story of God. Using the imagination in this way 'puts us in the picture' with the Gospel characters in first-century Palestine or helps us to see the Gospel stories played out in our own homes and neighbourhoods.

It's not hard to see that praying with the Scriptures, using our imagination in this way, is going to bring us closer to Jesus. While it's natural to think we would all welcome that opportunity, the truth is that for many people, getting closer to Jesus is a scary prospect. We don't want him to see our faults and failings or to know that we are far from the 'ideal Christian' who lives a life full of good works. But remember – Jesus already knows us and **accepts us as we are**. Think of the range of people who came to him and the people whom he sought out – *(invite examples)* – those on the margins, those who didn't live an exemplary life but who could see, in him, a living hope for transformation. So there is no need to be afraid. Trust that God will take us gently closer to Jesus, who will be tender with our frailty and kind to our trembling hearts.

Pause and then hand out sheet 2.17 and the reflection sheet, ready for them to use in silence once you've read the Scripture.

Just before we begin our time of praying with Scripture using the imagination, I'd like to emphasize that while this works well for many people, there may be some who struggle to form recognizable images in their mind – they may get more of an inner impression about something rather than details. Don't worry about this – just trust that God will be present through the Spirit, and believe that God is at work in your life right now, or you wouldn't be here!

So let's move to the story of blind Bartimaeus. It's familiar to us all, but I'm going to read it through for you twice, quite slowly. As I do so, don't strive to 'make anything happen', just get a sense of what is going on with Jesus, Bartimaeus and the bystanders. Then you can move into silence for about 30 minutes to spend more time with the passage, inviting the Holy Spirit to help you enter the story – it doesn't matter what part you take, just picture yourself there on a dusty road in the Middle East, or in your own High Street or somewhere else familiar to you. Let the story unfold as it will. Then when you are ready you can do some writing or talk to God or whatever helps you take the story deeper into your heart.

When it's time to join the group again, I'll put some music on.

Read Mark 10.46–52 twice and then get up and move away so people know it's time for their personal silent reflection.

It may take a few minutes for people to settle into their reflection. If anyone is obviously struggling after 10 minutes, you may need to take them aside and see what's going on – or not going on – for them. If they can't seem to use their imagination, suggest they try one of the other exercises on the reflection sheet. Reassure them that God will honour their desire for more of God and is already present in their lives.

When the half hour is up, put on one of the following Taizé chants, 'The Lord is my light' or 'Within our darkest night' or some other suitable piece of music while people come back to the group.

Concluding comments:

Let the music come to an end and then invite brief sharing about the experience in pairs, before asking the whole group:

What was that like for you?

What was difficult?

What surprised you?

Over time this way of praying can enrich your relationship with God, or with Jesus. Praying with the imagination can help you learn more about yourselves too, as you become part of the living Word.

Even familiar passages of Scripture can take on new meaning as you become one of the characters in the story – you may even find yourself seeing things from Jesus' perspective – giving you some insight into what it might mean to put on 'the mind of Christ'.

Closing prayer:

God of new beginnings,
continue the work you have been doing in us today.
Illuminate our awareness so that,
as we bring our whole selves,
including our imagination
to you, we may come to know
the wonder of your love for us
and for all people;
through Jesus Christ, our Lord.
Amen.

Entering the story – reflection sh[...]
Praying with Scripture using the imag[...]

Using imaginative prayer, pray with the story of blind Bartimaeus, which you will find in Mark 10.46–52	Ask the [...] as you engage [...] What, or who, do you have trouble 'seeing'? (not literally but in terms of really paying attention to an individual or a situation) What are your 'blind spots'? (for example what do you know you avoid – conflict, deep emotion?) Talk to God about what you've discovered and listen for God's response over the next few weeks.

How might you get involved with supporting those who are visually impaired?

Use a scarf to make a blindfold.  Tie it around your eyes and sit or stand still for 10–15 minutes, paying attention to what your senses tell you about what is around you. Listen closely, smell the air, touch the fabric of the chair you are sitting on – you may even have a snack with you that you can open and taste. When you are ready, take off the blindfold and look with new eyes at what and who is around you. In your journal, write some thoughts about this experience, before giving God thanks for the gift of sight.	Jesus inaugurated his ministry with words from Isaiah 61: The Spirit of the Lord is upon me, because he has anointed me to bring good news to the poor. He has sent me to proclaim release to the captives and recovery of sight to the blind, to let the oppressed go free, to proclaim the year of the Lord's favour. Read Luke 4.16–30 which describes the scene when Jesus reads these words from the scroll. Then imagine yourself in the synagogue. Let the action unfold before you as you listen, watch … When you are ready, make a few notes in your journal about what you have noticed. Talk to God about your questions or wonderings.

Snack 3.7 The extraordinary in the ordinary – symbols and spiritual growth

Suitable for an established evening women's group with a two-hour time-frame, but could easily be adapted for an all-male or mixed group.

Leader's preparation:

- make large (A4) laminated copies of the symbols below and place them in an opaque plastic bag
- gather some familiar Christian symbols such as a cross, bread, wine, etc.
- find and print off pictures of boats: container ships, tugboats, a ship in dry dock, fishing boat, pilot boat, etc., to use for the everyday symbol reflection – if possible have some smaller copies made in colour for the retreatants to use in their time of reflection
- make enough copies of handouts for every retreatant
- read L&F resource sheet '2.20 Using everyday symbols to aid spiritual growth'
- obtain a whiteboard (an A3 size is adequate) and a couple of dry markers
- type and print off (in font size 14 or 16) copies of the text of John 4.1–30, 39–42 (NRSV), enough for each retreatant
- pray with John 4, paying particular attention to the deepening meanings of the 'water' symbol
- reflect on the part that symbols have played in your own spiritual life so far.

Focus:

Put a large, clean sheet or cloth on the floor with a central candle. Spread the pictures of boats and the familiar Christian symbols across the cloth, but leave some spaces.

Gathering:

As this is an established group they will all know each other but may not know you, so it is a good idea to introduce yourself briefly and to thank them for the opportunity to join them. Outline the shape of the evening and give people a chance to ask any questions. Explain that there will be some time spent in silence for them to work as individuals on the material, and there will also be a time of sharing later for those who wish to do so.

O God, we know you as our shield and defender, ancient of days.
But we also know you as Father, Friend, Lover of our souls.
No description can come close to the mystery of your Love
made visible in Jesus Christ.
Help us tonight as we recall how the symbols of our faith have spoken to us.
Help us too, to be open to new symbols which may speak to us in unexpected
  ways,
revealing more of the wonder of who you are and who you want to be for us to-
  night.
We pray this through Jesus Christ, our Lord. Amen.

Leader's input:

As a light-hearted introduction, invite those present to take turns pulling a symbol
from the plastic bag and trying to think what their chosen symbol might convey
about God or about themselves! Give them a bit of help if necessary! Some ideas
or associations are given below with the symbol but they may well come up with a
completely different list.

☺	God loves each one of us	☹	Sometimes we stuff up!
🕯	The light of Christ	⚑	His banner over me is love
▤	God keeps no record of wrongs	👓	Jesus made the blind see
⧖	My times are in God's hands	✉	Love letters from God
△	The Trinity	⬆	Conversion or 'metanoia'

It's easy to see from this exercise that even the simplest symbol taken from a Wingdings
file in a Word document can say something to us about God, or about ourselves, or
even our world. It's not surprising then that symbols are such an important part of
the spiritual journey, part of our faith. Of course, Scripture is full of symbols: many
of the stories and parables of Jesus contain symbols to help teach listeners about the
nature of God and the Kingdom, for example the sower and the seed; the pearl of
great price; the fig tree.

Invite further examples of symbols from Scripture which carry special meaning for
those present.

On this focus cloth we have three of the key symbols of our Christian faith – the cross, the bread and the wine.

For us as Christians each of these has a sacred meaning, a particular way of helping us connect with the stories of our faith and the work of Jesus Christ. But for those who don't have such a connection, they can mean something different.

Invite them to suggest possible other meanings of the cross, bread and wine.

It is natural to want to work with familiar scriptural symbols but *any* symbol which has caught our attention can be explored and can provide 'food for the journey', no matter where we are. Just as familiar Christian symbols can change meaning in a non-Christian context, so ordinary items from everyday life can take on new meanings for us if we take the time to contemplate them – to look at them slowly and deliberately, listening for the voice of the Spirit. Here's what happened with a very ordinary kitchen object – as you listen, keep in mind it's a true story:

For a warm-up exercise at a workshop she was leading, Alice brought 12 clean(!) items from her kitchen drawer – things like a tin-opener, measuring spoons, a whisk, and so on. When the group had committed the day to God, each participant pulled something from the opaque plastic bag Alice handed round, and began to reflect on what the item might symbolize. Alice came to the last person, Maisie, who drew out a kauri wooden spatula, looked at it, then gasped and fled from the room, the spatula held tight to her heart. Alice suspected that God was at work, so after a few minutes she went out and found Maisie, who was holding the spatula tightly, with tears pouring down her face. She beamed at Alice and said, 'How did God know?' Wisely Alice didn't answer and soon Maisie went on ... 'I have always loved the touch of kauri – my dad used to work with it and sometimes he'd let me touch a bowl that was almost finished. They were really special times with him – there were lots of us kids and I didn't get time alone with him often. Dad's been dead for years now but for some reason, I was really missing him today – now somehow I can feel his presence with me – God is so good – it was just what I needed.

Give a bit of space for people to take the story in, and then ask if anyone wants to say anything – someone may have found the story triggered a memory, someone else may have another example of something ordinary being a vehicle of grace.

Once you sense that no one else wants to speak, continue with whichever group exercise you think will suit the group.

You have a choice here – you can do the John 4 exercise (1) if you sense the group would enjoy the more academic focus and still have time to do the boats exercise (2); or, depending on how much time is left, go straight to the boats exercise.

Group exercise 1:

⚜ We're going to turn to the familiar story of the woman at the well in John 4.

Distribute copies for people to read as you are reading, so you all have the same translation. Then read the Scripture aloud reasonably slowly. Give them a few minutes to read it once more and use the time to draw up the headings of the *chart below on the whiteboard. Then begin to 'unpack' the symbol of* water *which is central to the whole story. Speak briefly about each of the columns, and then ask them to contribute their ideas. Don't worry if they are not in the 'right' order – just write them in the appropriate column, based on the following (there may well be other offerings but these will help show the expansion of meaning of the symbol 'water').*

Literal	Symbolic	Spiritual	Personal	Communal
Water in a well compared with 'living' water, i.e. water that runs in a spring or stream. Accessible only by bucket; people could carry only enough for one day. Shared thirst brought a Jewish Rabbi and a Samaritan woman together when custom dictated they should never meet.

Satisfies physical thirst. (vv. 6–12) | 'Living' water symbolizes the life-giving water that will quench her spiritual thirst.

Jesus announces himself as the giver of this 'living' water. (v.14) | The connection with Jacob, their mutual ancestor, who 'gave us the well'. (v.12)

The water becomes 'a spring gushing up to *eternal* life'. (v.14b)

The woman reveals her spiritual longing. (v.15) | Evidence of the effect of the 'living water' already at work in the woman's life as she acknowledges her difficult personal circumstances. She and Jesus have a theological discussion AND Jesus shares the truth of his identity, one of the first – if not *the first* time – he tells anyone who he actually is. (vv.16–26) | The wider community is touched by the woman's transformation, and invites Jesus to stay with them. They want what they see in her ... the 'living water' which Jesus himself now symbolizes. (vv.29, 39–42) |
| | ⇨ THE EXTRAORDINARY BEGINS TO EMERGE FROM THE ORDINARY | | | |

End this exercise by emphasizing that while it may take time for the richness of even a familiar symbol to unfold, with attention and patience the extraordinary (the spiritual, personal and communal) will emerge from the ordinary.

Any thing around us can then become a potential bearer of God's communication and grace.

Group exercise 2:

✤ When we work with symbols over time, or when we are drawn to a symbol rich with potential, its meaning can expand if we are expectant and invite God into the process. One symbol that has a great deal of potential is the boat (or 'ship' as a nautical friend pointed out if thinking about a LARGE vessel!).

Hand out copies of the reflection sheet 'The extraordinary in the ordinary – boats' and go over the exercises to ensure that all the retreatants are 'on board' before they move into a time of personal silent reflection. Assure retreatants that if something in the reflection time touches or unsettles them, you are there to listen to them in private if necessary. As this is an established group, the group leader may also want to be available for support.

Concluding comments:

Provide time for sharing in pairs or with the whole group depending on numbers. Then draw the evening together by reiterating the value of being alert for anything in the midst of ordinary life that draws our attention. It may well be a cue from God to explore the different levels of meaning available to us through contemplating a symbol with the guidance of the Holy Spirit.

Closing prayer:

Take a minute's silence before asking each retreatant to say a word about their experience. Say the Grace together:

May the grace of our Lord Jesus Christ, and the love of God and the fellowship of the Holy Spirit be with us now and for evermore. Amen.

The extraordinary in the ordinary – boats – reflection sheet

Ask the Holy Spirit to guide your time of reflection.

What do 'boats' mean to you, i.e. what memories, emotions, family stories are linked to a boat of any shape or size?

If there is sadness, pain, anger or guilt in your remembering, bring that all to God whose heart is open to your need right now.

If the memories and associations are of adventure, thrills, holidays or friendships, bring that all to God too, for God shares our joy.

If you are in a time of transition, (such as between jobs, adjusting to illness or ageing) imagine you are **a ship in 'dry dock'.** You are 'high and dry', away from the sea.

Spend some time visualizing the scene before engaging with the questions.

You are there for a 're-fit' – what might have to be 'stripped away', or 'remodelled'?

What 'parts' of you do you want to keep and use for your next voyage?

What does it feel like to allow this process to happen under the careful eye of the Master of the ship, Jesus?

What do you want to say to Jesus about the next stage of your life, your next voyage?

Choose one of the 'boat' pictures.

Spend 10–15 minutes slowly looking at the picture, letting yourself notice the details but also alert to the thoughts and feelings which are surfacing.

Then consider the following:

What memories come to mind?
What questions emerge for me?
What is this 'boat' saying to me about my life at the moment?

Then consider:

Where is God in this picture?
How might God want to be in my 'life'-boat?

Read Matthew 14.22–33 s-l-o-w-l-y and imagine yourself in this story of the swamped boat and the storm stilled.

How does this story connect with your life?
What does Jesus say to you?

Churches were built modelled on boats, with a 'nave' holding the bulk of the congregation.

What sort of 'boat' is your church?
Who is its Master?
Where is it going?
What is its cargo?
What powers it?

© Sue Pickering 2010

Snack 3.8 Gardening with God

Suitable for people who enjoy gardening and want to deepen their connection with God; for example with a group of retired people, those who tend the church's garden, any group meeting in a private home with a lovely garden, or those working in a community garden or allotment. It would also be suitable as an introduction to 'Care of Creation', gently helping people start to address the issues of climate change and the environmental impact of development and poverty. The retreat could be held for a couple of hours in the morning or afternoon during the week or at the weekend depending on people's availability.

Leader's preparation:

- read L&F resource sheet '2.5 Caring for Creation' and sheets '2.16 and 2.17 Praying with Scripture, 1 & 2'
- visit the location of the retreat to check suitability, availability, etc. If you've chosen an outdoor venue, have a 'wet-weather' alternative planned just in case!
- print off (in a large font) both the quotes on pp. 95–6 so each retreatant can take a copy home if they wish
- have ready enough copies of the L&F resource sheets 2.5, 2.16 and 2.17, the exercise and Scripture sheet, and the reflection sheet.
- have ready small, empty pots, potting mix and common herb seedlings (such as parsley, sage, mint, rosemary, lavender or thyme), so each retreatant will be able to pot up a seedling to take home OR, if you have more resources, make available some larger window boxes and flower plants
- pray with the John 15 passage – 'I am the vine ...' (vv. 1–11, especially 4–5)
- reflect for yourself on what part the natural world plays in your life and prayer
- read Peter Harris, *Kingfisher's Fire: A Story of Hope for God's Earth*, Oxford, UK: Monarch Books, 2008 OR visit the website of A Rocha, a Christian nature conservation organization www.arocha.org.

Focus:

This will depend on where the retreat takes place. If in someone's garden or other outdoors location, there will be no need to provide a central focus as the garden bears witness to the Creator's hand. If you begin indoors, you may want to set up a focus table or cloth with, for example, grapes and vegetables, packets of seeds and gardening tools.

Gathering:

Affirm those present for taking the time to come to this retreat and assure them that it will be a mix of input and reflection, including time to get their hands in the earth they love.

Opening prayer:

In *the* beginning you, O God, created ... we do not know how, or even why, but deep within Your Mystery, you desired this world into being.
In *our* beginning, you formed us in our mother's womb, creating us to enjoy this beautiful world, to share responsibility for stewardship of the world's resources and to grow in your love.
Give us now, we pray, a fresh awareness of your life expressed through the natural world, so that, with opened eyes, we may see this world for what it is:
your precious gift to us. Amen

Leader's input:

To bring everyone on board, start by giving some time for people to share a little of their own 'gardening' stories in pairs, followed by a brief bringing together of some of the principles gathered from those present, for example trial and error, joy and relaxation, effort and success/disappointment, seasons of life, growth, flowering and decay, weeding and feeding, etc.

In the next hour and a half we are going to reflect on the place of the garden and the natural world in our spiritual lives. There will be time for you to go out and get your hands into the soil if you want to, and there will be time to invite God into your gardening practice in an intentional way.

All of us here today have something in common – our love of gardening and the outdoors. Some of us may be very experienced gardeners, some of us may be willing but untutored, wanting to learn more. We may have seen references in the media to a discernible shift towards people growing their own vegetables. There are even waiting lists for allotments in some areas because a new generation of people is starting to realize the benefits of working together and sharing ideas, information and wisdom – as well as the products of their labours. Gardening gurus on television and the persistent popularity of events such as the Chelsea Flower Show, illustrate a growing need for information and experience of gardening and gardens.

Last century, Dorothy Frances Gurney, wrote those now familiar lines in *Garden Thoughts*:

The kiss of the sun for pardon,
The song of the birds for mirth,
One is nearer God's Heart in a garden,
Than anywhere else on earth.

Less well-known, but similar in its theme, is George Bernard Shaw's:

The best place to seek God is in a garden. You can dig for him there.[18]

Hand out copies of the two quotations and then invite comments and discussion using the following to get started.

✻ Why have Gurney's simple lines survived to this day?
    What is there about Shaw's words that surprises you? touches your heart or mind?

Perhaps part of the reason these quotations still speak to us, is that the Creation, sometimes called 'God's second book', is a visible reminder of complexity of form, of a persistent drive for growth, of exceptional beauty, of mystery and of power beyond belief, an ever-present link with the One whose Word brought all things into being. But perhaps this closeness to God also has something to do with the *process* of gardening itself:

• the hands-in-the-earth practicality of it
• the seasonal changes
• the waiting and the hoping
• the vulnerability to the elements, to forces outside our immediate control
• the need for regular care by the gardener: we don't just plant and walk away
• the partnership that develops between a garden and the gardener
• the wonder of a bud bursting into bloom or vegetables ready for the table.

Invite other possibilities or add some of your own ...

Over time, as we work in a garden, getting to know the rhythms of the seasons, the needs and uniqueness of each plant, something special happens. We find ourselves moving away from being uninvolved observers of flower and vegetable plants, and begin to fall in love with the plants we tend faithfully: feeding, watering, weeding, watching, celebrating growth and fullness of fruit, flower or flavour. Somehow as we do this, we also begin to sense something of the deep commitment of our God

---

18 In *The Adventures of the Black Girl in Her Search for God*, 1932 http://www.quotegarden.com/gardens.html accessed 13.9.09

to the whole of Creation – to its restoration and renewal through partnership – God and people working together.

Depending on the group and the time available, you might introduce the John 15 passage – read it through to them twice and ask them what they notice. Make sure that the concept of partnership with God, the necessity of staying connected to God, the purposeful pain of pruning, etc. are covered before moving on to the practical section of the retreat.

Explain the next part of the retreat time – there are a number of activities to choose from here, but you could add different activities depending on the group and the gardens/outdoor sites to which you have access. It's important that people don't rush and don't talk to each other during this time – it is time for them and God alone, so they can meet God's world directly in the window box, garden or the woods nearby. Give retreatants a copy of the options and a portion of John 15. Tell retreatants that you will be out and about with them if anyone has any questions or wants to talk, so there is no need for them to talk to each other. ☺

Reflective activities:

⚜ Go outside and take a 'long, loving look' at the natural world around you. Do this in silence, asking God or Jesus to be present, perhaps even imagining him walking or sitting beside you as you look at the Creation. Stay with anything that draws your attention, letting yourself be absorbed in the detail, colour and mystery before you. When you are ready, talk or write or sing your response to God.

⚜ Choose a seedling and very S-L-O-W-L-Y put it into a new pot, ready to take home. Take a few minutes to pay attention to the process – what that was like, and how you felt as you did this activity *slowly* instead of at your usual, quicker pace.

⚜ Make up a planter box for an elderly or unwell neighbour – pray as you put the flowers into the earth that they may bring joy and colour into the person's life.

⚜ Do some weeding – s-l-o-w-l-y. Imagine Jesus kneeling beside you as you do this. If you want to, read Jesus' words about the tree and its fruit, think how it might apply to your life, and then talk to God or Jesus about what you have discovered.

Concluding comments:

Welcome everybody back and, once they are settled, invite them to share something of their experience with one or two others (depending on the numbers), and then invite people to give a little feedback about how they found that experience.

Summarize what you've been hearing from the retreatants, picking up what seem to be common threads. For example:

The natural world is full of wonder and we've experienced something of that today. We may also have noticed some of the environmental impact of human beings' drive for consumption, etc.

Then continue:

The question now becomes: What can we do to help care for Creation?

What can you and I do so that we make a gentler imprint on the earth and encourage others to do the same? Although we may not be as influential as the people whom we thought of earlier today, we can still be actively engaged in the great work of literally saving the planet for those who will follow us in generations to come. We can begin by brainstorming some ideas.

Write ideas up on whiteboard as they are offered, for example:

- make compost
- start recycling rubbish
- walk or cycle instead of taking the car all the time
- establish a worm farm
- start a community garden or help others to establish gardens at home
- make up plant boxes or small container gardens for those who have no garden space at home.

There is energy among us for change, there is hope for the future as we trust God's grace to sustain us. So let us gather the thoughts and feelings and discoveries of this time spent 'Gardening with God'. Let us pray:

Patient and loving God,
you build times of waiting into the cycle of nature and into our lives,
although we struggle to see the wisdom, sometimes, in the waiting.
Help us face the bits of ourselves that need
the firm yet gentle touch of your pruning.
Increase in us the good fruit so that, to those around us,
we may be vibrant and attractive signs of your presence.
Help us step beyond apathy, beyond our comfort zones, as we respond
to your call to care for Creation. Amen.

Gardening with God – exercises and Scripture sheet

Go outside and take a 'long, loving look' at the natural world around you.
Do this in silence, asking God or Jesus to be present, perhaps even imagining him
walking or sitting beside you as you look at the Creation.
Stay with anything that draws your attention, letting yourself be absorbed in the
detail, colour and mystery before you.
When you are ready, talk or write or sing your response to God.
(There is no need for embarrassment, God delights in you just as you are.)

Choose a seedling and very S-L-O-W-L-Y put it into a new pot, ready to take home.
Take a few minutes to pay attention to the process – what that was like, and how you
felt as you did this activity *slowly* instead of at your usual, quicker pace.

Do some weeding – s-l-o-w-l-y. Imagine Jesus kneeling beside you as you do this.

Choose one of the following portions of psalms. Read it several times slowly,
think how it might apply to your life, write your thoughts, feelings and questions
in your journal, and then talk to God or Jesus about your situation.

The righteous flourish like the palm tree,
and grow like the cedar in Lebanon.
They are planted in the house of the LORD;
they flourish in the courts of our God.
In old age they still produce fruit;
they are always green and full of sap,
showing that the LORD is upright;
he is my rock, and there is no
unrighteousness in him.
Psalm 92.12–15

Happy are those
who do not follow the advice of the
wicked,
or take the path that sinners tread,
or sit in the seat of scoffers;
but their delight is in the law of the LORD,
and on his law they meditate day and
night.
They are like trees
planted by streams of water,
which yield their fruit in its season,
and their leaves do not wither.
In all that they do, they prosper.
Psalm 1.1–3

Gardening with God – reflection sheet

Jesus said to his disciples:

'Abide in me as I abide in you. Just as the branch cannot bear fruit by itself, unless it abides in the vine, neither can you unless you abide in me. I am the vine, you are the branches. Those who abide in me and I in them bear much fruit, because apart from me you can do nothing.'
John 15.4–5

To engage with this Scripture passage, use *lectio divina* (slow reading, making connections with your own life, talking to God about your discoveries, and then resting in God) or imaginative prayer (putting yourself in this Gospel story hearing Jesus speak to you OR seeing yourself with Jesus in a vineyard you know or can imagine in this time and place).

Seeds

What grows in the grounds of your neighbourhood, in the varied soil of family, and friends, workmates and shopkeepers?

Are you active in the garden of their souls or interested only in self-protection, paying no attention to veiled appeals as worldly weeds and thorns pierce the fragile walls of their well-being?

Where are the seeds of love waiting to be sown, and tended with all your willingness and wisdom? Are you waiting for a special moment to start your planting programme? Are you waiting for 'just the right mix' of time and place, for the 'right word', or signs of interest in the process of growth?

Wait no more

Your family need the seeds called 'You matter'.
Your friends need the seeds called 'Compassion'.
Your community need the seeds called 'Hope'.

Now is the time for planting, for courteous, daily watering; for compost of encouragement and forgiveness-fertiliser, dug in with the respect and reverence due the growing soul as it reaches for the light of the Son.

Now is the time for planting the seeds of love.

Spend time with God reflecting on your own part of this world – your home and neighbourhood.

How might you begin to be a Christian in conservation?

Snack 3.9 One picture tells a thousand words

Suitable for any group including young people or the elderly as a 1½ to 2-hour retreat time.

N.B. If the group includes many elderly, tactfully check that none has visual limitations that would affect their ability to see the sort of pictures you will be using during the retreat.

Leader's preparation:

- read the L&F resource sheets '2.16 Praying with Scripture 1 – sacred reading/ *lectio divina*', '2.18 Praying using an art work as a starting point', '2.9 Keeping a spiritual journal, and writing as prayer', and '2.19 Silence and solitude'.
- familiarize yourself with the range of pictures available on pp. 107 and 108 or downloaded from the Canterbury Press website. These can be used as focus images for retreat or personal prayer and reflection, without having to seek further permission so long as you acknowledge the source
- print off a large (A4) copy of the Pentre Ifan Burial Chamber, and the 'light' and 'ducks' pictures (or put them onto PowerPoint or a similar computer programme to display them using a computer and data projector)
- have enough small (A5) coloured copies of 'light' or 'ducks' for retreatants to have their own copy or, if you have decided to use other pictures, print them off on photo quality paper
- make copies of the relevant L&F resource sheets for each retreatant
- depending on the age and mobility of the group have either a large table, or a large cloth on the floor, on which to put the pictures so the retreatants can reach them easily
- ideally, read Nouwen's *The Return of the Prodigal Son* or watch Sr Wendy Beckett's interviews
- work through the *lectio divina* process with the 'light' or 'ducks' picture yourself
- because this particular 'snack' can raise deep personal issues for retreatants, find out who could be available as a listening ear, counsellor or spiritual director to whom referral could be made if you don't have the time or the skills to support retreatants yourself.

Focus:

Copies of the selected photographs spread out on a large table or on a cloth on the floor. In the centre you could put a vase of flowers, a large candle or a cross AND a pile of Bible study books ...

Gathering:

Welcome everyone. If the group is meeting for the first time, allow a little time for simple introductions. If there are young people present, ask them to turn off their mobile phones and then, as part of the opening prayer, they can put them on the focus cloth for the duration of the retreat. If this is the first time that participants have spent time in silence, give them the L&F resource sheet on 'Silence and solitude', and take time to ensure that everyone is clear that there will be time for silent reflection, followed by time for processing in pairs as little or as much as they wish. And, as always, take a few moments to talk about confidentiality.

Opening prayer:

We begin with some silence so our busy minds can begin to slow down a little as we come together to learn more about ourselves and the various ways God communicates with us.

Allow at least a full minute's silence so retreatants are introduced to silence in a manageable 'snack' before the longer silence later in the retreat – then advise them that you will be inviting them to lay down their mobile phones on the central table or cloth as you come to the end of the prayer:

Creator God, you have given us eyes to see the world around us, minds to help us explore and understand the things we see, and hearts to respond to the love you hold out to us each day. Guide our reflection, so our seeing and thinking and loving may be enlivened by your Spirit, as we spend time in the silence with you.

As a way of demonstrating our intention to listen to you O God, we lay our phones down, fasting from texting or calling others, so we can pay attention to what you have to say to us today. Amen.

Leader's input:

You'll see a whole pile of books here, books written to help people learn more about the Bible and God.

Briefly describe them.

Some of you may have used books like these or you may have searched the internet for help with understanding God and faith and Jesus ... Today we're not going to look at any of them. Instead, we're going to experience how the visual arts can help us draw closer to God.

Using a starter question such as, 'Over recent years, what picture has made an impression on you?' *Facilitate a discussion on the pictures they mention, and try to elicit some ideas about what made them memorable, for example graphic depiction of war themes; something that evoked an emotional response; someone whom the retreatant knew well; amazing use of light or colour; beauty; human relationships; humour, etc.*

Showing the large Pentre Ifan Burial Chamber picture, ask:

What's your initial response to this picture?

Take a few answers and then tell the following story:

A woman was attending a two-hour retreat a bit like this one. Although the afternoon was shaped around praying with Scripture, several photos were available for people to work with, if nothing from Scripture had touched their hearts that day. At the end of the afternoon, the woman told the facilitator what had happened for her as she reflected on this photo. She said she had been thinking about her family situation and how it felt as if she was trying to hold up the large stone all by herself. As she spent time thinking and listening prayerfully, it became clear to her that God was inviting her to ask others to help her with the difficulty she was facing. She was a very self-sufficient person, used to coping alone, but she realized that she needed other people and, what was more important, there were others with whom she *could* share this load – *if* she was prepared to ask for help. It was a significant discovery – and exactly what she needed to hear from God that day. She faced her tendency to take on too much and the pride which got in the way of asking for help; she also learned that God was interested in the details of her life and would provide her with practical suggestions if she took the time to be still and to open her heart to God.

We see so many images on television and in the media; we might take loads of pictures on our phones or digital cameras but, because the majority of these images never occupy the centre of our attention for any length of time, they rarely become a vehicle for God's communication with us. The sort of response experienced by the woman I've just told you about, happened because she took the time to 'contemplate' one picture. She looked at it closely for a long time with an open mind and an attentive heart, listening for the 'still, small voice of God'. She discovered the wonderful truth that, when we give God our time, we learn something about ourselves as well as about God's love for us.

So how do we begin? One basic way of working with pictures like these, or with any other visual medium such as sculpture, tapestry, weaving, porcelain, architecture, carving, painting, etc. is similar to the *lectio divina* process.

Go briefly through the lectio divina *process if the group is unfamiliar with it, ending with:*

This approach allows us to engage deeply with the art work, *'reading it'* like a piece of holy text. This practice is not unlike the Russian Orthodox Christian way of praying with an icon. An icon is *not* considered something to be worshipped in itself, rather it helps believers fix their attention on some characteristic of God. Believers are invited to 'read' the icon – not simply look at it – because an icon is a window into the divine which has to be opened slowly, respectfully and expectantly. Gradually the icon reveals layers of meaning, much as our understanding and appreciation of a passage of poetry or prose is deepened as we spend time lovingly with the text.

Practical exercise:

⁑ There are two photographs for you to contemplate or 'read' during the time of silent reflection. *(One was taken by Phoebe Harrop during a school photography course; the other by me near a local beach.)* Both reflect the elements of ordinary life which, if contemplated, can be bearers of the sacred all around us. You can work with one or both, as the Holy Spirit leads you.

These pictures are available in colour to download from the Canterbury Press website. Give copies of the two pictures to each retreatant. Take the group through the following process, details of which are also on the L&F resource sheet 2.18. Give the group 45 minutes to an hour to work on their own in silence before returning to the full group.

Lectio	look closely at the piece of visual art for *at least* 15 minutes, longer if you want.
Meditatio	invite the Holy Spirit to help you 'chew over' or make connections with your own situation, your community, and with God. Consider what the various elements in the picture might symbolize for you. You may like to write a few notes in your journal or do a mind-map, or brainstorm ideas, feelings, questions.
Oratio	respond to God: talk, draw, dance, walk, cry, sing, whatever seems best. Share your feelings, thoughts, worries and dreams with the God who loves *you*.
Contemplatio	rest in God, let God love and be with you, enjoy God and take time just to 'be'.

For your information, some of the connections other retreatants have made with these particular photographs are listed below each picture. You'll notice a mixture of literal, symbolic and highly personal responses. Be prepared for this exercise to touch some people deeply. If that happens, ensure that you are able to offer time with the person individually or that you have arranged for others to be available by phone or in person after the retreat.

'Light'   'Ducks'

Hands catching drops of water   Mother duck leading her ducklings away
Christe lux mundi (Taizé chant)   from danger
Christ the light of the world   Mother duck abandoning her ducklings
Being receptive   Mother duck with TWO ducklings (response
Fire and water   of a woman who was able to have only ONE
Not wanting to waste water   child)
Bearing the light of Christ   The narrow margin between death and life
                                         The risk we have to take to get to 'green
                                         pastures'
                                         Always tagging along behind my older sister

Concluding comments:

The Bible is full of visual references that would have immediately engaged the listeners' imagination, drawing them into the story and reminding them of their connection to God. Our daily lives are full of images too, and whenever one catches our attention we know that, through it, the Spirit of God can draw our attention to some new awareness of God, building our confidence in a God of grace and goodness, helping us get closer to Jesus.

What can also happen, and a number of you may have experienced this today, is that sometimes the power of a picture to reach deep inside us can take us by surprise.

If a difficult memory or emotion has surfaced during this retreat, it has not happened by chance. It has happened because God wants us to be whole and is always drawing us towards healing, whether of old hurts or present difficulties. If you have discovered a part of yourself that is tender, vulnerable or touchy, instead of pushing this feeling underground, continue to take it to prayer as honestly as you can. If you need some help or would like to talk to someone in confidence, then I am available directly after this retreat; I also have the names and numbers of several people who have offered to support and listen if that would be helpful. We are here to help each other 'walk the journey and share the load'.

Closing prayer:

**God of growth and healing,
God who comes to us through other people's creativity,
be with us now as we go from this place and pick up our busy lives.**

Invite any who've laid down their mobile phones to pick them up again.

**May your gentle Spirit touch our yearning hearts.
May your joyful Spirit warm the days ahead.
May your compassion soothe our memories.
May your love remind us of our beauty.
May your hand hold us as we journey on.
trusting that you are with us always. Amen.**

Note: If you want to use specifically religious art, then you will enjoy Joanne Garton's paper, *Responding to God through religious art*, Spiritual Growth Ministries, New Zealand, 2009, available on the Spiritual Growth Ministries website: http://www.sgm.org.nz/research_papers.htm.

Colour versions of all these pictures are available to download from the Canterbury Press website.

1 The towpath near Shugborough, UK

2 Monarch Butterfly emerging from chrysalis

3 Whale sculpture, New Plymouth, NZ

4 Poles marking the pilgrims' path, Lindisfarne

5 A pohutukawa tree clinging to the cliff, NZ

6 A modern children's playground – anywhere

7 A little doll named 'Zoe' – abundant life

8 St Teresa's convent courtyard, Avila, Spain

Colour versions of all these pictures are available to download from the Canterbury Press website.

9 *Pentre Ifan Burial Chamber, Wales*

10 *Coughton Court gardens, UK*

11 *Autumn splendour, Taupo, NZ*

12 *Central Birmingham*

13 *Memorial, Warsaw*

14 *St Paul's, London*

15 *Mary's garden*

16 *St Cuthbert's Island, Northumbria*

Reproduced by permission

© Sue Pickering 2010

Snack 3.10 A half-day hike for the fit and faithful
OR a stroll round city streets for the slow and sleepy!

I've left this 'snack' until last as, being 'on-the-move', it is a bigger undertaking than the preceding 'snacks'. Either option is suitable for people who have a lot of energy or who might describe themselves as 'practical' Christians who don't think they can 'sit around in silence', so the shorter silences, sharing and group prayer provide a balanced introduction to how contemplative prayer practices can be integrated into ordinary activity.

Retreat 'A' – a half-day hike for the fit and faithful

While it's reasonable to think that people who choose this option will be able to complete the hike, it pays to make sure that everyone who registers can walk for up to three hours without becoming exhausted! As this retreat will probably be offered/ advertised through a church, talk to the vicar, wardens or others in authority to see if there are any legal, insurance, or health and safety issues that need to be attended to before you go any further with the planning.

Retreat 'B' – a shorter stroll round city streets for the slow and sleepy

As the name of this retreat implies, this is pitched at the fitness level of the ambling shopper. Retreatants need to be able to walk (or use a mobility scooter) for about an hour and a half in total, depending on the route you choose. You could choose to pray your way around the edges of the parish. If a shorter option is needed, look within your immediate community (or one within car-pooling distance) to choose areas of need – for example a prison, areas of obvious economic deprivation, a school or kindergarten, a hospital, an aged-care facility, factories, etc. Plan a route that takes in several of these sites where you can stop for prayer and reflection. (But – don't forget to include a good cafe!)

Again, run the retreat past those who have ultimate responsibility for a church-promoted event.

Leader's preparation (appropriate for either option):

- read L&F resource sheet '2.13 Moving – meditative walking' and '2.1 Attitudes and expectations – waking up to God'
- pray with Luke 24.13–35 (the walk to Emmaus) – the pattern for BOTH retreats
- find someone who has nursing or medical experience, and a first-aid kit, to go with you

- prayerfully choose where you will go, and then walk the route yourself. Decide where you are going to stop for prayer and reflection (four stops evenly spaced if possible)
- gauge the level of difficulty of the terrain and what sort of footwear, etc. people might need
- select a place to stop for refreshments in town, like a local cafe (check whether there are any toilets available). Those taking the rural option will need to bring their own food and water, but it's important that you know where shelter and toilet needs can be accommodated.
- check that there is mobile phone coverage and if not, arrange an alternative communication option; carry a GPS or locator if your chosen rural route is well off-road or rugged
- send to those who register a description of the retreat, a copy of L&F sheet '2.13 Moving – meditative walking', and a list of what they will need to bring with them
- have available copies of the Scripture passages for each person. For the rural option, make up your own questions and prayers; for the urban option, these are provided.
- have a map of the route for each person, showing the four places you're going to stop at
- for either retreat, make sure that you give a responsible person a map of your route, estimated time of return, a list of names of participants and a next-of-kin contact number 'just in case'.

Once you get under way, the following pattern is the same for BOTH retreats:

☺ personal reflection during the meditative walk, then, at each prayer-post:
☺☺ leader facilitates brief sharing of experience – in pairs and /or whole group if numbers are small
✦ leader summarizes the emerging themes/observations, offers a prayer and then,
📖 leader reads aloud the Scripture for the next stage of the journey …

At the end of either retreat, offer time for individual and group reflection and, if it's part of your tradition, you may also like to celebrate the Eucharist together, focusing on the final passage:

'... how he had been made known to them in the breaking of the bread.' (Luke 24.35)

Hike for the fit and faithful –
prayers and leader's guide-sheet

This option does not include a lot of detailed reflection questions or prayers at each stopping post. If you'd like to include these, then adapt those in the prayer and reflection sheet for the 'slow and sleepy' option to relate to a rural rather than an urban context.

Read from this text or use your own words to begin the process.

Welcome to this opportunity to spend time out in the beautiful natural world, with each other and with God. There is a map for each of you clearly marked with the four places where we are going to stop for prayer and reflection. So that we can really listen to God as we walk, we're going to walk in silence until we reach a prayer-post.

Remind people of the key points from '2.13 Moving – meditative walking'

When we stop at each prayer-post we'll spend some time sharing what we might have noticed, just in pairs. We'll pray together, hear the next portion of Scripture, and begin the next period of meditative walking. When we reach the third prayer-post we'll stop for a drink, share a little with each other and pray before beginning our return journey. Any questions?

We're going to use the story of the two disciples walking the road to Emmaus as touch-points for our reflection as we walk – you'll see some focus verses for you to think about on the accompanying sheet. *Hand this out to everyone.* I'm going to read the story aloud and then we'll ask for God's guidance and grace as we set off today.

Read the story from Luke 24.13–35 aloud and then pray:

Loving Creator God
as we set out on this hike today,
we ask that you will help each one of us
to see the natural world afresh.
Help us to walk with greater awareness of
where our feet fall and where our eyes rest.
May we be open to the miracle of life around us,
and the wonder of the world,
your gift to us, this day.
We pray this in the Spirit of Jesus
who walked the hills and paths of Palestine
and keeps us company today.
Amen.

Focus verses for use with 'Hiking option'

The story of the disciples walking on the road to Emmaus: Luke 24.13–35

Base to prayer-post 1: vv. 15–16:

While they were talking and discussing, Jesus himself came near and went with them, but their eyes were kept from recognizing him.

(Jesus walking with them unrecognized)

Prayer-post 1 to prayer-post 2: vv. 17b–21a:

They stood still, looking sad. Then one of them, whose name was Cleopas, answered him. 'Are you the only stranger in Jerusalem who does not know the things that have taken place there in these days?' He asked them, 'What things?' They replied, 'The things about Jesus of Nazareth, who was a prophet mighty in deed and word before God and all the people, and how our chief priests and leaders handed him over to be condemned to death and crucified him. But we had hoped that he was the one to redeem Israel.

(Jesus listening to their stories and feelings)

Prayer-post 2 to prayer-post 3: vv. 29–31:

... they urged him strongly, saying, 'Stay with us, because it is almost evening and the day is now nearly over.' So he went in to stay with them. When he was at the table with them, he took bread, blessed and broke it, and gave it to them. Then their eyes were opened, and they recognized him; and he vanished from their sight.

(Jesus known in the breaking of the bread)

(refreshment stop)

Prayer-post 3 to prayer-post 4: v. 32:

They said to each other, 'Were not our hearts burning within us, while he was talking to us on the road, while he was opening the scriptures to us?

(disciples remembering their response to Jesus)

Prayer-post 4 – return to base: vv. 33–35:

That same hour they got up and returned to Jerusalem; and they found the eleven and their companions gathered together. They were saying, 'The Lord has risen indeed, and he has appeared to Simon!' Then they told what had happened on the road, and how he had been made known to them in the breaking of the bread.

(sharing their experience with others)

Home base:

• talking about their experience with each other
• wondering together about 'what next'
• closing with prayer, and sharing the Eucharist if that is available.

Stroll for the slow and sleepy –
prayers and leader's guide-sheet

Welcome to this opportunity to spend time getting to know our wider community and the places where people gather for all sorts of reasons/the boundaries of our parish (choose one).

There is a map for each of you showing the route and marked with the five places we are going to stop for prayer and reflection.
You may like to describe each one briefly if people are not familiar with the area.

So that we can really listen to God as we walk, we're going to walk in silence.
Remind people of the key points from '2.13 Moving – meditative walking'.

We're going to use the story of the two disciples walking the road to Emmaus as touch-points for our reflection as we walk – you'll see some focus verses for you to think about on the prayer and reflection sheet.

As you pass the houses or shops, inwardly pray God's blessing on each one, listening for any prompts from the Spirit for particular prayer needs.

When we reach a prayer-post, we'll spend some time sharing what we might have noticed, just in twos or threes. We'll pray together for the needs of those at the site where we've stopped, hear the next portion of Scripture, and begin the next period of meditative walking. When we reach the third prayer-post we'll stop at the cafe for a while, share a little with each other and pray again, before beginning our return journey. Any questions?

I'm going to read the story and then we'll ask for God's guidance and grace as we set off today.
Read the story from Luke 24.13–35 aloud, and then pray:

EITHER 'Parish boundary' option

**God who formed the hearts and minds
  of all people**
be with us as we move around the
  edges of our parish.
Help us to notice your Spirit at work
in the ordinary and the seemingly
  simple.
Make us slow to judge, and quick to
  affirm the good we see,
the grace we glimpse.
May your love and light fill the lives
of those within our boundaries.
May they, and we, be blessed this day
and every day.
Through Jesus Christ our Lord. Amen.

OR 'local or wider community sites'
option – amend as needed
**God who formed the hearts and minds of
  all people**
be with us as we walk around our
  community today.
As we stop at sites of education, and of
  growth,
at sites of ageing, pain, grief or struggle,
may we be aware of your love and light
dancing with the children in their
  learning,
moving through the darkness and despair,
bringing hope and healing to all who
  turn to you.
May we be bearers of your peace
to all we meet this day.
Through Jesus Christ our Lord. Amen.

113

The walk to Emmaus, Luke 24.13–35 –
prayer and reflection sheet

Home base to prayer-post 1:

📖 *Scripture for prayer and reflection*
While they were talking and discussing, Jesus himself came near and went with them, but their eyes were kept from recognizing him. (vv.15–16)

Prayer-post 1:

☺☺ What did I notice/what drew my attention?
What am I finding difficult at the moment? What difficulties do I see in other people's lives?
Where have I seen signs of Christ's light on this walk so far/in my life?

☥ **We give you thanks that you walk alongside us always, O Lord.**
Even when we don't recognize your presence, your Spirit
knows us and all that we worry or wonder about.
Help us to be open to that same Spirit, as we walk
the next part of our journey today. Amen.

📖 *Scripture for prayer and reflection*
They stood still looking sad. Then one of them, whose name was Cleopas, answered him. 'Are you the only stranger in Jerusalem who does not know the things that have taken place there in these days?' He asked them, 'What things?' They replied, 'The things about Jesus of Nazareth, who was a prophet mighty in deed and word before God and all the people, and how our chief priests and leaders handed him over to be condemned to death and crucified him. But we had hoped that he was the one to redeem Israel.' (vv. 17b – 21a)

Prayer-post 2:

☺☺ What drew my attention?
Where do I see signs of hopelessness? signs of hopefulness?
What do I hope Jesus might do, or be, for me? for those whom I love?

✙ Loving God, we all have our hopes and ideas about
   how you might work in our lives. Sometimes we are
   disappointed, because what we think is best, doesn't happen.
   Help us to share our feelings and thoughts with you honestly,
   trusting that you listen to us, love us and always want the best for us.
   Give us the patience to wait, and the wisdom to see,
   the ways of your kingdom unfolding around us. Amen.

📖 *Scripture for prayer and reflection*
   ... they urged him strongly, saying, 'Stay with us, because it is almost evening
   and the day is now nearly over.' So he went in to stay with them. When he was
   at the table with them, he took bread, blessed and broke it, and gave it to them.
   Then their eyes were opened, and they recognized him; and he vanished from
   their sight. (vv.29–31)

Prayer- post 3 (refreshment stop):

As you sit down with your food and drink, visualize Jesus sitting with you, wanting
to be recognized, wanting to help you see the truth of his love for all people, including you.

☺☺ What did I notice on this section of the walk?
   What has this experience been like so far?
   What questions have arisen? What has surprised me? challenged me? excited
   me?

✙ God of journey, as we turn for home, refreshed
   by food and friendship, help us recognize you
   in each other, and in the people we see around us.
   Make us aware of the needs of the many,
   broken open by the greed of the few.
   May we respond to these needs,
   with the guidance and courage of your Spirit. Amen.

📖 *Scripture for prayer and reflection*
   They said to each other, 'Were not our hearts burning within us, while he was
   talking to us on the road, while he was opening the scriptures to us?' (v. 32)

Prayer-post 4:

☺☺ What has caught my attention?
    What has been my experience of the Scriptures (reading/praying/learning) so far?
    What might it be like to have my heart 'burn within me' as I read/pray the Word?
    What has been opening up for me as I've walked this path today?

✤ **Lord God, you have given us your Living Word**
   the sword of the spirit, rich in meaning and hope.
   Help us to be open to your particular word for us,
   given to guide, console, reassure, or invite us deeper
   into the fullness of your abundant Life,
   so we may be equipped to serve you and your world. Amen

📖 *Scripture for prayer and reflection*
    That same hour they got up and returned to Jerusalem; and they found the eleven and their companions gathered together. They were saying, 'The Lord has risen indeed, and he has appeared to Simon!' Then they told what had happened on the road, and how he had been made known to them in the breaking of the bread. (vv.33–35)

Return to base

You will have the chance to say a word or two about what you have discovered/experienced either as part of a Eucharist or closing prayers.

☺☺ What has emerged for me as a result of this time of meditative walking, reflection on Scripture?
    What do I want to take home from this retreat time for myself? for family? for my neighbours?
    What might God be inviting us to consider as a group, as an outcome of this experience?

✤ **O God, just as your disciples walked and listened to you, so may we faithfully**
   walk with you each day, and listen to your voice, however it comes to us.
   Just as they came to recognize your reality in the breaking of the bread,
   may we come to see you wherever heart-felt hospitality is shared,
   whenever we meet with others in love.
   Use us as agents of your grace to reach out to those around us.
   In Jesus' name. Amen

Part 4
Light meals – full Quiet Days

These opportunities for a longer time with God, usually have a simple structure, with various elements selected to suit the group and their familiarity with prayerful silence and reflection. For those totally new to this experience, a Quiet Day might look something like this:

9.30 am	Gather, welcome and settle
9.45 am	Opening worship and input from the leader to unpack the theme for the day
10.15 am	Personal silent reflection with optional individual spiritual direction if offered
11.45 am	Brief optional sharing
12 noon	Midday prayer
12.15 pm	Lunch (quiet conversation or silent or with music to act as a backdrop)
1.00 pm	Input from the leader
1.15 pm	Personal silent reflection and optional individual spiritual direction continues
2.15 pm	Gather for closing
2.30 pm	Closing liturgy which may include sharing and Eucharist
3.00 pm	Home-going

For others who may be more experienced, all the input for the day's theme could be offered at the start of the day, after the opening worship. Retreatants would then be free to use the rest of the day until 2.30 pm as they and God see fit.

It is really helpful if the leader/s of the retreat get to the retreat venue a good half to three-quarters of an hour before the advertised starting time. This will help you to:

- have five or ten minutes to bring the retreat once again to God, and then to sit in silence, drawing on God's strength and calming presence – particularly necessary if you are feeling a little stressed or nervous
- set up your resources and the centrepiece related to the theme
- arrange the seating in a circle or horseshoe-shape
- check on temperature, glare, draughts, toilets, kitchen, etc.
- put out items for any activity
- prepare refreshments
- on each chair place a copy of the opening worship/liturgy, a brief schedule of the

event's shape and content, and the initial reflection sheet – this minimizes disruption later
- provide a list of those attending, and space for unexpected people to give their details so they can be included in any distribution list advising of future retreat opportunities
- if you are providing one-to-one spiritual direction/holy listening, have another page on which people can tick a box to secure a nominated time slot – twenty minutes per person is realistic.

In my experience, it's unusual for every participant to arrive on time for a Quiet Day so it's important to have some way of managing the staggered arrival times without disruption and incorporating latecomers without embarrassment, for example put some reflective instrumental music on in the background so, as people arrive, they will be encouraged to slip into a quieter space themselves while they are waiting for others. Ask early arrivals to leave the chairs closest to the entrance for latecomers.

For each Quiet Day you will need to have:
- copies of reflection sheets or other handouts for each retreatant
- items for the opening liturgy/worship focus
- paper, felt-tips, crayons, etc. for drawing
- Bible, concordance, prayer book, etc.
- key additional elements related to the theme
- whatever you need if you are offering a Eucharist or other liturgical closing.

Notes for each of the Quiet Days

4.1 Hope and the Christian journey – emerging from the doldrums of our lives

Focus:

- symbols of winter and spring, like old leaves and new spring flowers (pictures will do if there are none to hand)
- a seed hidden in a pot with a label to show what it will become, and a seedling just emerging from a pot.

Materials:

- whiteboard, markers and eraser for brainstorming
- a map of the world, globe or atlas; large infinity symbol ∞ (A4 size); a large candle
- DVD of *Amazing Grace* to offer as a follow-up for discussion for those who wish.

4.2 May I have this dance? – the invitation to intimacy

Focus:

A selection from the following:

- an old gramophone; vinyl record covers for a range of dance music like ballroom, jazz, rock and roll, etc.
- a string of paper cut-out figures, linked together as if they are dancing in a line
- a few pictures of people dancing in different contexts, for example ice skating, tango, etc.
- a pair of ballet shoes or other type of dancing shoes; musical instruments associated with dancing, for example piano accordion, violin, a piccolo for a jig.

4.3 Bodies and blessings – the Word became flesh

Focus:

- a set of bathroom scales
- a number of items associated with particular parts of the body chosen for relevance to the group you are working with, for example walking stick, false teeth in a glass of water, spectacles
- jewellery, slippers, a box marked 'sanitary pads'/or 'condoms'
- some different representations of the baby Jesus, for example contemporary Christmas cards, fine art, etc.
- birthday candles – if possible in letters to spell out the name – JESUS – or else ordinary candles with the letters J-E-S-U-S cut out in card and taped to a toothpick for use as each candle is lit.

Materials:

- if you choose to do the HANDS exercise, gather some pictures of close-ups of hands of various ages and ethnicities
- several tubes of a pleasant hypoallergenic hand cream
- A4 paper, crayons and scissors
- any music relating to hands which appeals to you, for example Louis Armstrong 'He's got the whole world in his hands'.

4.4 Everyday God

Focus:

- name of each day of the week printed large on different colours of A4 card (landscape)
- the word 'EVERYDAY' printed on another piece of A4 card
- a clock with a large face – preferably one that has a seconds hand
- a wall planner for a year; a lectionary or Bible reading plan for a year.

4.5. Mud and mystery

Focus:

- a bottle of water with some sand or soil in it
- a couple of murder mystery novels
- several large question marks cut out in different coloured card.

Hope and the Christian journey – emerging from the doldrums of our lives

Opening Worship

SENTENCE OF THE DAY

Rejoice in hope, be patient in suffering, persevere in prayer.
Romans 12.12

Leader   When we see murderous acts on our screens
and we wonder just where the world's heading …

All   **You O God are our hope,**
for you stand for justice and peace.

Leader   When the climate around us is changing
and we don't know how we can stop it …

All   **You O God are our hope,**
for in you the round earth is held fast.

A globe, map of the world, or atlas is placed on the altar.

Leader   When our retirement savings have vanished
and our children have moved overseas.

All   **You O God are our hope,**
for in you we are all held, kept safe.

Leader   When we care for the church and those around us
yet the numbers attending are down …

All   **You O God are our hope,**
for you are at work in all people.

An infinity symbol (∞) is placed on the altar to symbolize the eternity of God's care for us.

Leader   When the strength of our youth is behind us
and we worry about our slow dying …

All   **You O God are our hope,**
for you walk us gently towards home.

Leader   When the dark of the night closes around us
and we wonder where light shall be found …

All   **You O God are our hope**
for in you all is light, all is well.

A symbol of light – a large candle – is placed on the focus table and lit.

Hope and the Christian journey – short talk 1

Begin by brainstorming words to describe DOLDRUMS, for example sadness, melancholia, depression, despair, pessimism, etc.

Then encourage retreatants to think of people in the Bible or in the Christian tradition who experienced 'being in the doldrums' – times of darkness, hopelessness, separation from family or friends – you may like to think of a few beforehand so you have ideas to share if the group doesn't offer much.

Depending on how well the group members know each other, you may also go on to invite simple personal sharing of a 'doldrums time in your life' in pairs for five minutes each – no obligation and no feeding back to the full group.

Then continue with a discussion ...

At the core of our tradition is the trinity of faith, hope and love. Many sermons talk about faith and about love but not a lot about *hope*.

🕯 **What do *you* think about when you hear the word 'hope'?**

Gather a few ideas before continuing ...
How loosely the word 'hope' can be used in the community:
    I hope I win the Pools or Lotto.
    I hope it's dry tomorrow so I can get my washing done.
    I hope I won't make a fool of myself at the meeting tomorrow night ...
Such uses point to a transitory, superficial or highly personal hope, rather than a hope that is deeply founded in God, lasting, enriching, confidence-building – the sort of hope that God offers to us all.

🕯 **What works against/undermines our hope?**

Discussion, make sure the following are mentioned:
- the media – crime, violence
- experiences of abuse, neglect, indifference
- our personality or upbringing – pessimism/optimism
- fear – about the future, climate change, money, race relations, the economy
- not knowing God's character and the truth that God will never leave us.

🕯 **What Gospel stories relate to the theme of hope?**

Some examples are:
- sometimes hope is born out of desperation:
    the woman who reached out to touch the hem of Jesus' garment (Luke 8.43–48)

the Syro-Phoenician woman who argued with Jesus, asking for the 'crumbs' (Mark 7.24–30)

the lepers or social outcasts seeking acceptance as well as healing (Luke 17.11–19)

- sometimes someone else hopes for the person who is in need:
    the friends of the person who was let down through the roof (Luke 5.17–26)
    the centurion who asked Jesus for healing for his servant (Luke 7.1–10)
    those who called blind Bartimaeus forward to meet Jesus (Mark 10.46–52)
- often hope is long-term, proclaimed prophetically:
    the sign given to Ahaz (Isaiah 7.14)
    the ministry of John the Baptist (John 1.19–34)
    a new heaven and a new earth (Revelation 21.1–4).

Introduce spring flowers – as a symbol of greening, blossoming, promise of new life and then discuss the following question:

🕯 What makes Christian hope unique?

Christian hope is found in the stories of the Gospels, in the life of Jesus, in the fruit of the Spirit, in the welcome of God. Jesus comes among us as the hope-bringer – not the bringer of the superficial hopes our society promotes, but the deep, enduring hopes made possible by our Lord's work on the cross and the action of the Holy Spirit in our lives here and now: our deep hopes for connection, for freedom, for healing and for peace of mind.

We can come to God no matter how small our hope may be, because even a thimble-full of hope can be transformative. Consider the story of the man who brought his son to Jesus in Mark 9.14–29. The disciples had been unable to cast out the offending spirit, but the man persisted and made sure that Jesus saw the boy himself. We glimpse the desperate father's state of mind as he tells Jesus:

'It has often cast him into the fire and into the water, to destroy him; but *if you are able* to do anything, have pity on us and help us.'
Jesus said to him, 'If you are able!—All things can be done for the one who believes.'
Immediately the father of the child cried out, 'I believe; *help my unbelief!*' (vv. 22–24, *my italics*)

Twice *(see italic print)* the father reveals his ambivalence, the mixture of hope and despair, which had brought him to Jesus. He is like so many of us today, wanting to believe in the Christ, wanting to hope for a good future for our children, but distracted by world events, suffering and personal tragedy, or by rational or scientific arguments that challenge the very existence of mystery or miracle.

123

Provide an opportunity for people to respond to this story – perhaps sharing their own mixtures of faith and doubt, of hope and fear, etc.

'If you are able ...' the man says to Jesus. Do we really believe that God can do the impossible? Do we know God so well that we can trust God to move the mountains of our relationship difficulties, push back the waters of fear as we age or lose loved ones? Can we hope that God has the power to do 'all things ... for the one who believes'?

In the silence this morning, you will be able to consider the implications of these questions for yourself as you work with some of the suggestions on the reflection sheet provided.

May God bless this time and bring you closer to that Love which passes all understanding.

Hope and the Christian journey – reflection sheet 1

What have been some of the 'doldrums' times in your life?

What would *you* like to say to God about those times?
What might *God* want to say to you about those times?
What helped you to emerge from those times?

If you are currently in a 'doldrums' place, spend some time with God reflecting on your current situation – then talk* to God about what is happening – be as honest as you can, as if talking to your best friend.

Ask the Holy Spirit to help you choose one of the Scripture stories below; enter into it **with your imagination,** as an onlooker or letting yourself meet Jesus, seeing what he might say to you, or what he might do.

The woman healed: Mark 5.25–34

Jairus' daughter: Mark 5.22–24, 35–43

The anointing at Bethany: Matthew 26.6–13

'I believe; help my unbelief.' *Mark 9.24*

With the Holy Spirit's guidance, spend some time reflecting on this verse.

What situations are you facing that cause you tension between being hopeful of God's grace and mercy, and doubting whether God can make a difference?

Bring your hopes and your doubts to God with confidence, knowing that God can transform your fledgling belief into something shining and strong.

We have waited eagerly for you O Lord, for you are our help and our shield.
Our hearts shall rejoice in you, because we have hoped in your holy name.
Psalm 33.19–20 (New Zealand Prayer Book, p. 233)

What 'doldrum' times are visible around your neighbourhood?

What signs of hope do you see in your community of faith, in your family, in your workplace or town?

Talk to God about what you notice.

(* You may prefer to write, draw, sing, dance or move to express your prayer.)

Hope and the Christian journey – additional resource sheet

We have this hope, a sure and steadfast anchor of the soul,
a hope that enters the inner shrine behind the curtain,
where Jesus a forerunner on our behalf, has entered,
having become a high priest forever according to the order of Melchizedek.
Hebrews 6.19–20

Hope and the Christian journey – short talk 2

This afternoon's input explores three qualities of Christian hope: realism, optimism, future-focus. [19]

Realism

When people are terminally ill, hope can 'take a back seat' as treatments come and go and the disease process continues relentlessly. A point may be reached when hope of a cure may well be unrealistic, but the dying person – and his or her family – can still hope: for effective pain relief, for loving hands to care for the diminishing body, for laughter and humour to lift the spirit, for time for reminiscence of all that life has been, for freedom from regret or guilt, for a peace-full dying. Hoping in this way does not deny the reality of the person's condition but offers a way of living their dying with grace and gratitude.

As Christians, we cannot deny the challenges to the institutional Churches as we have known them. We cannot pretend that ministry is easy or resources adequate, when the contrary may be patently obvious. We have to be realistic: prepared to critique what we are doing and how we are doing it, making space for the Spirit of God to enter our challenges, listening together in prayer until we find God's way forward for our parish, our community and our world. This 'way forward' may be small to start with, realistic in terms of the amount of time and energy we have to give, but trusting that, if what we are beginning is from God, then God will give it increase and bring it to completion (Philippians 1.6).

As Christians, we cannot deny the poverty we see in the slums of our cities, or the suffering produced when natural disasters devastate parts of the planet, displacing the marginalized. But nor can we deny the outpouring of support, practical help, financial resources and ongoing reconstruction provided by aid agencies, governments and individuals in response – surely God giving hope to those who seem to have no hope. God's creative Spirit will bring hope into any situation when we acknowledge the reality of what we are facing and our need of God's guidance and grace.

We hope in spite of difficulties, in spite of failure or tragedy, because our hope lies in and with God, not in ourselves. Above all, as Christians, we cannot deny that God can work even in the most intractable situation, for 'nothing will be impossible with God' (Luke 1.37).

---

19 Terms used by Rob Yule: http://www.stalbans.org.nz/teachings/rob_yule/power_of_hope/ power_of_hope_.htm.

Optimism

Begin with a question and discussion ...

🕯 **How have you seen the impossible become possible?**

Responses may include a mixture of the personal, regional or global, for example:

- reconciliation when a marriage was under threat
- conceiving a child after years of infertility
- recovery from an addiction
- local protest to protect part of the environment or to ensure wise management of resources
- the Abolition of Slavery Act in Britain in 1833
- the fall of the Berlin Wall over 20 years ago
- redemption of those who have been oppressed in some way, for example the Bible Society's work with former child soldiers in the Congo
- the Civil Rights Movement and the election of Barak Obama as President of the United States
- the end of apartheid in South Africa in 1993
- the first steps to the closing of Guantanamo Bay prison.

Social justice remains an essential focus for all of us, because there is so much more work to be done. The film *Amazing Grace,* for example, not only told the remarkable story of William Wilberforce's fight to abolish slavery in Great Britain, but also helped to heighten our awareness that slavery continues today – sweatshops in Third World countries, people trafficking, child soldiers, girls and women trapped in prostitution ... media reports keep these issues in the public arena and we are called to response, not apathy.

Invite the retreatants to add other examples of social justice issues of which they are aware/in which they are involved.

God is always at work bringing healing, order and hope. Along with others of good faith who have been prepared to take a stand, ordinary Christians like you and me have opposed unjust structures. Over 30 years ago, for example, a group of artists, students and Christians, including students from St John's Theological College in Auckland, invaded the pitch at a rugby game between the Springboks and the All Blacks in Hamilton, NZ in 1981. It was dangerous, it was unpopular, but it helped to publicize opposition to apartheid and brought pressure to bear on the South African government. With protest mounting within South Africa too, apartheid ended 15 years later.

When we are confronted by seemingly hopeless situations – things which seem far too big for us to tackle – we have only to remember the changes we have seen to political systems and structures in the last 50 years, to remind ourselves that entrenched attitudes and systems can be dismantled. We can remind ourselves too that our God is *Creator*; God's loving energy and creative intelligence find expression through people of good will everywhere, so problems can be solved, new ways forward found, and justice done for the poor, the homeless and those who are in prisons of their own or others making. This must give cause for optimism.

Future focus

God's kingdom is both here and now, *and* still unfolding, *fully* realized only in some future time. It is the 'both/and' nature of the kingdom that makes facing the future with confidence possible. Scripture paints a picture of what the future might look like in God's time, with God's love, peace, wisdom and justice spread like banners over the whole of creation. Rob Yule writes:[20]

> As a child I loved the biblical prophecies of a coming age of universal peace on earth. I continue to be stirred by their glorious vision of the nations going up to Jerusalem in the latter days to learn the ways of the Lord, of weapons of destruction being made into agricultural machinery, of war being studied no more, of animals and humans living in harmony, of the desert blossoming like the rose, of the whole earth being full of the knowledge of the Lord as the waters cover the sea (Isaiah 2.1–5, 11.1–9, 35.1–10, 65.17–25, Micah 4.1–3, Habakkuk 2.14).

If we truly believe that God is at work in the world, visible in all acts of mercy, active wherever there is goodness and love, consoling whenever there is pain and grief; if we truly believe that God is God, able to do far more than we can ever imagine (Ephesians 3.20) then, rather than being disempowered by current trying circumstances or threats of global catastrophe, we can choose to live hopefully in and with Christ. We can dream of a kingdom to come, 'a new heaven and a new earth' (Revelation 21.1–5) in which there will be no more tears or suffering. But we can also remember that Jesus told the Pharisees (Luke 17.21): 'The kingdom of God is among you.' 'Among' is sometimes translated 'within', but either way, it's clear that Jesus is talking about the *present reality* of the kingdom of God, a way of living which can change the world – if we would but live it out day by day.

May this afternoon's reflection give you some space to discover more of the kingdom of God within you, among you.

---

20 See Rob Yule, http://www.stalbans.org.nz/teachings/rob_yule/power_of_hope/power_of_hope_.htm.

Hope and the Christian journey – reflection sheet 2

'Hope is realistic. Hope is optimistic. Hope is futuristic.' (Rob Yule)

Spend some time thinking about this description –
ask the Holy Spirit to help you see where these three aspects of hope link
to your own life and the lives of those around you.

How might you begin to live as if the kingdom of God were with you in your
present reality?

You may like to do some journalling to help you express
what you are discovering about yourself, about God, and about hope.

Meditate on Jeremiah 29.11

I know the plans I have for you,
says the LORD,
plans for your welfare and not for
harm,
to give you a future with hope.

Almighty God, give us such a vision of
your purpose and such an assurance of
your love and power, that we may ever
hold fast to the hope which is in Jesus
Christ our Lord.
Amen.

A New Zealand Prayer Book,
p. 623

Write your own prayer or song to God
about hope.

How might you be a bearer of hope in your family, among your friends, in your
community?

What do you need from God to help you be a hope-bearer with Christ?

Closing prayer:

O Jesus, you brought hope to the hopeless:
people who were on the margins,
people who were at the limits of their resources and energy,
people who were confined by convention
or imprisoned by illness.
Stay with us through the power of your Spirit, we pray.

When we feel hopeless, or on the edge,
may your clarity flow through us,
bringing a vision of new life in your love.

When we are sick and suffering, confused and uncertain,
may your wisdom inform our understanding,
assuring us of your compassion and companionship.

When we fall short of the fullness of life you want for us,
may your Word come to live in us,
teaching us more of your faithfulness and love.

Help us begin to live the Kingdom now,
for you are our Hope, for today and all time.
Amen.

May I have this dance? – the invitation to intimacy

Opening Worship

You have turned my mourning into dancing.
Psalm 30.11a

Leader We come as we are Loving God,
thankful that we can spend time with you this day.

All **We come with our preoccupations,**
the humdrum and the humorous,
the boring and the challenging,
the ups and downs of life,
known and held by you.

FIRST CANDLE IS LIT

Leader When the world would have us limp
under the strain of debt and doubt;
beneath the worry of the present
and concern about the future …

All **We choose to stand tall in you,**
to let your light and love,
reveal to us the wonder
of the dance divine within us.

SECOND CANDLE IS LIT

Leader Thank you God for loving us
so much that we are breathless –
in wonder and in silence,
we will listen to your voice.

All **We will wait upon your word**
hearing your invitation
to the closeness lovers share
as we give you all we are.
Amen.

THIRD CANDLE IS LIT

May I have this dance? – short talk 1

Dance is part of many – perhaps most – cultures … if we've travelled we may have had the treat of seeing intricate Thai dancing or Spanish flamenco, or of joining in Russian Cossack dancing or a Hawaiian hula! *(See if people want to share any of their experiences.)*

🕯 **When you think about dancing, what comes to mind?**
Spend a moment with the person next to you and share a little of your own experience …

Perhaps you recalled dancing with others or by yourself; perhaps you danced at competitions or in a relaxed homely environment where nobody minded whether or not you stood on people's toes. We can dance in a group, square dancing for example or line dancing. We can dance on our own too – it helps with the housework, keeps us supple and is a beneficial way of enjoying our bodies if we live alone.

But what about dance and our spiritual journeys – literally and metaphorically?

When we look at most institutional Church environments today, dance is literally absent from our worship services; in some denominations it's been actively discouraged. Occasionally we might see a liturgical dance as part of a special service – or chance upon a circle dance in a Christian setting, as I did one memorable year when most of the people attending a conference at Swanwick, joined hands and danced around the grounds singing. To the Hebrew people, singing, making music and dancing, have always been part of everyday life. People set their faith stories to music, sang psalms to maintain their relationship with God, and used dancing to express their joy and celebration:

- Ecclesiastes 3.4b speaks of there being both 'a time to mourn *and* a time to dance'.
- The psalmist writes 'Praise his name with dancing' (Psalm 149.3).
- King David 'danced before the LORD with all his might …' (2 Samuel 6.14), as the ark was brought to the city of David.

One of the first miracles Jesus did took place at a wedding – where the men would have danced together and the women would have danced together – as they do in Jewish weddings to this day.

- Dancing helped people in biblical times to **worship** God.
- Dancing helped people in biblical times to **build their relationships and communities**.
- Dancing helped people in biblical times to **express their joy**.

Including dance or movement in our worship services and in our own times of prayer and praise at home may not be easy and won't happen without some compromise or resistance. Even in biblical times, not everyone wanted to join the dance. Michal, daughter of Saul, disapproved of David's display of joy and thanksgiving as he danced, accusing him of showing off to the women (2 Samuel 6.20–21):

> 'How the king of Israel honoured himself today, uncovering himself today before the eyes of his servants' maids, as any vulgar fellow might shamelessly uncover himself!'

But David was very clear for whom he was dancing, replying:

> 'It was before the Lord, who chose me in place of your father and all his household, to appoint me as prince over Israel, the people of the Lord, that I have danced before the Lord.'

Perhaps it's time to begin reintroducing movement and rhythm to our liturgies – or at the least to our own prayer lives – reclaiming our body's capacity to express itself physically not just with words or art.

I am not talking about highly energetic leaping about but about gentle bodily responsiveness to help us express our love and longing for God, our thankfulness or even our lament.

For the rest of the morning I invite you to work with the reflection sheet being passed around – ask the Holy Spirit to help you choose a starting point and to guide you as you pay attention to what is going on in your interior life, as you spend time in silence with God this morning.

Remind people to get a drink whenever they want to, lunch is silent with music as we munch, individual spiritual direction times are available, and we gather at 1 pm for the second part of the day.

May I have this dance? – reflection sheet 1

'I am the Lord of the Dance,' said he. (Sydney Carter)

Ask the Holy Spirit
to help you choose one of the Scripture
stories below.

Enter into it
with your imagination,
as an onlooker or letting yourself meet
the welcoming father in Luke 15,
or the generous provider Jesus in
John 2, seeing what they might say to
you or what they might do.

The celebration when the prodigal
returned home. (Luke 15.25–32)

The wedding at Cana. (John 2.1–11)

Spend some time with the question,
'Did Jesus really dance?'

What would it mean for you if
the answer was 'Yes'? Or if it was
'No'?

Spend some time reflecting on your
experience of dance and dancing.

If your experience is generally positive,
begin to remember before God
those situations and people who
helped you learn about your own
ability to move to the rhythm of
the music, to feel comfortable in
your own body.

If, however, you believe you have
'two left feet' and no sense of rhythm,
ask the Holy Spirit to bring to mind
any hurtful or embarrassing memories so
that the healing light of Jesus can
touch the tender spots
and bring some peace of heart and mind.

What is your experience of dancing with others – square dancing, line dancing,
Scottish country-dancing or even competition ballroom dancing?

What cultures in your neighbourhood dance as part of their community life?

How might dancing with others become part of your life/your church's life
if it hasn't been so far?

© Sue Pickering 2010

May I have this dance? – short talk 2

This morning we've focused on dancing at the literal level, and what our particular 'dance history' might be. We've also begun to think about what part dancing might have played in the lives of Jesus and the people of his day. This afternoon, we'll consider the way our desires and will relate to the will and desires of God. What are the dynamics of this metaphorical 'dance of the soul'? Is there a battle for supremacy, or is there a gentle yielding, so the One who knows the dance of life best, can lead us? Which raises the key question: 'How willing are we to let go of control and allow God to be God?'

This true story (with some details altered for confidentiality) says something about dance in both a literal and metaphorical sense:

A young man whom we'll call Tom had a bad accident and was left paralysed from the waist down. Although he made good progress and had even begun to join in wheelchair sports, two years later he still felt awkward and angry if faced with social situations, especially those which involved dancing.

One day Tom agreed to attend a youth camp as one of the young adult leaders. Everything was going well until the Saturday night when there was a disco. Before the music even started, Tom told the others that he was feeling a bit tired and went back to his room.

He had hardly closed the door when he felt God urging him to go back and join in. Instantly Tom started to think, 'I can't dance, what's the point of going back? They'll all be having fun and I'll be stuck in this thing!' He slapped the arms of his wheelchair in disgust. But the invitation came again ... and again ... 'Go back to the disco, Tom.'

Somehow Tom found himself going out of his unit in his wheelchair and over to the main hall. The door was open, he could hear the music – and he ventured inside. As his eyes adjusted to the dimmer light and he could see what was going on, he began to realize that he could somehow actually *feel* the music. Before he knew what had happened he found himself moving his chair in time with the rhythm, and using his hands to express the music's energy and fun.

A minute or two later, a girl came over and, without any pitying looks, smiled and started dancing with him, matching her movements to his. Tom was both stunned and delighted – things changed for him that night – a huge hurdle had been overcome – he felt less isolated and more connected to the others, he began to feel better about himself and he was awed by God's care for him ... God was turning his mourning into dancing.

The pivotal point in the story is the moment when Tom becomes aware of God's invitation to him to 'join the dance', to be part of, rather than separate from, the community. Although we can't know exactly what Tom was going through, we can understand that he may still have been trying to come to terms with his loss of mobility and freedom, and with his changed view of his attractiveness to others. For him 'dancing' could have become a metaphor to symbolize all that he had lost ... that is until God stepped in with that gently insistent invitation, offering the chance for Tom to begin to 'refresh' his self-image, and reconnect with others.

God invites us to dance too – we don't have to be famous or influential – we don't have to be clever or beautiful – we only have to be ourselves. But often, the first response to God's invitation is 'Who me? Look for someone else'.

Give examples: Moses, Exodus 3 or Peter in John 13.6–9.

A notable exception was Mary, the mother of our Lord. Her initial response was to wonder about *how* the Son of the Most High could take flesh and form in her womb, *not* whether she would agree. In Luke 1.38, she says, 'Here am I, the servant of the Lord: let it be to me according to your word.' In effect she is saying, 'I will dance with you, my God.' There is a stunning openness to the work of God in her life, and a clear-hearted willingness to align her will with the will of God – for the eternal benefit of humanity. We may be a bit afraid of the intimacy of the close relationship which God offers to everyone in Christ, but we can be encouraged by the example of Mary and countless others, people who have said 'Yes' to God and who, having joined the dance, have lived in a way that made a difference to others. God and a willing soul can do amazing things together.

For the next hour, choose a focus from reflection sheets 2 or 3; consider how you might respond to the Spirit's invitation to 'join the dance'. We gather for the closing prayers *(or Eucharist)* at 2.30 pm.

May I have this dance? – reflection sheet 2

David danced before the Lord with all his might …
2 Samuel 6.14

Using 'dance' as a metaphor for your spiritual journey and connection with God, spend some time reflecting on your own 'dance' history with God – your times of feeling connected with others, in your faith community, and your times of feeling more isolated.

What would help you to 'join the dance' and get closer – to God? to others? to yourself and your own needs?

How might you help others 'join the dance'?

Spend some time with God reflecting on your current situation –
then talk* to God about what you desire most – be as honest as you can be, as if talking to your best friend.

(* You may prefer to write, sing, dance or move to express your prayer.)

We hear the Spirit's music in Creation, in our own gifts, in life as it unfolds in us and in the world around us, and in the word of God.
God's gracious invitation is that we dance to that music. Jesus, as the song says, is the 'Lord of the Dance'.
True freedom and discernment mean that, while keeping our eyes on him, we create, not in isolation but together, our own gestures and movements in tune with the Spirit's music.
Those who really listen to the music have the freedom to invent their own steps and movements, and then they find that in fact they are all dancing in unison.

David Lonsdale,
Listening to the Music of the Spirit, pp. 65–6

Draw or write your response to Lonsdale's statement.

You have turned my mourning into dancing;
you have taken off my sackcloth and clothed me with joy,
so that my soul may praise you and not be silent.
O Lord, my God, I will give thanks to you forever.
Psalm 30.11–12

Pray with this Scripture and make some notes or drawings about your experience.
How does this Scripture apply to your life now?

IMAGINE JESUS INVITING YOU TO DANCE WITH HIM …

How do you feel? What do you think?

If you say 'Yes' what sort of dance do you do? What happens? How do you feel?

If you say 'No', how does Jesus help you face your fears?

Record something in your journal about this experience.

May I have this dance? – reflection sheet 3

Spend some time with this poem and picture and see what God might be saying to you through them.

The dance ...

I lean against the wall and watch
the swish of silk and satin;
others are chosen, but
no one asks for me.
My dancing dreams are dashed
and, alone, I turn away.

If only there were someone
to bring to life my longing,
to clasp me close and
hold me to his heart,
to help me dare to dance
with joy and with abandon,
careless of other's sighs
and crinkled brows.

Then will I know I am
both blessèd and beloved,
free to be myself
for all of time.

If you haven't already done so, you may like to consider one of the following themes: freedom and risk, youth and ageing, trust and letting go, joy and delight. How do these themes relate to your spiritual journey and your relationship with God?

Closing dance (!)

Following the pattern suggested in Part 1.7 Sharing (p. 11) bring the group together and allow half an hour for a gentle processing of some of their retreat experience.

Somewhere in that half hour, offer the retreatants the chance to experience a simple circle dance as part of the closing. By then they should be relaxed and a little adventurous!

Choose a Taizé chant like *Christus resurrexit* or any other suitable lively chant or song with a 4/4 rhythm.

A basic dance starts with all people holding hands facing inwards towards the centre of the circle.

Two paces to the left, that is left foot moves, right foot joins it; left foot moves, right foot joins it *(repeat)*.

Two paces to the right, that is right foot moves, left foot joins it; right foot moves, left foot joins it *(repeat)*.

Two paces into the centre, two paces out to the edge again, both starting with left foot *(repeat)*.

REPEAT above movements if you want to keep it basic.

Aim to go into the circle AND lift your hands, as the song comes to the ALLELUIA.

Play around with a few basic steps and you will soon come up with an original circle dance that all can enjoy. Just make sure that you have worked it all out beforehand and you have someone else who is willing to give it a go with you to demonstrate.

If you feel this is too scary for you, let alone for the group, then a simpler alternative would be to stand in a tight circle, put your arms around each other's waists/or hold hands and gently sway in time to some music with a regular beat, listening to the words, which could reflect the theme of walking with God, drawing closer to God, etc.

Closing prayer:

Loving God,
you call us closer to you in love,
you invite us to lay down our burdens,
and dance with you through life.
Help us to recognize our resistance,
and let ourselves be led
by your strong hand,
as the melody of
your mystery enfolds us.
Amen.

Bodies and blessings – the Word became flesh

SENTENCE OF THE DAY

For it was you who formed my inward parts;
you knit me together in my mother's womb.
Psalm 139.13

All standing, the candle for letter 'J' on the birthday cake is lit.

Leader   We gather this morning, away from the crowds,
             away from attitudes that demean the body
             and make it an object to be used, a commodity to be exploited.

All   **This body of ours we have borne**
             since our beginning
             a gift and a grace to express you in our lives.

With your eyes closed, gently touch your forehead, trace the shape of your ears, nose, cheeks, lips and chin. When all are ready, the candle for letter 'E' is lit.

Leader   This body of ours has become our home,
             we are used to its miracle, accustomed to its form.

All   **This body of ours is made with your love.**
             We are belovèd, we are precious, we are *your* life here on earth.

Gently touch your arms, feeling their shape, the bones and muscle. When all are ready, the candle for letter 'S' is lit.

Leader   Although we are ageing, although some are struggling
             to get through the days without potions or pills,

All   **this body of ours is still made for your love.**
             You see deep inside to the truth of our longing
             for more of your loving and more of our dying
             so we may make space in our being for you.

Gently place your hands over your heart and hold them there while the candle for letter 'U' is lit. Sit for the reading.

Leader   In the beginning was the Word, and the Word was with God,
             and the Word was God … And the Word became flesh and lived among us,
             and we have seen his glory, the glory as of a father's only son,
             full of grace and truth. (John 1.1, 14)

All   **Blessèd are you Lord God, in your son Jesus, who chose to come to us,**
             not with the pomp and splendour of an earthly king, but in the vulnerable,
             ordinary miracle of a baby; Love in a form we can embrace. Amen.

The candle for letter 'S' is lit; silence is observed.

Bodies and blessings – short talk 1

As we approach Christmas and the busyness of end-of-year celebrations, family gatherings and, for those of us in the Southern Hemisphere, the complicating factor of the long summer holidays, it is very easy to lose sight of the mystery of the incarnation, the indwelling reality of God fully present in a vulnerable human baby. But, if we set aside, even temporarily, the Christmas tack and tinsel, we can begin to ask ourselves: How can the presence on earth of 'God with us', 'Immanuel' (Isaiah 7.14) so long ago, so briefly, make a difference to life in our fast, complex, recession-struggling, climate change-deluged, contemporary world?

You may want to stop and give people time to give their own thoughts – this will depend on the group.

It makes a difference because Jesus lived a human life in a human body perfectly, more fully than anyone before or since. He was born of Mary, nursed at her breast, toddled along after Joseph, grew stronger as any active, healthy boy would grow. He experienced the challenge and joy of studying the Torah, the uncomplicated pleasure of working with wood, of walking and fishing, and being alive, just as we are alive today.

The incarnation is uniquely Christian and makes a difference because, as the Scripture says:

> ... Christ Jesus, who, *though he was in the form of God*, did not regard equality with God as something to be exploited, but *emptied himself*, taking the form of a slave, *being born in human likeness*. And being found in human form, he humbled himself and became obedient to the point of death— even death on a cross. (Philippians 2.5b–8, *my italics*)

Central to Jesus' identification with humanity, was this 'kenosis', this 'emptying himself', choosing *not* to avail himself of all the power, knowledge and resources at his disposal. We see this highlighted in the 'temptation in the desert' narrative (Matthew 4) and, at his arrest, in the poignant comment made to one of his disciples:

> 'Do you think that I cannot appeal to my Father, and he will at once send me more than twelve legions of angels? But how then would the scriptures be fulfilled, which say it must happen in this way?' (Matthew 26.53–54)

The incarnation makes a difference because Jesus *went through* what many people go through today as their lives take sudden turns, as illness or accident rip certainty from their vocabulary. He didn't theorize about human life from the safety of the

142

Trinity's loving community, he chose to *experience* it directly: physical thirst (John 4); gutting grief (John 11); betrayal at the hand of a friend; bloody-sweated fear; the desperate need for the support of sleepy friends; imminent death; excruciating pain; the paralysis of the cross … (Matthew 26.36–27.50).

Jesus did not speculate about the human condition, he chose to live it as a human being, undefended. Were we only to consider Christ's divinity, we would miss out on some of the core concepts of our faith. If we pay attention to the humanity of Jesus, it will help us to:

- come closer to him and to increase our understanding of just how much Jesus chose to give up so that he could walk the path to the cross
- treat our bodies with care, knowing that we share this flesh and form with the Son of God
- remind ourselves that we are the hands, feet, voices, hearts and minds of Jesus today
- know that our sufferings are held in the love of a God who is not remote or indifferent but who knows, in and through Jesus, what it is like to be human.

The reflection sheet being handed out now has several options designed to help you explore more deeply both the mystery of the incarnation and your own embodiment – ask the Holy Spirit to guide you as you spend time with the God who 'knit you together in your mother's womb'.

Give details of next activity – midday prayer if you are having that, or lunch with music while they munch.

Bodies and blessings – reflection sheet 1

¹In the beginning was the Word,
and the Word was with God,
and the Word was God.

¹⁴And the Word became flesh and lived
among us,
and we have seen his glory,
the glory as of a father's only son,
full of grace and truth.
John 1.1, 14

◆

Reflect on this Scripture passage,
using the *lectio divina* pattern to help you
read slowly.
Consider how these lines connect with
your life, tell God how you are at the
moment or give God thanks for the body
you have, and then rest in God's love.

Blessèd be:

each curl of toe, stretch of finger
orgasm's peak, frustration's sigh

each curve of breast, cell for thinking
tear for grieving, strength of thigh

each sniff and taste, yawn and swallow
touch and tender, hallowed breath

each one a precious incarnation
until our spirit soars at death

◆

Ponder this poem, noticing what you are
drawn to and what you pull back from.

Talk to God about your discoveries, or
about anything that has affected
how you see your physical self.

What does this
picture spark off
in your mind?

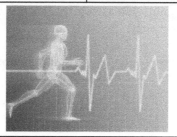

Or do you not know that
your body is
a temple of
the Holy Spirit
within you,
which you have from God,
and that you are not your own?
For you were bought with a price;
therefore glorify God in your body.
1 Corinthians 6.19–20

What is this Scripture saying to you today?

Read the Birth narrative from Luke
2.1–40.

Notice to which part of the story you
are drawn, and enter that scene with
your imagination.

Be one of the characters, sense the
environment as best you can, let
yourself be open to the unfolding
mystery of this little baby's birth.

Make some notes, share your response
with God, and then simply rest in God
for as long as you want to.

Bodies and blessings – short talk 2

Our bodies are a mystery to us sometimes. Some of us may be very fit and physically capable of anything we want to achieve. Others of us need medication to keep us ticking over; find muscles beginning to lose their strength as we age, or have to accept changes in vision and suppleness – even in height as we begin slowly shrinking! The miracle of *simply being* is a daily gift.

Our bodies were not just made for *individual* engagement with life, but also as vehicles for *community* connection, *community* building. We are made for loving, touching, singing, caring for creation, comforting, storytelling, celebrating ... and of course praying and praising the One who made us.

In short, we are made for relationship, God loving us through our interactions with each other:

- for the shy, God provides the first timid invitations to conversation and fun
- for the robust, God provides the strength to reach out to those in need
- for the young, God provides energy and the time to help others
- for the elderly, God provides warm hands and a warm heart in memory-rich reflection.

One well-known passage in the New Testament highlights our inbuilt need of each other, and exposes the lie behind our western preoccupation with stoic individualism and making our own way in the world, often at other people's expense. I am going to read from The Message version so that we can have a fresh experience of this familiar passage, 1 Corinthians 12.12–13, 25–27a. The text is written on one of the reflection sheets for your further reflection, along with some other suggestions for your time with God this afternoon.

Read the passage, give a little time for processing and then invite any comments.

Here the Church is metaphorically described as a body, helping us appreciate the interrelatedness of the various roles and leaders and followers. Each one is a key to the well-being and effectiveness of the whole. No one part or job is more important than any other and we do well to keep that in mind.

We are clearly told that no one part of our bodies is more important than the others – and that is of course true. However, so that we can begin to pay quality attention to our *bodies*, honouring the fact that they are the temple of the Holy Spirit, we do have to begin somewhere, so we are going to start with the hands.* We'll consider how our hands connect us with others *and* carry us through our days.

(But you could choose another part of the body and arrange a set of reflections on heart, feet, lungs, ears ... your choice.)*

As a baby, Jesus would have gone through the wonder of discovering that he had hands and fingers which could be used for all sorts of things – especially to suck, pick up interesting things, and find other parts of his body such as his nose, ears and toes … and other bits in between!

Our hands play a significant part in how we interact with others (see 'Many hands make light work' reflection sheet) AND how we live as individuals (see 'Hands' reflection sheet), so* you have a choice this afternoon of which focus you want to make – there are reflection sheets for both and you can decide which one might suit your situation right now.

(* Unless as a leader you decide to do only one of the following two group exercises and leave the other for another time.)

Group exercise 1 – many hands make light work

This old saying has been around for an age, but it still 'rings true'. However, it is not so much that the actual work itself becomes different, it is that our attitude to it does. The purposeful activity, the laughter, the problem-solving, the shared cuppa or two, the presence of friends and the inviting in of strangers, weave some sort of lightening of the load. And this should come as no surprise. After all, Jesus told us that wherever two or three people are gathered in his name – in a loving, peaceful, other-centred group – he would be there in the midst of us (Matthew 18.20), AND that the 'yoke' he places on us is 'easy, and [the] burden is light' (Matthew 11.30). This lightness comes from the power of God at work in and through each one of us, as we work together for the good of those around us, in obedience to the guidance of the Holy Spirit.

In terms of working for the good of those around us, our hands might, for example, make and deliver a meal to a bereaved neighbour, hold someone's hand if they are in hospital, or build a toy-box for the back of the church ... deceptively simple activities in themselves, but taken together and multiplied across a congregation, we can begin to see how 'the body of Christ' can grow and strengthen. A network of care, hand to hand, begins to develop and so does the church's capacity to reach out to its neighbours and those in the community who are in need.

Notes:

Bodies and blessings – reflection and activity sheet
Many hands make light work

Have a close look at this picture, notice your response and the thoughts that emerge.

Spend some time making connections with your own community of faith, of work, of family, of friends …

What might you want to write or draw in the sand?

Think about the last time you were part of a group of people working together for a common purpose. Let yourself imagine the scene in as much detail as you can and get in touch with any feelings that are clearly connected with that event. Where do you think God was in that context? Where would you like God to have been? How might you help others be aware of God's presence and provision in the midst of such a project?	*Spend some time with this passage from The Message, letting the Spirit guide your reflection.* Your body has many parts – limbs, organs, cells – but no matter how many parts you can name, you're still one body. It's exactly the same with Christ. By means of his one Spirit, we all said good-bye to our partial and piecemeal lives. We each used to independently call our own shots, but then we entered into a large and integrated life in which *he* has the final say in everything … Each of us is now a part of his resurrection body, refreshed and sustained at one fountain – his Spirit – where we all come to drink. The old labels we once used to identify ourselves – labels like Jew or Greek, slave or free – are no longer useful … *1 Corinthians 12.12–13* The way God designed our bodies is a model for understanding our lives together as a church: every part dependent on every other part, the parts we mention and the parts we don't; the parts we see and the parts we don't. If one part hurts, every other part is involved in the hurt, and in the healing. If one part flourishes, every other part enters into the exuberance. You are Christ's body – that's who you are! *1 Corinthians 12.25–27a* Eugene Peterson, *New Testament Edition*, pp. 422–3

Group exercise 2 – hands

One of the privileges of being in ministry is to give people the bread during communion – to see people come up and hold out their hands for spiritual food that can transform their lives.

Sometimes we might wonder what these hands have been doing over the last week or two …

Sometimes these hands have touched others – lovingly, impatiently, perhaps even in anger.

We are all a mixture – light and shadow – some of the things we have done with our hands we might think are 'acceptable', some 'unacceptable' – but, all are known to our Lord – and we are still loved and welcomed to the table because of God's great love for us.

Sometimes we face hardship or loneliness and we need reminding that *God's* hands reach out to us – in the form of a neighbour's unexpected visit, a distant daughter's phone call or a smile from a 'stranger'.

In the next half hour you are invited to move through several exercises focusing on your hands. There is no rush. If you don't 'get finished' you can always continue in your own time at home. Do these in silence, offering the time to God that the Holy Spirit may guide you and offer you hope and comfort.

Notes:

Bodies and blessings – reflection and activity sheet

Hands

On a piece of A4 paper, trace around the hand you normally write with. Then write on it *all* the things that hand did yesterday. Remember this is not going to be seen by anyone so you don't have to censor it! When you are ready, take a 'God' colour crayon and put God on the page somewhere. Then in prayer, bring to God all of it – things of which you are proud and anything of which you are ashamed. Leave them all in God's hands – they are big enough to hold your life and the whole world's pain and joy.	Choose one of the close-up pictures of hands. Spend at least ten minutes contemplating it. Then make a few notes in your journal about your choice, what drew you to that picture, what it has shown you about yourself, your community or your God.
Choose a tube of hand cream and gently and slowly rub the cream into the fingers, palms and backs of both of your hands. Give God thanks for each finger, tendon, each joint and muscle. If you have arthritis or some other damage to your fingers, talk to God about this and how it affects your life.	Pray with one of these Scripture passages: If I take the wings of the morning and settle at the farthest limits of the sea, even there your hand shall lead me, and your right hand shall hold me fast. *Psalm 139.9–10* Can a woman forget her nursing child or show no compassion for the child of her womb? Even these may forget, yet I will not forget you. See, I have inscribed you on the palms of my hands … *Isaiah 49.15–16a*
Write your own psalm, song or poem about 'hands'.	

Bodies and blessings – closing prayer poem

(For leaders – not for distribution)

Hands

This morning, Lord,
these hands planted silver beet,
fed chooks, children, cats, sparrows,
and skimmed pips off a batch of plum jam.
This morning, like any other day,
there were beds to make, washing to be done,
and a patch sown on the knee of a child's jeans.

This afternoon, Lord,
one of these hands got a blister from the axe handle
and the other, a splinter from kindling wood,
but the afternoon brought deeper pain
when my hands closed tight to hide anxiety
then later opened to brush away tears
before anyone could notice.
It's been a day of ups and downs
with not much quiet in between.

Now, this evening, Lord,
I come forward to receive you
and hold out these hands like a cup
for the bread of your sacred body.

And I discover
that as you bless my hands with your presence,
so do you bless all their efforts.
All the planting, baking, cleaning, mending,
everything touched, everything tended,
all my fears and tears, my loving, my hurting,
the whole-up-and-down day, Lord,
is suddenly Eucharist.

Amen.

Joy Cowley
Aotearoa Psalms: Prayers of a New People,
Pleroma Christian Supplies, New Zealand, 2004.

Everyday God

Opening Worship

SENTENCE OF THE DAY

In your book were written all the days that were formed for me,
when none of them as yet existed.
Psalm 139.16b

FIRST CANDLE IS LIT

Leader   The days of our lives,
the hours of our days
are more than our minds can contain.

All   **O God, you have numbered them.**
In your heart they are held;
By your love they are warmed.

Leader   In spite of our wandering
away from your side,
every morning your mercies are new.

All   **When we wake you are waiting**
to lighten the day;
wherever we go, you invite us to see
your presence in people, whoever they are.

SECOND CANDLE IS LIT

Leader   If our eyes can be opened
to the truth of your being,
woven in wonder throughout life on earth,

All   **our lives will be marked, by the signs of your love.**
Free from fear of the future,
free from pain of the past,
we will walk with you daily,
in service and song.

THIRD CANDLE IS LIT

Everyday God – short talk 1

As a focus, in the centre of your gathering space, arrange the cards with the names of the days of the week, the clock, a wall planner or calendar, and lectionary or Bible reading plan for the year. Add some tea-light candles if you wish.

How often do we hear people say 'the year has flown', or 'I don't know where the day's gone' or some other saying that implies we have no control over time. How often do we feel caught up in the accelerating pace of modern life, unable to 'stop the world' just because we want to get off for a minute to catch our breath – literally and metaphorically?

One of the consequences of this headlong rush through life is that time with God can get squeezed out, no matter how well-intentioned we are about regular prayer and Bible reading, or attendance at our local church. Responsibilities for young children, caring for ageing parents, maintaining business profitability, managing illness, or simply surviving recession or redundancy, all compete with time for family, for connection with others, for sleep and re-creation and for the daily tasks that need doing.

It's not surprising we can find ourselves wondering, 'Where is God in the midst of this muddle?'

Give each retreatant a copy of reflection sheet 1. Invite them to take the next ten minutes to choose a typical weekday, put details of what they normally do during each hour in the left-hand column, and notes about when/how they engage with God in the right-hand column, for example times when they currently pray, read Scripture, think of God, etc. Don't give too many examples at this stage. When they've finished ask the following question:

What did you notice as you did that exercise?

Encourage a discussion around the following themes:

- use of time
- what occupies the most time
- time for their own needs and inner resourcing
- God space/s
- How do the retreatants feel about their attempts to find space for God?
- What do they think God expects of them?

Note: Although a few people may consciously integrate God into their lives so the whole day becomes a 'God-space', it's more likely that, especially if most are new to retreats and contemplative spirituality, the majority will see 'God-space' as dedicated time set aside to be with God once or twice a day, and will be less aware of God's presence in their whole day ...

Many of us find it hard to keep to a regular prayer time, we may be so tired at night that we fall into bed without a moment's reflection or thanksgiving, we rush through meals without saying grace ... It would be easy to get discouraged, but the good news is that God is the fountain of all encouragement:

- Where we might see our failure, God sees our heart's intention.
- Whenever we turn to God, there is rejoicing in heaven.
- When we might chastise ourselves for our weakness, God sees our pain and loves us.
- When we compare ourselves unfavourably with the 'saints', God welcomes us just as we are.

God is also faithful, promising to be with us, if only we have eyes to see. To encourage Joshua as he was about to cross over the Jordan and enter the promised land, God said: 'Be strong and courageous; do not be frightened or dismayed, for the LORD your *God is with you* wherever you go' (Joshua 1.9, *my italics*). As part of the commissioning of his disciples, Jesus said, 'And remember, *I am with you always*, even to the end of the age' (Matthew 28.20b, *my italics*).

These words of assurance spoken millennia ago, are also spoken to us today. No matter what we do or who we are; no matter whether we know God well, or are just beginning to find out about the One who loves us so patiently, we can be confident that God *is* with us in all circumstances, in all our days and all our nights.

Draw people's attention to the text of 'Everyday God'. If you have the music, this is a good time to play it before handing out reflection sheet 2 and guiding the group into silent personal reflection.

Everyday God – reflection sheet 1

DAY OF THE WEEK	NOTES
1 am	
2 am	
3 am	
4 am	
5 am	
6 am	
7 am	
8 am	
9 am	
10 am	
11 am	
12 noon	
1 pm	
2 pm	
3 pm	
4 pm	
5 pm	
6 pm	
7 pm	
8 pm	
9 pm	
10 pm	
11 pm	
12 midnight	

'And remember, I am with you always, to the end of the age.'
Matthew 28.20b

Everyday God

Earth's creator,
Everyday God
Loving Maker,
O Jesus,
You who shaped us,
O Spirit,
Recreate us.
Come, be with us.

In your presence,
Everyday God
We are gathered.
O Jesus,
You have called us
O Spirit,
To restore us.
Come, be with us.

Life of all lives,
Everyday God
Love of all loves,
O Jesus,
Hope of all hopes,
O Spirit,
Light of all lights,
Come, be with us.

In our resting ...
In our rising ...
In our hoping ...
In our waiting ...

In our dreaming ...
In our daring ...
In our searching ...
In our sharing ...

God of laughter ...
God of sorrow ...
Home and shelter ...
Strong and patient ...

Way of freedom ...
Star of morning ...
Timeless healer ...
Flame eternal ...

Word of gladness ...
Word of mercy ...
Word of friendship ...
Word of challenge ...

Gentle father ...
Faithful brother ...
Tender sister ...
Loving mother ...

Our beginning ...
Our unfolding ...
Our enduring ...
Journey's ending ...

Alleluia ...
Now and always ...
Alleluia ...
Through all ages ...

from 'Restless is the Heart', Bernadette Farrell, OCP Publications, CD reference number 10827, published in 2000. Used with permission.
Text for use ONLY at the 'Everyday God' Quiet Day

Everyday God – reflection sheet 2

Everyday God

Ask the Holy Spirit to guide you.

Then, slowly read through the text of the song, two or three times, letting your attention be drawn to a line or a verse.

Sit with this line or verse in prayer.

Meditate on it, making connections with your life, responsibilities and longings.

When you are ready, express your thoughts to God in whatever way seems right.

And then just rest in God, making space for God's love to enfold, warm and welcome you.

Choose from one of the Scripture passages below, which show Jesus in the midst of everyday life

Matthew 19.13–15
(the little children are brought to Jesus)

Mark 8.1–8
(the feeding of the four thousand)

Luke 21.1–4
(the widow's mite)

John 6.16–21
(Jesus walking on the water)

Read the passage two or three times and then imagine yourself in a **contemporary setting** as the central character with Jesus perhaps, or as a bystander or disciple.

Be aware of the 'everyday nature' of the location and see how the story unfolds.

Much of what we've looked at so far relates to *chronos* time and the arbitrary divisions of time which our calendar and modern living impose upon us, although not always without a struggle. Our lives revolve around *chronos* time – eating at set times, watching certain TV programmes, keeping or missing appointments, using public transport, making deadlines and so on. Our days are shaped by the clock and often relationships suffer.

To what extent are *you* bound by a timetable set by others, such as employers, teachers, shop-owners, law-makers, media, family habits?
How free are you to make changes to your daily schedule?
Talk to God about what you have discovered … and listen too!

Everyday God – short talk 2

Make sure that you have coloured pencils/crayons/or felt-tips and copies of reflection sheets 1 and 3 and L&F resource sheets mentioned below for each retreatant.

God's approach to *time* is different from ours. From God's perspective, time is *kairos* not *chronos*:

> ... with the Lord one day is like a thousand years, and a thousand years are like one day. The Lord is not slow about his promise, as some think of slowness, but is patient with you, not wanting any to perish, but all to come to repentance. (2 Peter 3.8–9)

Kairos time is more to do with waiting, unfolding, coming to fullness and birth, deepening, being and becoming, opening, and 'things falling into place' at the appointed time which God alone knows. From this perspective, trusting in God and developing loving relationships are paramount: quality time spent with people is time spent with God in whose image we are all made; trusting in God means letting go of striving and anxiety, and becoming free.

Ask if anyone has any questions or can give an example of 'kairos' time, before continuing:

As we learn to dance to God's music in the midst of everyday life, we change our perspective, and stop having to make things happen to calm our worrying mind. Gradually God begins to occupy the centre of our lives, and we begin to make ourselves available to God, ready to notice the God-moments, and God's presence in the day.

You can either begin the next section by asking the retreatants for their ideas on how they might notice the God-moments, etc. and then move on to include anything from the list which has not been mentioned already. Or you can offer the listed ideas first – perhaps using a whiteboard if that would be easier – and asking for any other ideas later.

We can, for example:

- remember that each person is made in the image of God and so are we
- be expectant (see L&F resource sheet 2.1)
- accept that, as St Teresa of Avila[21] taught, we are God's hands and eyes and feet

---

21 James E. Kiefer, *Teresa of Avila*, www.justus.anglican.org/resources/bio/268.html.

and voice as we reach out to people AND that God reaches out to us through those who touch, look lovingly, meet us, speak to us
- be alert for the creation to be a vehicle of grace to us as God uses something from the natural world to help us reflect on our daily life
- notice synchronicity – those unexpected moments of graced connection, like a phone call from a distant friend that comes as we think of her, or 'bumping into' someone who needs encouragement or a hug.

God is always turned towards us, drawing us to experience love which is beyond all understanding. There are all sorts of ways in which we can respond to that love, ways of turning towards God during a day. Whether or not we are somewhere 'religious' like a church or cell-group meeting, there are opportunities even in the midst of busy office schedules or commuting to draw from the source of all inspiration and compassion.

- We can use the positives of modern technology and go online to connect with prayer resources designed to fit into a short break in work, for example the Irish Jesuit's site: http://sacredspace.ie/, or we can download a short prayer reflection with music and a spoken passage of Scripture for our MP3 players or iPods so we can tune in as we commute, such as the UK Jesuits' site: www.pray-as-you-go.org.
- We can learn to 'practise the presence of God' (see L&F resource sheet 2.4) – turning our minds towards God in love often during the day.
- We can let natural breaks in our routines become times of praise or thanksgiving. As we sit in the doctor's waiting room, we can be conscious of God's presence through the care we are offered. As we wait for the lights to change or the train to arrive, we give thanks for a mercy received or a prayer answered.
- We can begin to read our Bible daily, preferably in the morning so we can carry with us some of its wisdom, be consoled or strengthened for whatever the day may hold – every day.
- Whenever people we know come to mind, we can hold them in our heart, in God's heart for a few moments, a prayer made for a purpose we cannot know, but which may be life-preserving.
- We can begin to give thanks before bedtime (see L&F resource sheet '2.7 Examen – a simple review of the day') and offer a simple grace at dinner or when most of those with whom we live are present.

There are many ways to be open to God's presence in our lives, as the above examples begin to illustrate. Over time, if we are faithfully following our Lord's invitation to grow and to become more like Christ, we will be aware that no matter what we are doing, God is present; no matter who we are with, God is present. Instead of 'fitting' God into a few minutes of hasty prayer here, or a quick chapter of Scripture reading there, we begin to recognize a God who weaves through our lives – in and out of our worries and wonderings, through the circles of our doubt and decision-making, always offering the guidance of the Spirit and the example and sacrificial love of Jesus.

We may even discover that the monastic practice of living a Rule of Life, a regular rhythm of prayer, work, study, rest and recreation, takes shape in our lives naturally under the guidance of the Spirit.

If that happens we will indeed be living, moving and having all our being in God (see Acts 17.28).

Hand out reflection sheet 3 and any L&F resource sheets if you are using them.

Before going into the time of personal silent reflection, give each retreatant a clean copy of reflection sheet 1. Invite them to consider what might work for them as a little rule of life (one of the options on reflection sheet 3, and take a crayon, felt-tip or coloured pencil in what they consider a 'God-colour' and during the afternoon – as part of their reflection – put God on the page in any way that makes sense to them.

Closing prayer:

O God who made the universe
and set the stars and seas and life in place,
help us to recognize you in the circumstances
   of our everyday lives,
help us to invite you into all that we do, rather than
   exhausting ourselves striving to be independent,
help us to see your presence in all the little acts of love
   which make this planet holy.
May our whole life –
each second, each minute, each hour and each day
be saturated by your love and shared with those around us.
Amen.

Everyday God – reflection sheet 3

A Book of Hours

days
hours
minutes
seconds.
smaller, and smaller
the splinters of time,
imprisoning years,
capturing moments
in case they might
somehow
take on a life of their own –
in case they might choose to
s-t-r-e-t-c-h life's balloon until it pops!!!
burst *open* the barred doors of convention
dance their own way against the rat-race
skip on home to love and laughter and joy
where time has no name
apart from
I AM

Pray with one of these sayings
and see how it relates to your
own life and awareness of Christ.

Christ in mouth of friend and
stranger …
St Patrick's Breastplate

To see Christ in his distressing
disguise …
Mother Teresa

Christ has no hands on earth but
yours …
Teresa of Avila

Christ behind me, Christ before
me …
St Patrick's Breastplate

When you look at your day set out on a sheet, what might work for you as a 'little rule
of life': times when you pray, study, work, rest and are recreated?

When could you anticipate the most difficulty in maintaining
some awareness of God in the midst of everyday routines and demands?
Ask the Holy Spirit how that difficulty might be overcome.

Kairos time is more to do with patience, unfolding, coming to fullness and birth,
deepening, being and becoming, opening, things falling into place at the appointed
time, which God alone knows.

What *kairos* moments, or examples of God's timing, have you noticed in your life?
What have these moments taught you about God, about yourself ?

Mud and mystery

Opening Worship

SENTENCE OF THE DAY

In the beginning was the Word, and the Word was with God,
and the Word was God.
John 1.1

Leader How can we speak of what we cannot comprehend?
Even when our hearts are turned to you,
our words are stumbling sentences.

All **You are so much 'more',**
You are so far and yet so near,
You are eternal, yet present in us now.
You are mystery, you are miracle
You *are* ...
You simply *are*.

THE FIRST CANDLE IS LIT

Leader In the life of Christ
you walked this earth
and chose to be with us.

All **In Christ you touched the poor**
In Christ you laughed and sang
In Christ you healed the sick
In Christ you faced dark death
In Christ ...
In Christ you simply saved.

THE SECOND CANDLE IS LIT

Leader Through the Spirit's gifts
you stay with us always,
guiding, encouraging, enlivening us.

All **The Spirit builds our faith**
The Spirit brings us joy
The Spirit helps us grow
The Spirit tends our soul
The Spirit ...
The Spirit simply loves.

THE THIRD CANDLE IS LIT

Mud and mystery – short talk 1

Have handy a bottle with water with some sand/soil in it – hold it up so retreatants can see it, and give it a good shake so the contents become cloudy. Then set it aside while you talk.

We've probably all done this with our children or grandchildren – helped them to see the way water and sand or soil works when mixed. But, while the word 'mud' may take us back to childhood discoveries in murky ponds, or games played in winter wetness, as adults most of us avoid mud and try to keep our children and dogs out of it because it makes more work for us!

But that's not a choice for millions of people around the world. All too frequently, modern communications bring us news of rivers breaking their banks, devastating floods, village after poor village wiped out by mudslides in the space of a few hours. We see scenes of heartbreak and loss on a scale we cannot imagine. Mud then becomes associated somehow with the sorry state of survivors and destroyed homes – mud oozing through toes, mud caked on meagre possessions, mud on the drawn faces of those trying to make something out of the nothing left of former lives.

We cannot know how we might react to the cumulative loss of family members, of homes and incomes, of lifestyle and location. We cannot imagine the scale of the sadness that must pervade whole neighbourhoods and regions faced with massive reconstruction and resettlement. But, from our own experience of loss, we may know that several things make a difference in how – or even whether – we recover and find the strength to pick up the pieces of our lives. Let's consider these now:

- our attitudes and resilience
- our faith in God
- being part of a close community which cares for its members.

People react differently to adversity – we all know that suffering can bring out the best or the worst in people. Some struggle with the loss, anger surging to the surface as they search for someone to blame; others by contrast seem to connect with an inner strength which enables them to find a way forward. An old verse by Frederick Langbridge reminds us:

Two men look out through the same bars;
one sees the mud and one the stars.[22]

It is natural for us to 'see the mud' as we start to mourn our losses; it takes time to begin to recover from the exhaustion of grieving and the rollercoaster of emotions we experience. But sooner or later, life draws us back to daily routines and the

---

22 http://www.famousquotesandauthors.com/authors/frederick_langbridge_quotes.html.

demands of family or finances. We have the choice then of how we re-engage with those around us, what attitude we bring to each day. We may ask ourselves how can we begin – literally and symbolically – to 'look up' again, for when we are sad, or ashamed, or confused or grieving our body language conveys our mood with lowered eyes, and drooping heads.

> Psalm 3 speaks of God *raising our heads*:
>> But you, O LORD, are a shield around me,
>> my glory, and the one who lifts up my head. (v.3)

Let's just stay with this a moment and imagine it.

Offer a minute's silence for the retreatants to engage with this image unhurriedly.

With tenderness of touch, God raises our heads, gently lifts our chins, so we may come to see the possibility of a new life, different from the old life of course, but still potentially hope-full, in time. And how does God do this? Through the little acts of kindness we share with other people; through a small smile from a child, hinting at life beyond the 'mud'; through the support of our community – each for the other; through the generosity of friends and strangers; with the comfort of the Sacrament and the familiarity of liturgy; with the gathered community of faith sharing losses, sharing stories, sharing resources; and with an inner knowing that the Spirit holds us still and sure. Such graced moments, such gracious people are the 'stars' which become visible as God raises our heads.

This pattern of possibility, happens all around the world when unexpected events take their toll, for in the wake of each tragedy, countless 'stars' – acts of compassion and people of good will – begin to shine. In the Pacific* for example, in September 2009, island communities were literally rocked when an earthquake measuring 8 on the Richter scale struck Samoa, American Samoa, and Tonga. In the midst of a multitude of losses, in the midst of the destruction of homes and businesses, there emerged stories of selfless courage, resolute faith, and determination to rebuild shattered lives. Communities around the Pacific raised money, sent goods and troops and aid workers, and volunteered to be part of the reconstruction. There was an outpouring of *alofa* – unconditional love – which is helping to begin to ease some of the pain.

*If you prefer, you could use an example closer to home or one with which you are personally connected.

Early in Christian history, St Irenaeus spoke of the glory of God being revealed in a man or woman who was *fully alive* ... and surely that is what God desires for us. While events around us may throw us into the mud, we do not have to stay there.

God invites us to 'wait patiently for the Lord' so we may be restored to completeness of being:

> I waited patiently for the LORD;
> he inclined to me and heard my cry.
> He drew me up from the desolate pit,
> out of the miry bog,
> and set my feet upon a rock,
> making my steps secure. (Psalm 40.1–2)

Draw the retreatants' attention to the bottle of sand and water – by now the sand should have settled in the bottom of the bottle, leaving the water clear.

The sand has settled – the water is clear.

As you move into the morning, don't worry if it takes a little while for your mind to settle into the silence of God. Just trust that, as you spend time waiting on the Lord in openness, the Holy Spirit will help you focus on whatever is right for you today.

The reflection sheet offers a number of possibilities for you so, with God's help, you can consider both the 'mud' in your life *and* the 'stars' which become visible when God lifts your head.

Mud and mystery – reflection sheet 1

*Two men look out
through the same bars;
one sees the mud –
and one sees the stars.*
Frederick Langbridge

What do you see?

How do you respond to adversity?

If you are 'stuck in the mud'
feeling trapped by circumstances,
or sense that you are, in some way, not free,
know that God is beside you and wants
to help you.

Talk to God about your situation;
write in your journal;
or put colour on the page to express your
feelings, then,
prayerfully,
add a 'Christ colour',
letting the Holy Spirit bring you
an awareness of God's peace
and love.

 Recall those people through whom you have seen God's care for you –
shining examples of God's grace or provision or love.

You may like to draw some stars and enjoy choosing colours to
reflect the gift of each person/event.

But you, O Lord, are a shield around
me, my glory,
and the one who lifts up my head.
Psalm 3.3–4

I waited patiently for the Lord;
he inclined to me and heard my cry.
He drew me up from the desolate pit,
out of the miry bog,
and set my feet upon a rock,
making my steps secure.
Psalm 40.1–2

Spend some time in silence with either or both of these Scriptures,
letting the words touch your heart.
You may like to let these take shape in your imagination, or to journal your response.

May these words be a comfort to you, bringing you
reassurance of God's desire to bring you to a place of renewal
and reconnect you with the love of those around you.

Mud and mystery – short talk 2

Mystery – what does that word mean to you?

- A detective story with a complex plot that twists and turns?
- Something that is hard to understand?
- A puzzle that needs to be solved?

In the New Testament the word 'mystery' signifies a divine secret which is being (or has been) revealed in God's good time, so while it might seem odd, 'mystery' comes paradoxically close to the word for revelation. Paul uses the term most frequently in reference to God's purpose or plan of salvation revealed in Jesus Christ. But, for the apostle Peter, the inclusion of the Gentiles as well as the Jews in the divine purpose of salvation was a great mystery. It took an unexpected spiritual experience while in prayer *and* a direct request from Cornelius to begin to dissolve his prejudice (see Acts 10).

Initially this inclusiveness may even have been a mystery for Jesus. As his ministry unfolded and he had to come to terms with the religious hierarchy's resistance to his ministry, the revelation of God's greater purposes was visible in Jesus' exchange with a Canaanite woman seeking healing for her daughter:

> ... a Canaanite woman from that region [Tyre and Sidon] came out and started shouting, 'Have mercy on me, Lord, Son of David; my daughter is tormented by a demon.' *But he did not answer her at all.* And his disciples came and urged him, saying, 'Send her away, for she keeps shouting after us.' He answered, '*I was sent only to the lost sheep of the house of Israel.*' But she came and knelt before him, saying, 'Lord, help me.' He answered, '*It is not fair to take the children's food and throw it to the dogs.*' She said, 'Yes, Lord, yet even the dogs eat the crumbs that fall from their master's table.' Then Jesus answered her, '*Woman, great is your faith! Let it be done for you as you wish.*' And her daughter was healed instantly. (Matthew 15.22–28, *my italics*)

Allow time for a discussion of this passage if people want to explore it in more depth.

Another area of mystery relates to the unconditional love of God poured out on the undeserving and the faithful alike – the mystery of grace. Unmerited kindness is something we may not often experience but, in his book *What's So Amazing about Grace?*, Philip Yancey tells the true story of a woman who, left with an expensive wedding banquet booking when her fiancé got cold feet, decided to hold a party anyway, but *not* for the original guests:

Ten years before, this same woman had been living in a homeless shelter ... Now she had the wild notion of using her savings to treat the down-and-outs of Boston to a night on the town.

And so it was that in June of 1990 the Hyatt Hotel in downtown Boston hosted a party such as it had never seen before. The hostess changed the menu to boneless chicken – 'in honor of the groom', she said – and sent invitations to rescue missions and homeless shelters.

That warm summer night, people who were used to peeling half-gnawed pizza off the cardboard dined instead on chicken cordon bleu. Hyatt waiters in tuxedos served *hors d'oeuvres* to senior citizens propped up by crutches and aluminium walkers. Bag ladies, vagrants, and addicts took one night off from the hard life on the sidewalks outside and instead sipped champagne, ate chocolate wedding cake, and danced to big-band melodies late into the night. [23]

Invite the retreatants to respond to the story. Some may want to share their experience of 'unmerited kindness'.

And then of course we have the mystery of suffering and healing. We have only to look among our own families and friends to find memories or stories of accidents, painful illness, untimely death, and prayers that seem to go unanswered. It is when we are challenged by such events that our faith can begin to crumble or even disintegrate, unless we have the chance to talk honestly about our feelings, and about how we see God at work in the world. A wise friend, a minister or a spiritual director can listen to our pain and our disappointment or anger with God, without trying to rush us through to a 'happier place'. They can also encourage us to talk to God *directly* – even if that means yelling at God in the frustration and terror of loss. Over time, they can help us work out who we think God is and how we think God should have responded. Communication with God is maintained while we work through our grief, and so we are open to the 'small mercies' that God makes available to us if we *have eyes to see them*.

'Seeing' and 'perspective' are brought into the spotlight with the Gospel story of a man born blind who waits until he can get a chance to catch Jesus' attention as he passes by on the road. The whole of John 9 explores the man's healing, the subsequent argument he has with the Pharisees, and his acknowledgement of Jesus initially as a prophet and later as worthy of worship. We see the man grow from dependency and alienation to strength in the new life Jesus has opened up for him. He moves from literal blindness to spiritual sight as he acknowledges Jesus as the Son of Man and worships him.

What is intriguing here is that Jesus did something unusual to effect the healing – instead of a simple touch, he spat onto the ground and made *mud*, which he then

---

23 Philip Yancey, *What's So Amazing about Grace?*, Strand Publishing: Sydney, 1999, pp. 48–49.

spread over the man's eyes, before telling him to go and wash it off in the pool of Siloam (John 9.1–7).

We have no way of knowing but it's worth wondering whether, as Jesus did this, he was thinking of the Creation story, for there are echoes of it in his actions:

> then the LORD God formed man from the dust of the ground, and breathed into his nostrils the breath of life; and the man became a living being. (Genesis 2.7)

Both these creative acts are deeply evocative – a mixing of the ordinary and the sacred, the stuff of earthly life with the mystery of divinity. And the result in both stories? Mud and mystery combine to bring life, hope and the promise of new relationship with God.

We are going to use the central portion of this story for our guided meditation this afternoon, as a way into a deeper appreciation of the connection Jesus makes with the blind man.

Hand out reflection sheet 2, which will be needed for the reflection time after the guided meditation.

Guided meditation

For details on how to prepare and present a guided meditation in the context of a longer retreat or quiet day, please refer to Appendix 8.

Before we begin, let's remind ourselves that, like our intellect and our feelings, our imagination is one of our God-given faculties and can help us as we seek to listen to God. However, if you are a bit uncertain, or if you prefer not to participate, that's absolutely fine.

For some people, forming pictures in the mind comes quite naturally; others find it easier to form an 'inner impression' without a lot of detail; and there are some for whom it's a struggle. Don't worry – just trust that whichever group you fall into, the Lord will honour your attentiveness and your intention. Whether or not you experience anything profound, the Holy Spirit is at work in you and the benefit of the exercise may become clearer later. Something good has happened in your spirit even if it defies description.

I'll outline the process, and then we'll start with prayer.

- I'll read aloud the portion of Scripture first so you can get a sense of the story and context
- then I'll invite you to imagine the scene and where you might be in relation to Jesus – an onlooker, one of the disciples, the blind man, even Jesus himself …
- when we reach the meeting point with Christ, I'll invite you to be open to what Jesus might say or do
- once I've stopped speaking, take your time to let any dialogue unfold, see what happens next, and let the encounter come to a natural conclusion
- it's a good idea to spend some time afterwards making a few notes or mulling over in your mind what you have experienced so the blessing of it is not lost.

I suggest you put aside any of your papers or journal or Bible for the meantime. Just settle yourselves comfortably, close your eyes, make sure your feet are firmly on the floor, and let your breathing form a steady and slow rhythm.

Let us pray:
Loving God, as we begin this guided meditation we ask for your grace and the guidance and protection of the Holy Spirit.
Take away from us any fear, any striving to make things happen.
Instead, give us a confident openness to your work in our imagination and in our lives. Through Jesus Christ our Lord. Amen.

Read the passage on reflection sheet 2.

Now re-tell the story, inviting the retreatants into the scene:

Imagine that you are walking with Jesus and his disciples – let the details of the scene unfold – get a sense of the heat, what you are wearing, the dust on the ground, the smells around you and the noise of people and donkeys, maybe the birds or goats in the distance – or – just allow an inner impression to form.

Pause for a couple of minutes to allow this reflection.

Notice where you are in relation to Jesus – who you are with – what you are doing.

Now you hear someone asking Jesus what caused this man's blindness – his own sin or that of his parents? And you hear Jesus' reply – not his own sin, nor that of his parents – but that the glory of God might be revealed in him.

What happens in you as you hear that question and response – what memory or question of your own pops to the surface?

Again pause for a couple of minutes to allow the story to unfold.

And now you watch as Jesus moves – you see him spit on the ground and begin to work the moist dust into mud.

How long does this take?

Where is the blind man?

What are you thinking?

Time for reflection.

Jesus stands up and approaches the blind man.

What does Jesus say?

What does the blind man say?

Jesus reaches out and touches the man's eyes – spreading the mud over them.

What do you notice about Jesus? about the man? about the disciples? about yourself?

Time for reflection.

Finally Jesus tells the man to go and wash in the pool of Siloam.

What does Jesus ask you to do?

What is your response?

Just let the meditation come to a natural conclusion when you are ready.

The retreatants can leave the group when they are ready and take reflection sheet 2 with them as material for use until it is time to gather for the closing.

171

Mud and mystery – Closing Prayer

O God of mystery,
just as the mud from flooded rivers
flows out to sea,
dissolving in the wide waters of the ocean;
so may our failures and times of struggle
be absorbed in the depths of your love.
Gift us with the capacity to see
you at work in unlikely places.
Help us recognize your light
shining in our darkness, so we may
be light-bearers to those in need.
We ask this for Christ's sake,
who was made of dust like us,
and of divinity like you.
Amen.

Mud and mystery – reflection sheet 2

As he walked along, he saw a man blind from birth.
His disciples asked him, 'Rabbi, who sinned, this man or his parents,
that he was born blind?'

Jesus answered, 'Neither this man nor his parents sinned;
he was born blind so that God's works might be revealed in him.
We must work the works of him who sent me while it is day;
night is coming when no one can work.
As long as I am in the world, I am the light of the world.'

When he had said this, he spat on the ground and made mud with the saliva
and spread the mud on the man's eyes, saying to him,
'Go, wash in the pool of Siloam' (which means Sent).

Then he went and washed and came back able to see.
John 9.1–7

After the guided meditation using this Scripture, you may want to re-read it slowly, letting the words touch your heart.

Let the Holy Spirit guide your reflection and bring this passage to new life for you.

Go for a walk and ask God to show you something which represents the mystery of Creation.

What aspects of your faith are a mystery to you?

Think back over your life, noticing anything which has caused you pain
or made you doubt God's goodness and provision.

Talk to God or write in your journal about anything which puzzles you or anything
which makes you angry with God or anything for which you are thankful.

Re-establishing communication with God will begin the healing and
recovery from old hurts.

Part 5
Dinner – overnight or weekend retreats

There is no doubt that when people attend a longer retreat, they are giving themselves more opportunity to get a sense of the calm to which we are all called, even in the busyness of our very full lives. From this central place of stillness, where God's Spirit touches and guides our spirit, flow all our acts of compassion and service. If our centre is hectic and 'running on empty', compassion fatigue and 'burnout' are likely; if our centre is regularly nourished by the loving energy and silence of God, we carry this inner peacefulness with us wherever we go; from it we can speak, discern, respond, and enable the best in others to find expression. So, although running residential retreats is a lot more work for the leaders, the benefits to the retreatants are worth the effort.

At this point, you may find it useful to re-read Part 1 to refresh your memory about the way a contemplative retreat moves from the gathering and early input, through the deepening times of silence and personal reflection, and then to shared conversation and preparation for the return to the normal rhythms of life. Keep in mind that while this dynamic has been present in the shorter retreats and Quiet Days, retreatants are more likely to go 'deep' on longer retreats because there is more silence and more opportunity for personal time with God.

In this part there are three residential retreats:

1 *Unfolding* – an overnight retreat with detailed descriptions of the process to help leaders who have not led this type of retreat before.
2 *Four seasons in one life* – a weekend retreat which introduces some spiritual practices for the retreatants to use (referring to the L&F resource sheets where applicable) and gives retreatants choices about where they want to focus. Full details for each address and all the group prayer times are included.
3 *Do not be afraid!* – a weekend retreat with resources and four addresses. The group prayer times use accessible morning and evening prayer options or you could put together a simple service with an opening and closing chant, and time for praying with a verse of Scripture on the theme. Overall, this lessening of detail more clearly shows the dynamic of longer retreats for retreatants who already know how to listen to God, and want to make the most of space for prayer and reflection. While we prepare thoroughly, the Spirit of God often shapes the available input and resources; and so we may find that some are not needed, while others assume greater significance.

General points for residential retreats:

When planning a residential retreat, there are issues to consider that do not apply to shorter retreats:

- Selecting the type of accommodation (single/twin/bunk/cabin/retreat house/ country cottage/access for those with mobility limitations, etc.), meal arrangements (catered/provision for special diets/self-catering), costs for venue hire including any deposit required/cancellation costs/minimum numbers/venue restrictions/any safety issues.
- Arranging additional facilitators/spiritual directors so you don't work alone.
- Deciding on levels of remuneration for leaders/cooks, etc., and setting the total cost to retreatants.
- Having the contact details of any local Christian counsellor/psychotherapist/ spiritual director to whom referrals can be made should the need arise.

Without going overboard about it, we must be prudent and note some further 'cautions' – these can apply to any retreat but are especially important for the longer retreats:

- The physical safety and comfort of retreatants – it pays to find out as much as possible about the venue beforehand, especially if it is new to you. Visiting the site yourself is really the best way to note any environmental hazards so, for example, you know whether there is limited access for people with hip or mobility problems, etc. Those people who have back injuries or a degenerative disease can be encouraged to bring their own seat/chair to ensure comfort.
- The mental health of participants – it would be unwise to use guided meditation with anyone whom you know has a history of psychosis or any problems distinguishing between what is real and what is not.
- On an overnight or weekend retreat it is possible that material from the unconscious might surface and cause initial alarm in the retreatant; this is where the importance of having someone else working with you on overnight or weekend events is clear, as he/she can support the retreatant, help her/him connect with where God's invitation (or the person of Jesus) might be in the midst of this eruption, and explore together what possible healing may be being heralded.
- It pays to spell out that the term 'confidentiality' means that what is said in this retreat stays in this context and is not repeated by anyone to anyone once the retreat ends. We have no right to tell someone else what another retreatant has said or shared with us during that time UNLESS we have specific permission from that person AND/OR we are genuinely concerned for that person's safety or that they may harm someone else.[24]

---

24 It is a good idea to make sure that, in the context of supervision or your lay/clergy ministry formation group, you have discussed what you would do in either of these situations. This sort of

It is not uncommon for retreatants to weep and it is important that we don't rush in and *assume* that tears must indicate something is *wrong*, or that the retreatant is grieving a loss. This may be so in which case, the retreatant may welcome a sensitive enquiry about his/her well-being. But for some people, the relief of being able to spend time with God can itself trigger tears; sometimes the wonder of being loved by God is so breathtaking that tears and silence are the only response we can make. Sometimes, too, words are replaced by tears during times of confession, forgiveness and consolation.

In the closing liturgy, retreatants may be invited to share something of what has been happening for them during the retreat. Clearly this is not compulsory because we need to recognize that not everyone is able to speak aloud in a group situation. However, asking for a single word, or a phrase, or the placing of a symbol on the central focus table, can be an opportunity for people to name, and thereby deepen, what God has been showing them. If offering retreat time for a group that meets regularly, then this simple sharing can also help build a sense of community as people hear a little of the Spirit's movement in each other's experience.

Above all, longer retreats deepen the relationship between the retreatant and God in a unique way, and we are privileged to be part of that process.

---

dilemma can happen not only on retreat, but also potentially, in any pastoral encounter, so you need to know how best to respond. Options might include: contacting the person's GP, immediate referral to a counsellor, contacting the local Mental Health Crisis team if there is one, and/or contacting a responsible member of the person's family. Ideally, you would be able to work through the ethics and practicalities of any of the above decisions with your supervisor *before* the need arises.

Unfolding – overnight retreat

Preparation and resources

Focus:

Arrange on a low table: some flowers; a cross; the folded Scripture verses in a small basket (see Resources below); a candle to light before opening prayer; folded jersey/ pullover; folded map; folded letter (see 'Leader's input 3 – Saturday afternoon' for details); a fern plant that has some fronds open and some about to unfold (a photo of one will suffice if necessary).

Music:

The music for this retreat is selected to enhance the theme 'unfolding', and to match the time of day. If you don't have other relevant music, the following are suggestions:

- Keith Duke, *Sacred Dance*, Suffolk: Kevin Mayhew Ltd, CD 1490179, 2005, Track 9 'The Love of God'.
- Edvard Greig, 'Morning', from *Peer Gynt*, Incidental Music, Op.23 (widely available).
- Margaret Rizza, *Chants 1*, Suffolk: Kevin Mayhew Ltd, CD 1490102, 2002, for example track 4, 'Inpoured Spirit'.
- Secret Garden, *Songs from a Secret Garden*, Polygram Pty Ltd, 528 230–2, 1996, Track 1, 'Nocturne'.
- Taizé, *O Lord Hear My Prayer: The Songs of Taizé*, Kingsway KMCD 736, 1994, Track 4 'The Lord is my light', and Track 5 'Within our darkest night'.
- Vaughan Williams, *The Lark Ascending: Violin Showpieces*, Naxos, CD 8.553509, 1997, Track 3, 'The Lark Ascending' (widely available on classical compilations).

Resources:

- *Scripture verses* (see Appendix 1) – cut out enough for the number of retreatants, fold them up and put in a basket from which they can choose at the end of night prayer.
- *Loaves and fishes (L&F) sheets* – chosen for the experience level of the group and to introduce particular activities such as praying with Scripture, journalling, etc.
- *Copies of Night and Morning prayer*, any activities, reflection sheets, etc. enough for each retreatant.
- Coloured pencils, crayons and A4 or A3 paper.

Nuts and bolts:

- Any housekeeping issues – orientation to the retreat venue – check out anything which retreatants might need.
- Policy re mobile phones and silence – to be negotiated with the group before they actually arrive at the retreat venue.

Extension:

If you wanted to use this theme and give it a **Lenten** focus, then using the stations of the cross in your own church or a nearby Catholic church, could illustrate how the journey to the cross *unfolded*. The Scripture passages, music, leader's input and reflection material would then need to be altered to reflect the Easter story, but the basic shape of the overnight retreat could remain the same.

Similarly if you wanted to use this theme in **Advent**, in preparation for Christmas, you could gather a sequence of photos showing the gestation of a baby, or a series of pictures/postcards/Christmas cards showing: Jesus as a baby, infant, young boy, several as an adult man, then of Jesus crucified, and risen.

Unfolding

Welcome to this time of retreat. You have made a decision to put time aside to listen to God. For some of you that will have been difficult, because you have other responsibilities and calls on your time; for others the challenge may have more to do with wondering what you are letting yourself in for, especially the experience of silence, for so much in our world is noise and the busyness of other people.

Be assured that God has called you here because God wants the very best for you. Be assured that you are beloved of God, whether you have walked closely with God for many years or whether you are just starting to get to know God a little better. Be assured that God welcomes you and wants to bless you.

Pause for a few moments.

Before we have our time of opening prayer and reflection, we'll attend to a few 'housekeeping' matters and then do a little 'warm-up' to help us all make the transition from what we've left behind.

Go over retreat timetable and any practical issues relating to venue, meal times, room allocation, house 'rules', etc.

✵ 1 *Divide group into pairs. Each person finds out his/her partner's favourite tree and favourite song, and then introduces his/her partner to the whole group.*
  2 *Invite everyone present to line up according to the date of their birth – January at one end of the room and December at the other end. OR invite people to imagine the gathering space is a map of the world and to go to their approximate country of birth.*

It's also a good idea to make a few commonsense guidelines for our time as a group.
  Refer to Part 1.2 Gathering if you need to.

✵ EITHER *ask*: 'What guidelines can we establish so each person can get as much as possible from this time apart with God?' *(Put their ideas on a whiteboard.)* OR *have a list of what you think is important for a group already on a whiteboard and invite discussion, amendment and eventual ownership of the final set of attitudes and behaviours, for example:*

• maintain confidentiality – what is said here, stays here
• respect each person's position – theological, personal, etc.
• give each activity a try – come to it open-minded
• be prompt to group sessions

- respect the silence
- take responsibility for your own emotional well-being.

We're going to begin this time of worship with a prayer and then a time of listening to music that reflects our theme of 'unfolding'. This violin piece is 15 minutes long and is called 'The Lark Ascending'. It may take you a while to begin to slow down from the fast pace of daily life. You may even feel a bit impatient or restless. Don't worry if you struggle to pay attention at first – just come back to the present moment from wherever your mind has wandered to, and rejoin the music.

We light this candle as a symbol of the Christ Light present among and within us.

Let us pray:
Loving God,
We thank you for bringing us here today,
for helping us make this choice to step away from
all the other calls on our energy
so we may spend quality time listening to you.
While we are here, we ask for your provision and protection
for our families and those for whom we care.
May your Holy Spirit guide us, aiding our attentiveness
and harnessing our hopefulness, so we are open
to your unfolding work and tender touch.
Amen.

Depending on the group, you may also like to lead them in The Lord's Prayer, before continuing ...

Make yourselves comfortable, lie on the floor if you want to ... while the music unfolds ...

Start the music 'The Lark Ascending' – you can enjoy listening to it too, but be aware of what is happening among the retreatants, for example restlessness, sighing, even weeping. When the music finishes, allow another 30 seconds before inviting the retreatants to open their eyes and return to the here and now.

Creator God,
We thank you for this example of music and
the unfolding melody of the skylark's soaring song.
And now, O God of grace
we commit the rest of this evening and tomorrow to you,
mindful that we are held in your love,
that great love which is so clearly seen in Jesus.
Amen.

Leader's input 1:

You may be wondering about the items on the focus cloth – each of these items illustrates something about the process of unfolding, the theme of this retreat. We're going to talk about two of them tonight – the plant and the jersey; and the other two – the map and the letter – will have their turn tomorrow.

'Unfolding' is a reoccurring theme in the natural world. The unfolding of a fern frond or a bud for example is an everyday wonder.

Talk a little about the plant you have with you and any special features.

While flowers might sometimes be forced to meet consumer demands, home gardeners usually let nature take its course, allowing buds to unfold in their own time so the beauty is not damaged. We can think too about the miracle of transformation as a butterfly emerges from its chrysalis; how we've watched as the damp wings begin to unfold. We know that this process cannot be rushed or the tender wings will be damaged and the butterfly rendered flightless. **We cannot hurry growth.**

If we turn now to the jersey – it might look decorative folded up as it is, but of course it serves no real purpose until it is unfolded *(demonstrate)* and we put it on. Although we enjoy the colours and the complexity of the knitting or design, we know that the jersey's primary purpose for most of us is to provide warmth and protection from the cold.

Growth   Warmth   Protection

The Christian spiritual life – measured for many as moments of discovery amid years of struggle – moves at a pace at odds with the speed of much modern living with its fast food, speed dating, and instant gratification. Instead, our journey with God unfolds slowly over the course of a lifetime, as God's Spirit stirs within us, and as our spirit, mind and will gradually begin to cooperate with the work of grace in our lives. Sometimes there will be experiences of connection with God so profound that we think our faith will be cemented in place for all time; but then the days and months go by, and the growth plateaus and slows. When that happens and we begin to wonder or even doubt, then coming to a retreat like this, taking time to listen to God as well as talking to God, helps to nourish that fragile plant, our soul's yearning for God, until the shy bud of our love for God begins to unfold.

As we begin to face more of who we are and discover more of who God is, we are warmed. Just as the butterfly needs the warmth of the sun to become strong and capable of flight, so humanity needs the healing heat radiating from the heart of God. Through it we come to know ourselves to be children of God, precious sons and daughters who are deeply loved. No matter what our background, our weaknesses or our strengths; no matter if we have done things of which we are ashamed, the love of God is there for us, offering us forgiveness, peace of mind, a sense of meaning and purpose, encouragement, and expansion of our capacity for being, until **we are fully alive.**

As we continue to grow, guided by God's grace, warmed by the Spirit's action in our souls, we begin to discover the truth written in the Psalms:

The LORD is my strength and my shield;
in him my heart trusts;
so I am helped and my heart exults,
and with my song I give thanks to him. (Psalm 28.7)

We become aware of the way God has provided for us in difficult times, the people whom God has brought into our lives, the unfolding of events, the opportunities and challenges where we've drawn heavily on God's grace and God has been faithful. Through all of these, we come to know that our deepest self – our spirit – is sheltered, safe in God's keeping for all time, and we begin to say 'thank you'.

Pause.

Looking back over our lives can be helpful, because it is often only in retrospect that we realize God has been active in our lives, as we sense a greater purpose at work in some of the events we have experienced. We're going to do a reflective activity now in which you can think back over your spiritual journey to see where you have been aware of times of growth in your faith, conscious of some experience of the warmth and sheltering love of God.

Introduce 'Unfolding – spiritual journey – reflection sheet 1' and give the retreatants half an hour at least.

⁂ Share in pairs or in threes anything you wish about your journey to date.

God's invitation lies before you tonight – to allow the process of unfolding to enter a new stage and, in order to do that, we are going to fast from speaking to each other once night prayer is over, until we gather for the closing liturgy tomorrow afternoon.

If silence is a new experience to most of the retreatants you may like to have copies of L&F 2.19 available.
Go through the key themes with the group and then ask people to get into pairs and discuss the following question:

What does the word 'silence' mean to me/evoke in me?

Allow 10–15 minutes, and then draw the group together and have a brief plenary session in which people can share as little or as much as they prefer about their experience of silence.

We are going to enter a period of intentional corporate silence, a silence that has a different quality to it, which some might describe as 'numinous' or 'mystical'. In essence, it is the grace-full silence where God dwells. As such we need not be anxious; we need not fill the silence with our own interior chatter or exterior conversation or constant activity. We are simply to put ourselves at the disposal of God and listen, with the ears of our whole being.

Night prayer can be said either as a leader/group response litany or by dividing the group into two, and alternating column A and column B. Choose a suitable song from those suggested, or another of your favourites with a 'night-time' theme. Before beginning night prayer, just ask retreatants if they have any questions – reinforce the starting time and breakfast arrangements for Saturday morning, and the silence from night prayer to the closing liturgy tomorrow night.

So let us turn now to night prayer, offering all we are and all that we shall become to God.

Unfolding – spiritual journey – reflection sheet 1

Draw a road or a river to represent your spiritual journey so far – you can add rapids and rocks, potholes and cul-de-sacs, or whatever will illustrate the various parts of your experience. Place the following symbols on your road or river, to show times of spiritual growth, awareness of God's love and provision for you during your life so far:

✿ spiritual growth   ⚬ warmth   ⚑ provision

Reproduced by permission

© Sue Pickering 2010

Unfolding – night prayer

The unfolding of your words gives light; it imparts understanding to the simple.
Psalm 119.130

We listen to 'Nocturne' (*Songs from a Secret Garden*)

We pray this litany:

Leader	All
From conception to birth	**From toddling to teens**
From young adult's maturing	**to nesting and nurturing**
In changes and chances	**in ageing, in dying**
You hold us O God.	**We journey with Jesus**
Your Spirit enables	**Your Spirit consoles**
In the day	**in the night**
We are yours for all time	**We are yours for all time**

Silence.

Scripture reading:

The heavens are telling the glory of God;
   and the firmament proclaims his handiwork.
Day to day pours forth speech,
   and night to night declares knowledge.
There is no speech, nor are there words;
   their voice is not heard;
yet their voice goes out through all the earth,
   and their words to the end of the world. (Psalm 19.1–4)

Standing in a circle, turn to the person on your right and, just as you might offer the peace to them during a church service, instead offer the silence to them as a gift for this time.
   Then turn to the centre and hold your hands out, palms up, as if waiting to receive a treasure.
   The leader then says, on behalf of all present:

Tonight and tomorrow O God, we place our voices and
our words into your hands.
Hold us in the gentle silence beneath the shadow of your wings,
so we may know ourselves belovèd and safe,
as we spend time in silent reflection, alone with you.
Amen.

As you leave the group, take a folded Scripture verse from the basket ... and unfold it when you get to your room.

Unfolding – morning prayer

We listen to 'Morning' (Edvard Grieg).

Leader   For it is the God who said, 'Let light shine out of darkness,' who has shone in our hearts to give the light of the knowledge of the glory of God in the face of Jesus Christ. (2 Corinthians 4.6)

Cup your hands in front of your heart and, in silence, bring the following places, situations or people to God, as they are named:

Our planet and the needs of our environment.
All efforts to reduce carbon consumption and eco-destruction.

Countries where people are suffering – politically, spiritually, physically – as the result of violence, poverty and the abuse of power.

People, all whom we know or think about – a few particular people –
Lift them into the love of God

Ourselves as baby, toddler, school child, adolescent, etc.
Let a particular memory or incident or period in your life come to mind.
May Love which is at the heart of God, bring you healing and hope.

Silence.

Chant: 'The Lord is my Light' – Taizé – Please join in, if you wish.
The Lord is my light, my light and salvation.
In him I trust. In him I trust.

Scripture reading:

For it was you who formed my inward parts;
    you knit me together in my mother's womb.
I praise you, for I am fearfully and wonderfully made ...
My frame was not hidden from you,
    when I was being made in secret,
    intricately woven in the depths of the earth.
Your eyes beheld my unformed substance.
In your book were written
    all the days that were formed for me,
    when none of them as yet existed. (Psalm 139.13–14a, 15–16)

Reflect on the reading for five minutes.

We give you thanks for this day, O God, and for the chance to settle more deeply into your love. Guide us by your Holy Spirit and help us listen, and wait, and watch for your life, unfolding around us and within us. Amen.

Reproduced by permission

Leader's input 2 – Saturday morning:

Brief time for any housekeeping matters.

Last night we looked at the fern frond and the jersey and identified three themes associated with unfolding – growth, warmth, and provision. We spent some time considering where on our spiritual journeys we might have seen some of the activity of God. Now we're going to turn to the third item on the focus table – the map. When we try to find our way somewhere unfamiliar we might use a GPS (global positioning system) or even Google maps. But – we've probably all heard stories of unsuspecting drivers ending up stuck somewhere because the GPS in their vehicle took them on a circuitous route along tiny lanes, or the Google maps website showed a not-yet-completed road! The systems are not necessarily foolproof! Even if we have a physical map of some sort *(pick up and gradually begin to unfold it)*, maps need interpretation and an understanding of how to work out the coordinates before you can find the actual place you are looking for.

God's has designed a map for the spiritual journey – the Bible. And God has given us the means to understand and interpret it – prayer, study and discernment with the help of the Holy Spirit; conversations with trusted Christian mentors; commonsense; circumstances 'falling into place'; and a sense of 'rightness' or an inner peace when the call of God harmonizes with our personality, experience and giftings. But even though we have this map, even though we may sense God's call, progress on the spiritual journey is not necessarily smooth – there are cul-de-sacs and missed entry lanes to the motorway, puzzling roundabouts, steep, gut-sapping hills and dark, difficult tunnels when we cannot see our hand in front of our faces. There is for most of us a tension between call and response, cooperation and resistance, longing and avoidance.

Scripture refers repeatedly to the pattern of God calling an individual for a reason, for example:

- leadership (for example Gideon, Judges 6; Moses, Exodus 3)
- prophetic words to be spoken (Jonah 1.1–3; Jeremiah 1.1–10; Isaiah 6.1–8)
- birth-giving to a special child (Hannah, 1 Samuel 1; Elizabeth and Mary, Luke 1.26–80).

The responses of God's chosen ones varied: disbelief, argument, suggesting someone else for the role, outright disobedience, searing awareness of personal shortcomings, uncertainty about how God's vision might be fulfilled, and humble acceptance. Struggle was an inevitable part of most people's response as they wrestled with their inner inadequacy and what God was expecting of them.

God still calls men and women today, not often for the mighty purposes of the biblical characters but to the daily living out of our faith as followers of Christ, offering hope where there is hopelessness, love where there is loneliness, and a way of being that helps others see Jesus.

Even within the small sphere of our lives, God will unfold opportunities and challenges – ways of serving others that stretch us, that undo our complacencies and preferences. It's no surprise then that, when God invites us to take another step on the Way of Christ, our initial response is commonly one of resistance – we think that we are not worthy, or we lack the skills or haven't the time. Resistance can also be especially subtle, when we fill our lives with 'good deeds', burying God's 'still, small voice' under a pile of meetings, planning, and pastoral work. Sometimes we are afraid – of getting too close to God, of forgetting special spiritual experiences or of losing cherished notions about God. But God is always calling us to the 'more' – more love, more life, and much more of God than we can imagine.

Spiritual unfolding requires a willingness to take time to discern the way forward, and a certain degree of surrender, a readiness to forego our own desires and 'let go and let God'. By making the choice to be here, you have overcome the pull of questions, uncertainties or seemingly worthwhile alternatives – and you are here, now. And so is God.

May your time together this morning be blessed.

Give details of lunch arrangements, remind retreatants they can help themselves to tea or coffee, etc. any time, and all will gather at 1.00 pm for the second input of the day.

We maintain the silence so you and God may enjoy the morning together in this lovely place.

Unfolding – spiritual journey – reflection sheet 2

Using either *lectio divina*
(L&F sheet 2.16)
or imaginative prayer
(L&F sheet 2.17)
reflect on one of the following Scriptures
which show the dynamic of God's
invitation, and the person's response.

Ananias and Paul
Acts 9.10–19

The call of the first disciples
John 1.16–20

Zechariah and Elizabeth
Luke 1.5–25

With the guidance of the Holy Spirit,
revisit your spiritual journey diagram
from last night.

Add to it your own 'resistance' history
– times which, now you can look back,
proved to be moments of holding back
from God, going off on side-tracks or
wilful disobedience.

Talk to God about who you were then,
and who you are now.

Then pray with the following Scripture:

Do not remember the sins of my youth
or my transgressions; according to your
steadfast love remember me, for your
goodness' sake, O LORD.
Psalm 25.7

In some way, mark this new beginning
with God.

Read the book of Esther – the story of an
orphaned Jewish girl who, in the time of
the exile in Persia, is placed in the Persian
harem. As the story unfolds we see how she
is able to risk interceding for her people.

'Who knows? Perhaps you have come to
royal dignity for just such a time as this.'
(Mordecai to Esther, his niece –
Esther 4.14)

Reflect back over your life and notice
where some 'bigger picture' was
being painted, which you only became
aware of later.

Consider your current situation – your
work and family, friends and pastimes,
struggles and achievements.

What might God be inviting
you to do or be?
(Remember, it may mean doing something
that stretches you but makes a difference
in a person's life, such as picking up the
phone to ring someone.)

How might you respond to this call?

Consider your spiritual journey so far and identify a moment of significant
choice-making (such as a relationship, a career, where to live, whether to
proceed with a pregnancy ...)
To what extent has traditional Christian discernment (prayer, Scripture, trusted mature
Christian friends, common sense and your interior awareness of the Spirit's 'yes' or 'no')
been part of the process? Talk to God about what you discover. And listen too ...

© Sue Pickering 2010

Leader's input 3 – Saturday afternoon:

This morning we looked at the folded map and the unfolding nature of Christian discernment which helps us make life-giving choices so we can be free to follow the call of God without resistance.

This afternoon we come to the final item on the focus table – the envelope and its contents. Most of us receive letters each day, but if yours are anything like mine, the letters contain things like bank statements and bills for power or phone, or reminders of things to do or see or pay for. But, just occasionally, there will be something different – perhaps a note from someone giving feedback about something we've said or done... *(change this to suit your own details if you prefer)* or a card from a friend with an invitation to celebrate a special birthday or share a photo of a new grandchild ...

Like old people in a rest-home, we treasure these reminders of personal links and realize again the importance of keeping connected, and the need for us to do our part to sustain and deepen our relationships with those whom we love, those who love us. The more we put into these relationships, the more mutually satisfying they can be.

The same dynamic applies to our relationship with God who writes us letters too, but not generally on paper, nor sent through the post! They are usually invisible, often surprising and exquisitely timed.

How does God send us 'letters'/divine communications?

Give the retreatants a few minutes to talk about this in pairs before gathering their ideas or – if you prefer to maintain the silence – let them think about it and then continue...

We know that God reaches us through the Creation, Scripture and tradition – but God also sends us messages through other people, novels and films, music of all sorts, synchronicity of events, answered prayer, unfolding glimpses of grace at work, and direct experience of God's Being.

God's letters are coming to us all the time but often we don't open them. Why?
- because we are not 'going to the mailbox' often enough – not practising paying attention to what's around us, or reading our Bibles or praying or noticing what touches our hearts
- because we don't believe that God loves us and wants to communicate with us personally
- because we don't think we're worth much in anyone's eyes, not even God's
- because we're too busy ... *(you can add any other reasons you like or ask the retreatants).*

If appropriate, at this point introduce L&F resource sheet '2.1 – Attitudes and expectations', and go through it with the retreatants.

What does God want us to know? Perhaps this envelope holds a clue?

Pick up envelope, open it and take out the folded paper inside – unfold it and look at it for a moment before turning the paper around so everyone can see what is written there: MY DEAR ONE, I LOVE YOU (signed) GOD.

Look at the seven words one by one and you will see the gospel proclaimed in language we can all understand. The great I AM claims us as precious, as uniquely loved. We see God's heart intention towards us, God's committed faithful love. Once we know the truth of this love deep within us, how can we not share that knowing with others around us? By action, with compassion, we 'tell aloud' the good news that all are beloved children of God. We are blessed in order to be a blessing to others, that they may know the richness of God's love for humanity made visible in Christ.

This afternoon you have the opportunity to reflect on the unique way God communicates with you and to listen and respond to God's 'voice' no matter how it may come to you. As part of our closing liturgy, you'll have the chance to share a symbol which says something about your experience on this retreat.

Unfolding – reflection sheet 3

Take some time to meditate on
God's love letter to you:

MY DEAR ONE,

I LOVE YOU,

GOD.

In prayer ask the Holy Spirit to help you
listen for any other 'words'* God might
want to say and then make your own
response in whatever way seems best.

* Remember God might communicate
with you through the things and
people around you, as well as through
Scripture, creation and your faith
tradition.

In your imagination, enter the Gospel
story of the transfiguration of Jesus as
described in Mark 9.2–8.

Let the details of the scene unfold
before you.
Or – if you more easily form an inner
impression, just be still and quieten
yourself, and listen to your heart and
mind as you reflect on the relationships
represented here.

Take some time to allow this experience
to settle in your soul before you do a
little journalling or in some other way
begin to honour this 'letter' from God,
the Love that powers the universe.

Prayerfully consider the following and
notice what might apply to you and your
history of paying attention/not paying
attention to God:

God's letters are coming to us
all the time
but often we don't open them.

Talk to God about what you have
discovered.

Let God hear your desire to be more
aware of God's activity and presence in
your life – even if at the moment you can
only say that you want to want to have
some desire for God.

Write, sing, dance,
paint or doodle your own
'love letter' to God.
No one else
need see it.

When you are finished go outside and
take a walk with God in the Creation
– speak your love letter out loud and
rejoice in God's delight in you.

Reproduced by permission

Unfolding – closing liturgy

Set up the focus to represent 'unfolded' – the open letter, the unfolded jersey, map, fern or flower, etc.

We come together now to gather the gifts of this retreat. As we remember, listen, share symbols and words of thanksgiving, we honour the work of the Spirit among and within us.

Silence:

Let us hold a moment's silence as we reflect on the ways God has met us to console, affirm or challenge us over the last day and night. For some it will be just as important to acknowledge that God may not have been as present as you had hoped – notice this and name your yearning to God.

Recollection:

Think back over the retreat and, using the 'Unforgettable moments' sheet (see Appendices), make some notes about what stands out for you. Take ten minutes to do this and then share one thing with one other person for five minutes.

Music:

After 15 minutes, start a piece of reflective instrumental music to indicate a return to the group.

Listening:

Read a Scripture related to the theme, for example Luke 2.25–35 – Simeon.

Sharing symbols:

Invite each retreatant to offer a symbol of the retreat; they may choose to speak about it briefly if they wish or can 'pass'; it is an opportunity for leaders to share too.

Singing:

Choose a simple chant or song that all will know or be able to pick up easily, for example 'Be still and know that I am God'. Have the words written on the whiteboard if necessary.

Silence:

A period of silence long enough to allow you to set up quietly for the Eucharist if you haven't done it earlier.

Eucharist:

This may be offered if appropriate for your tradition and that of the retreatants.

Thanksgiving:

Invite each retreatant to offer a word or short phrase of thanksgiving – people are free to 'pass'.

Encouraging:

What God has begun today, will, through the Holy Spirit, continue to deepen in you as you return to your families and workplaces. Turn to God in faith each day so you can stay connected to God, the source of peace, joy and love no matter what you are doing or where you are …

We will let you know of other opportunities to spend time resting in God.

Have available details of any contemplative services or Quiet Days/Snack retreats, etc.

Music:

Stand in a circle, holding hands so you can sway to the music together if you want to!

Choose a song or chant that has a theme of moving out into the world, or being a bearer of the Christ-life, for example listen to 'The Love of God' (Keith Duke, 'Sacred Dance', Track 9) or sing the well-known 'Servant Song' (Brother, Sister let me serve you).

Sending forth and blessing:

We thank you O God for all your blessings and for our time together.
May the life of Christ continue to unfold in us and may the blessing of God, Creator, Redeemer and Life Giver be upon us all. Amen.

Four seasons in one life – weekend retreat

Preparation and resources

Focus:

This retreat looks at the four seasons of life. For the focus you will need to gather objects or pictures, etc. that illustrate both the *natural seasons* of winter, spring, summer and autumn, and *the seasons of the human life*: babyhood, childhood and adolescence; adulthood; middle age; and ageing. In addition, have a large central candle and smaller good quality candles for each retreatant, marked with their name so they can claim them again at the end of the retreat. Change the focus before each change of season, so the movement is reflected visually as well as in prayer and input.

Music:

You may have a range of music relevant to the 'Four Seasons' theme. However, if you don't, then Vivaldi's Violin Concerto *The Four Seasons* is a widely available option (EMI Red Line CD 7243 5 69873 2 6). Note: there are three movements in each 'season' so, when the Vivaldi music is indicated in the retreat, you may want to select one movement rather than play all three.

You will need the words of 'The day thou gavest Lord is ended' (Hymns A & M Revised, no. 33) and of the old hymn 'Great is thy faithfulness', which contains references to 'Summer and winter, springtime and harvest'. You can access a simple version sung by Chris Rice, by visiting http://www.youtube.com/watch?v=0k1WhFtVp0o (Lyrics: Thomas Chisholm, 1923. Composer: William Runyan).

OR ... for a bit of fun, and depending on the age of the group gathered, you may want to use the Frank Sinatra song 'It was a very good year'; Peter, Paul and Mary's 'Turn, turn, turn' (based on Ecclesiastes 3); Margaret Rizza, *Icons 1*, Kevin Mayhew Ltd, CD 1490109, 2003 (instrumental); Taizé, *Instrumental 2*, Ateliers et Presses de Taizé, GIA Publications Inc. CD 651, 2005; and O *Lord hear my prayer: The songs of Taizé*, Kingsway KMCD 736, 1994.

Resources:

- A copy of Shakespeare's *As You Like It*: Act II, Scene iii, vv. 139–66.
- Scripture verses (see Appendix 1) – cut out enough for the number of retreatants, fold them up and put in a basket from which they can choose at the end of Friday night prayer.
- L&F resource sheets to introduce particular activities, for example '2.19 Silence and solitude', '2.16 & 2.17 Praying with Scripture 1 & 2', '2.9 Keeping a spiritual journal', '2.11 Making – personal creativity', '2.8 Exploring our image of God', etc.

- Copies of night and morning prayers, any activities, reflection sheets, etc., enough for each retreatant.
- Coloured pencils, crayons and A4 or A3 paper. Whiteboard and markers for brainstorming or group discussion. Materials for collage or shoebox exercise, L&F resource sheet 2.11.
- The things you will need for the contemplative Eucharist (see Appendix 5).
- For short services of Holy Communion, see for example Andy Raine & John T. Skinner, *Celtic Daily Prayer: A Northumbrian Office*, Marshall Pickering, 1994, pp. 57–65 or *The Iona Community Worship Book*, Wild Goose Publications, 1991, pp. 48–51.
- The picture 'Autumn splendour' from the Picture folder, to be downloaded from the Canterbury Press website.

Nuts and bolts:

- Any housekeeping issues – orientation to the retreat venue – check out anything which retreatants might need.
- Policy regarding mobile phones and silence – to be negotiated with the group before they actually arrive at the retreat venue.

Extension:

You could choose to focus on one season depending on the group, for example with a group of elders focus on autumn, with a group of 25–40 year olds, focus on spring. OR this material could make up a series of Quiet Days over the course of a year.

Four seasons in one life

Friday evening

Gathering:

See Overnight retreat 'Unfolding' for details of the gathering stage of a residential retreat: Welcome, sample warm-up, guidelines/group 'rules', housekeeping.

⚘ Hand out retreat programme and discuss any issues arising from it.
  Hand out L&F '19 Silence and solitude' and confirm the time of silence – from after night prayer on Friday to lunchtime on Sunday.
  Music will play during meal-times. If people need to talk something over, the leaders are available for that purpose.

Opening prayer:

You may want to sing a hymn of praise or songs of thanksgiving according to your, and the retreatants' custom.

We light this candle to remember Jesus, light of the world, Jesus who shared our humanity and is present among us and within us, by the power of the Holy Spirit.

Silence.

God you created the seasons of the natural world
and the seasons of our human life.
Be with us now as we spend time with you
reflecting on our sane and silly seasons,
the ups and downs of a life, long or short.
As we rest in you may we come to know more fully
that in you, all our seasons fulfil their purpose.
Amen.

In a few moments of silence invite retreatants to connect with the hopes they have as they come to this time set aside for paying attention to God. When they are ready, they come forward and light their individual candles from the central candle. (These can be relit each time you gather for prayer – retreatants can take them home at the end of the retreat.)

Play Vivaldi's Four Seasons *– 'Winter' (RV 297 in F Minor); choose one or two movements.*

Scripture reading:

It is good to give thanks to the LORD,
to sing praises to your name, O Most High;
to declare your steadfast love in the morning,
and your faithfulness by night,
to the music of the lute and the harp,
to the melody of the lyre.
For you, O LORD, have made me glad by your work;
at the works of your hands I sing for joy. (Psalm 92.1–4)

Loving God, you know our hopes and our needs.
Be with us during this retreat time.
May your Holy Spirit aid our reflection;
may the wisdom and life of your Son help us go deeper –
in our relationship with you, in our self-awareness and
in our love for others and for the world. Amen.

Leader's address 1:

Winter

There are many ways of putting together an overview of human life from birth to death – including psychological, anthropological, social, spiritual and developmental frameworks. But for many of us, Shakespeare's description in *As You Like It* covers our lifespan well:

> All the world's a stage,
> And all the men and women merely players;
> They have their exits and their entrances;
> And one man in his time plays many parts,
> His acts being seven ages ...
> Act II, Scene vii, 139–43 *(read the* whole *section to verse 166)*

Let's begin our retreat with two questions focusing on the end of our 'three score years and ten'.

> When you think of 'ageing' what comes to mind?
> What *season* would you link to ageing?

Most of our responses are of the 'sans teeth, sans eyes, sans taste, sans everything' variety, concentrating on the losses inherent in ageing, the physical and intellectual creeping paralysis and the inevitable slide down the slope to death. With that in mind, probably most of us would link the season of 'winter' with ageing. However, another way[25] of looking at the human life cycle is to *start* with winter, moving through spring and summer until we reach autumn, the time for harvest and celebration.

Of course our lives don't always fall neatly into models – whether of living or of dying. Circumstances may propel us forward or backward, disconnecting us from the norms of our peers and demanding major life adjustments as we try to cope with accident, illness or major losses. Models are simply tools to help us work with our inner and outer realities.

Normal life expectancy in Schachter-Shalomi's model equates to 12 months spread over the four seasons. Whether we are living in the northern or southern hemisphere, in this model, the first three months January, February and March cover the ages 0–21 years, and correspond to winter. It is a busy period with many critical tasks and vulnerabilities: birth and infancy, early childhood, puberty, transition through adolescence to the 'coming of age' and first adulthood. This season is about potential

---

25 See, for example, the work of Rabbi Professor Zalman Schachter-Shalomi and Ronald S. Miller, *From Ageing to Sageing: A Profound New Vision of Growing Older*, New York: Grand Central Publishing, 1995, pp. 22–3.

and an emerging sense of identity, but much of the inner growth is 'below ground', hidden like *seeds in winter waiting* for the warmth of spring to make them visible.

Woven through these formative years are our experiences of God. Some of us will have been blessed with a personal awareness of Jesus at a young age, and a stable family life in which prayer, holy Scripture, hospitality and loving service were valued by parents and faith community alike. Others of us may have suffered at the hands of religious bigots whose abusive behaviour was 'justified' by Scripture and whose image of God was as a vindictive, unpredictable judge ready to pounce and punish. Our image of God is shaped during this period – for better or for worse.

We will also have been influenced during these years by events on a larger scale, as we became aware of people around us, in our country and the wider world. Our treatment at the hands of powerful others, the effects of natural disasters thrown daily across our television screens, the way we tried to make sense of injustice and apparently random violence – all will have left their mark on our becoming, as we journeyed through our winter towards our spring.

So the early stages of our life are where we begin this retreat. The reflection sheets being handed round now will help you work with this foundational season as you consider significant people, events, emotions and memories from this time, and invite God into those places which are still tender.

Four seasons in one life – reflection sheet 1

❄ Winter ❄
Conception to 21 years old

Ask the Holy Spirit to help you as you
think back to your early life from conception to 21 years old.

When you are ready, take an A3 page and divide it into three, covering:

conception, gestation, birth
infancy, and pre-school

early school experience, puberty,
sexual awareness, high school

later adolescence, higher education,
leaving home and reaching the
'key to the door' at 21

Then for each period, draw or note any significant people, events or memories.
Where there are things to affirm, give thanks.

Notice where and who God was for you during these years.

Where there is struggle, absence of affection, uncertainty or pain,
as honestly and as openly as you can, acknowledge these feelings before God.

Let Jesus be with you as you rest in his love.

Pray with one of the following passages,
using your imagination (L&F 2.17) to help you enter the scene
as fully as you can.

Luke 2.1–20: The birth of Jesus

Luke 2.41–52: The boy Jesus in the temple

Four seasons in one life – night prayer – Friday

The LORD *will keep you from all evil; he will keep your life. The* LORD *will keep your going out and your coming in from this time on and for evermore.*
Psalm 121.7–8

Leader We listen to/sing together: 'Within our darkest night', Taizé (KMCD 736, Track 5)
All **Within our darkest night,**
you kindle a fire that never dies away, never dies away.

Leader O God, light in our darkness,
All **You hold us in Winter, in strange startling places.**
You cherish the tiny seed of our soul,
knowing we need your nurture and love.

Leader O God, water for our dryness,
All **You bring us to life with your gentle-touch Spirit,**
breaking us open to sprout and to grow,
true to the form you have set in our hearts.

Leader O God, peace in our chaos,
All **You wait and you wait, patiently present,**
until our eyes lose their blindness and finally see
that you alone are the one in whom we can rest.

Leader O God, we are yours,
All **O God, we are yours.**

Silence.

Scripture reading:

Now the word of the LORD came to me saying,
'Before I formed you in the womb I knew you,
and before you were born I consecrated you;
I appointed you a prophet to the nations.'
Then I said, 'Ah, Lord GOD! Truly I do not know how to speak, for I am only a boy.'
But the LORD said to me,
    'Do not say, "I am only a boy";
    for you shall go to all to whom I send you,
    and you shall speak whatever I command you.
    Do not be afraid of them,
    for I am with you to deliver you, says the LORD.' (Jeremiah 1.4–8)

Silence.

The leader says, on behalf of all present:
O God, we place our voices and our words,
our hopes and our uncertainties into your hands.
You hold us in each season of our lives,
be with us now and through this night,
as we spend this time with you. Amen.

As you leave the group, take a folded Scripture verse from the basket ... and unfold
it when you get to your room.

Four seasons in one life – morning prayer – Saturday

Leader We listen to 'Spring' (Vivaldi – *Four Seasons* – one movement)

Leader O God, hope for new life,
All you watch us unfold as we step into Spring,
you hold us secure, reveal our vocation
and bring us to lover, to child and to home.

Leader Shepherd and servant,
All you guide our exploring and coming together,
you seek us when lost and take joy in our finding,
you help us see Jesus, alive in our hearts.

Leader O God you are with us,
All Jesus you are with us, Spirit you are with us.

Silence.

Prayer (as seems appropriate).

Leader We chant together:
'O Lord hear my prayer' – (Taizé, KMCD 736, Track 1)
All O Lord hear my prayer (2x) When I call, answer me.
O Lord hear my prayer (2x) Come and listen to me

Scripture reading:

For everything there is a season, and a time for every matter under heaven:
a time to be born, and a time to die;
a time to plant, and a time to pluck up what is planted;
a time to kill, and a time to heal;
a time to break down, and a time to build up;
a time to weep, and a time to laugh;
a time to mourn, and a time to dance …
a time to tear, and a time to sew;
a time to keep silence, and a time to speak;
a time to love, and a time to hate;
a time for war, and a time for peace. (Ecclesiastes 3.1–4, 7–8)

Leader We reflect on the reading for five minutes.

O God of the years, of the hours and of the silence,
we offer you this day, and give you thanks for life.
Be with us by your Spirit,
as we contemplate our journey.
Help us listen, help us open
our hearts and minds to you,
confident your love will more than meet our need.
Amen.

We listen to 'Summer' (Vivaldi – *Four Seasons* – one movement).

Leader's address 2:

Before looking at Spring and Summer, invite retreatants to comment on their experience of the Winter reflection. No obligation – just if they want to.

Spring and Summer

In Schachter-Shalomi's model, Spring equates to April, May and June, and the ages 22–42. In April we 'start cleaning up the emotional and intellectual debris ... acquired from parents, educators and friends ... pruning away certain goals and mind-styles ...; [we] retain what seems workable and proceed to the new challenges of the thirties. By May at the age of thirty-five, most people have settled into a career and family life. By June, at the age of forty-two, most have essentially finished the task of establishing their social identity and their place in the world.'[26]

This is a period of *budding and blossoming*, of finding a good match between abilities and meaningful employment, and of coming to a fuller appreciation of who we actually are. If we are willing to do the inner work of looking at earlier pain or trauma, of naming our fears, of facing our inadequacies or mistakes, new energy can be released for growth and relational deepening. If we cannot, our budding may dry up, our blossoming wither.

This can also be the time when we begin to reassess the place of religious affiliation and spiritual practices in our lives, re-examine our beliefs, and carefully consider our image of God, and the way we think God works in the world (see L&F 2.8). This is vital preparation for maturing and ageing.

The three months that relate to Summer, our July and August and September, 43–63 years, can be characterized by the word 'integration'. Ideally, we come to a point where our body, mind and spirit work in harmony, so that our full humanity can be applied to our faith, our work and relationships, and can inform our vision. We know we are in this place when we say things like: 'It's all coming together', or 'This role fits me like a glove', or 'I've found my niche!', or 'I feel truly myself'. Our experience, skills, spirituality and personhood find expression in service, in leadership, and the willingness to take on responsibility. In our summer season we may serve on community committees, we may take on leadership in our churches, mediate in restorative justice family meetings, or champion efforts to help the environment. Our worldview is expanding as is our capacity for spiritual growth. From seed to stem to flower to *fruit* – our mature lives can now be a blessing to others.

One practice which helps our spiritual deepening is the keeping of a spiritual journal. This can be a very useful tool for many reasons – particularly because we are notoriously forgetful, even of our experiences with God. Let's look at this spiritual formation sheet together *(hand round L&F 2.9)*.

---

26 Schachter-Shalomi, ibid. p. 22.

The next reflection sheet being handed round (reflection sheet 2) gives you some ways of working with your life seasons of Spring and Summer. Take your time, approaching these activities from a contemplative perspective, being alert for anything that catches your attention. As you engage in personal creativity, let your mind be open for the gentle touch of the Holy Spirit – a word or a picture might 'drop into your mind' or an old memory may surface. Trust God to help you do what is just right for you at this time.

Remind them briefly about the shape of the rest of the day – optional midday prayer, lunch, etc. and gathering together at 5.00 pm for a Contemplative Eucharist (see Appendix 5) – have the readings available on a separate sheet if you want to.

Four seasons in one life – reflection sheet 2

Spring: 22–42 years old

Before you begin, pray for guidance and then read the Personal Creativity resource sheet (L&F 2.11).

Note down the key events/people/discoveries/faith moments/losses, etc. experienced during your twenties and thirties as you established your home, relationships and work routines.

Then, use collage in any way you want to represent your personal 'springtime'. Add colour, words or symbols to show where and who God has been (or is) for you during these years

OR

Using the Shoebox exercise (see L&F 2.11), explore your inner and outer landscape, paying attention to the way your 'public self' and 'private self' developed over the Spring years.
Again, in some way, indicate where and who God was /is for you during this period of your life.

Talk to God about anything you discover and spend time listening too.

When you are ready, pray imaginatively with one of the following Gospel passages, bringing the context of the passage into your own setting (L&F 2.17)

Jesus calls the first disciples	Jesus heals an official's son
Luke 5.1–11	*John 4.46–53*

Summer: 43–63 years old

Quieten yourself and ask for the Holy Spirit's guidance.

Take some time to reflect on the Summer season of your life.

Read spiritual resource sheet (L&F 2.6) Drawing or doodling as prayer.

Then draw a mandala – a circular space within which you can use colour and symbols to represent the Summer season of your life.

Once you have finished that, spend some time with the following Scripture:

We are called to 'maturity, to the measure of the full stature of Christ' (Ephesians 4.13b).

Then rest in the God who loves you in all your seasons.

Leaders address 3 – Saturday evening

If possible, have a large copy of the photo 'Autumn splendour' as part of the focus. Provide some time for anyone who wishes to comment briefly on anything from the day's reflection.

Autumn

And now we come to Autumn – the last three months of October, November and December, and our years 64–85 and beyond. Traditionally, Autumn is the time of *harvesting* – an activity that is often accompanied by celebration to mark all that has been achieved.

Ask for examples, like church harvest festivals, wine festivals, etc.

In the autumn of our lives, harvesting involves looking back over our lives, allowing us to:

- reflect on what we have achieved
- acknowledge our contribution to the community, whether on a small or large scale
- gather the legacy to pass on to loved ones and colleagues
- begin to step willingly away from the compulsion of productivity.

Instead of ageing being a time of increased isolation and futility, *conscious* ageing can give us the opportunity to acknowledge our eldership and embrace our role as wise woman or sage – a kuia or kaumatua.[27] It may be hard to let go of all our busyness and learn just *to be*, but that is the invitation offered to us as we age. Part of this letting go involves making peace with others, with our past, with God and with ourselves; part of it means taking time to consider the big questions such as 'Why am I here?'; and part of it means consciously preparing for death.

The contemplative stream of Christian spirituality offers us a way into this 'letting go' through silence and solitude, deep prayer and meditation, forgiveness and reconciliation, journalling and life review, and learning to pay attention to the gifts of God, present in each moment of our existence. As we come to know God more intimately, our anxiety levels can decrease, our ability to stay in the moment with God begins to grow, and our confidence in God (literally con+fidere = with faith) allows us to trust God for all that lies ahead, including the timing and circumstances of our death.

---

27 In Maori society, a kuia is a respected older woman (cōō-ee-ya) and a kaumatua is a respected older man (coh-māh-to-ah).

As we age, the reality that we do not live for ever moves increasingly closer to home. We may have serious health issues; people in our circle of friends start dying; we are getting slower and it's clear that our bodies no longer have their former resilience. Although our western culture still routinely avoids the inevitability of death, we can choose to begin to face it by doing such simple things as planning our own funeral. While this might seem morbid, it can actually release some of the fear of death, while helping our loved ones know our preferences!

You will have a chance to begin some of this work tonight and tomorrow morning – even if elderhood is a long way away, adopting contemplative spiritual practices now means that you will be in a better place to make the rest of the journey, however long it may, or may not, be.

And just a reminder – the reflection sheet suggestions for prayer and journalling are *optional*. Feel free to leave any of them for a later date if you and God are working together on something else!

Four seasons in one life – reflection sheet 3

Autumn – 64–85 years old and beyond

Spend some time praying with this Scripture – draw or sketch the scene if you want to – or do some journalling about what you discover. Then enjoy resting in God!

> The righteous flourish like the palm tree,
> and grow like the cedar in Lebanon …
> In old age they still produce fruit;
> they are always green and full of sap,
> showing that the LORD is upright;
> he is my rock, and there is no unrighteousness in him.
> *Psalm 92.12,14–15*

Beginning to face our mortality.

Pray for the grace of God to be with you in this process.
Remember that these exercises are optional not compulsory –
if you are nervous about it then talk to one of the retreat leaders.

If you only had three months to live, what would you want to do/see/say?	Write your own obituary notice in no more than a hundred words.
What would you make your priority?	OR
Who would you want to share this precious time with you?	Plan your own funeral service.
Who would you like to be with you at the time of your death?	

Looking back over our lives.

Take a large piece of paper and divide it into four sections with the following questions. Use colour or diagrams or words or symbols to help you explore each question in turn.

What have I achieved?	How have I contributed to the various communities of which I have been a part?
What do I want to leave as a legacy to my loved ones or colleagues? How might I do this?	What am I being called to relinquish? What help do I need from God and others in order to 'let go' of those things/duties which are not God's call for me now?

Four seasons in one life – night prayer – Saturday

We listen to: 'Autumn' (Vivaldi – *Four Seasons* – one movement)

Silence.

We say Psalm 139.7–12 by alternate verses:

Where can I go from your spirit? Or where can I flee from your presence?
If I ascend to heaven, you are there. If I make my bed in Sheol, you are there.
If I take the wings of the morning and settle at the farthest limits of the sea,
even there your hand shall lead me, and your right hand shall hold me fast.
If I say, 'Surely the darkness shall cover me, and the light around me become night,'
even the darkness is not dark to you; the night is as bright as the day,
for darkness is as light to you.

Silence.

Prayer.

Scripture reading:

There was also a prophet, Anna, the daughter of Phanuel, of the tribe of Asher. She was of great age, having lived with her husband seven years after her marriage, then as a widow to the age of eighty-four. She never left the temple but worshipped there with fasting and prayer night and day. At that moment she came, and began to praise God and to speak about the child to all who were looking for the redemption of Jerusalem (Luke 2.36–38).

We reflect on the reading for five minutes.

We sing 'The day thou gavest Lord is ended' (Hymns A & M Revised no. 33).

Gracious God, the love from whom we came and to whom we shall return,
be with us this night and all our nights, here and in eternity. Amen

Four seasons in one life – morning prayer – Sunday

We listen to (*or sing*) 'Great is thy faithfulness'.

Leader In our Winter
All   you have named and nourished us.

Leader In our Spring
All   you have enlightened our adult becoming.

Leader In our Summer
All   you aid our maturing, all life lived for you.

Leader In our Autumn
All   you help us to gather, you help us let go.

Leader We trust you, O God.
All   **We trust you, O God.**

Silence.

Prayer.

We chant together 'The Lord is my light' (Taizé, KMCD 736, Track 4).

All   **The Lord is my light, my light and salvation.
In Him I trust.** *(2x)*

Scripture reading:

I remember the days of old.
  I think about all your deeds.
  I meditate on the works of your hands.
I stretch out my hands to you;
  my soul thirsts for you like a parched land …
Let me hear of your steadfast love in the morning,
  for in you I put my trust.
Teach me the way I should go,
  for to you I lift up my soul.
  (Psalm 143.5–6, 8)

We reflect on the reading for five minutes.

**O God, you have led us through the seasons of our lives
as we have spent time with you on this retreat.
Help us to gather the fruit of our silence and reflection
that we may see more clearly your loving presence
woven in threads of unbreakable Being
lighting all our existence.
May we bring ourselves more fully to you this day. Amen.**

Leader's address 4:

God has been at work with us and within us this weekend as we've reflected on our lives to this point, using the metaphor of the four seasons as a framework. Now we have arrived at the final session of our retreat time together, and it's appropriate to look in more detail at Psalm 92.14:

> In old age they still produce fruit; they are always green and full of sap.

This is a heartening description of the final season of our life – rather than talking about material productivity, the verse highlights the continuing growth possible in our spiritual lives, even if our bodies are failing. Instead of turning inwards, over-whelmed by our physical deterioration and the cumulative grief of loss upon loss, our lives can have meaning and purpose, our spirits can continue to grow in Christ. This is a work of partnership between our spirit and the Holy Spirit. Even as we age we can continue to deepen our prayer: sharing our innermost thoughts and feelings; listening, and waiting upon God in silence; praying for others as we are led; and adopting a contemplative stance – being alert for God in the midst of daily life, taking time to see below the surface to the truth of God's love for us all. As we learn to trust God with more and more of our lives, God's love and light begin to shine through us; all our comings and goings are in God's care. Guided by the Spirit, we can engage in a key task of ageing – *'putting things right'* – within ourselves and with others. We can:

- *Attend to the pain of the past.* This does not mean having to relive it as it was. Nor does it mean doing our inner work alone. As Christians, we ask the Holy Spirit to be with us as we *acknowledge* the hard places, such as times of failure, disappoint-ment, cowardice or grief. Acknowledgement *is not the same* as making excuses for our damaging or ungodly behaviour; nor does it mean condoning the hurt-ful actions of others. What it does mean is that we compassionately look at our younger selves from a viewpoint of maturity and wisdom. We accept that we did what we did, right or wrong. We may need to face the reality that others hurt us and we made the best choices we could at the time, in order to survive. In prayer, we can use our imagination and invite Jesus to be present with our younger self, trusting that the grace of God can transcend time and overcome all darkness, to bring light and healing.
- *Forgive.* Forgiveness does not come easily to most of us, yet without forgiveness we are at risk of carrying unnecessary burdens of bitterness, guilt, frustration and anger. We need God's grace to be able to forgive others; it takes time, courage, determination and skilled pastoral support, but without it our lives become stunted, and the flow of love from God through us to others is compromised.

Deeper healing can begin when we confess[28] before God, those things of which we are ashamed, those attitudes which lured us away from abundant life in God. But then comes the challenge – are we willing to *accept* God's forgiveness, so freely granted at such cost to Christ? There is a telling injunction in the rite of Holy Communion, when the priest pronounces the absolution and says: 'Take hold of this forgiveness and live your life in the Spirit of Jesus.'[29] For many, real freedom from guilt and regret is not dependent solely on God's forgiveness, gladly given, but also on our willingness to forgive ourselves for our 'sins of omission or commission' and to front up to those whom we have wronged, making a genuine apology and offering reparation or a new beginning where possible.

An example of the enduring, expanding spiritual life can be seen in the closing years of Corrie ten Boom, a Dutchwoman whose passion for God and people was sustained through war-time experiences, worldwide ministry and incapacitating illness which left her with limited movement and speech for several years before her death. Her biographer recalls:

I had always seen the Lord Jesus in her, but now in her present physical weakness, I see Him so much more clearly. She is always pointing Lotte and me to Him – sometimes literally with her hand as she points to heaven and says with a radiant face. 'I cannot ... but He ... He can.'
As people came into her home, their lives were changed by her attitude ... of faith, patience, gratitude and love for Jesus ...
As the months stretched into years and the great communicator remained mute, her body gradually becoming weaker as age and successive strokes took their toll, the lessons to be learned from this last phase of her long life became clearer. Through her example and the loving care of those who surrounded her, we were able to see God's view of human life. She was making an important statement in this humanistic world: that however limited physical circumstances may be, human life is made in the image of God, is precious and worth living.[30]

Provide time for any response to this reading or discussion if it seems appropriate, before continuing.

We don't have to wait until old age to have this sort of rich spiritual connection with God, for God offers to shepherd us through the whole of our lives, if we will but accept the invitation and let God lead us. But, if we are near the end of our lives,

---

28 Both the Church of England and the Roman Catholic Church offer services of 'Reconciliation' for people who wish to make a formal confession. See for example: http://www.cofe.anglican.org/worship/downloads/pdf/cirecon.pdf.

29 New Zealand Prayer Book, p. 460.

30 Carole E. Carlson, *Corrie ten Boom: her life, her faith*, Eastbourne, UK: Kingsway, 1983, pp. 208–9.

intentional prayer and reflection will assist our fruitfulness and 'greening' because it is never too late to get closer to God; never too late to welcome our brother Jesus into the centre of our being, into our hearts. As we do this, the answers to the great philosophical questions of humanity clarify, or, paradoxically, fade in importance as we come to know that 'we are profoundly loved and need never be afraid'.[31]

Whatever our age, we can live fully in the present moment which is, actually, the only time we really have. Through the grace of God, the example and redeeming work of Jesus, and the guidance of the Holy Spirit:

- we can offer nourishment to those around us as we share the gifts we've gained, our wisdom and life experience
- we can be 'fully alive' in our attitudes and relationships even if we are becoming physically limited
- we can do our part to encourage guardianship of our beautiful natural environment
- we can act as agents of peace and reconciliation
- we can trust that God dwells in the centre of our lives, in communion with our spirit, even if our minds are beginning to wander
- we can have the hope of the resurrection life – lived now in the love which surrounds us, lived in the life hereafter, in the 'dwelling place' that God has prepared for us (John 14.2–3).

Thanks be to God.

This morning you have the opportunity for further personal prayer and reflection and to consider some of the gifts of this retreat time. After we have had our midday meal, we will come out of the silence and gather for our closing liturgy. Then there will be time to share, with one other person, a little of what has been happening for you with God if you wish, using the Gathering the gifts worksheet. Towards the end of the closing liturgy there will be a chance to share, silently or with a few words, a symbol which represents something of this retreat for you.

Hand out reflection sheet 4 and a copy of 'Gathering the gifts of this retreat worksheet' (see Appendix 7) to each retreatant.

---

31 New Zealand Prayer Book, p. 163.

Four seasons in one life – reflection sheet 4

Think about the elders you know – who demonstrates for you the truth expressed in Psalm 93.14?

In old age they still produce fruit; they are always green and full of sap.

What is it about them, and their lives that brings you joy, hope or confidence in Christ?

To whom might *you* be a joy-bringer, an agent of reconciliation or hope?

Do some dreaming with God. ☺

Spend some time in silence before God. Ask for the grace of the Holy Spirit and the companionship of Jesus before you begin.

What memories/insights/opportunities come to mind when you think about the past and some of its challenges?

How might you – with Jesus beside you –
i. attend to the pain of the past?
ii. give and receive forgiveness?

Draw, write or otherwise express your feelings and thoughts.

Our **spiritual life**, represented by this line, can continue to grow, even as our physical, social or intellectual life diminishes.

To God we return

'Three score years and ten'

Reflect on this diagram.

What does it say to you about your life now, and about your life in the future?

From God we come

Talk to God about what you are discovering and what you hope for.

Four seasons in one life – closing liturgy

Set up the focus to represent all the four seasons – in nature and in our lives.
The retreatants' individual candles are lit and put in an easily accessible place so
participants can pick them up at the end.

We have considered the different aspects of our lives and the way God's life and love
are woven through our times and seasons.
We come together now to listen, to share symbols and words of thanksgiving, and to
honour the work of God's Spirit among and within us.

Pause.

> We hold silence as we reflect on the weekend, our hopes, any unmet expectations,
> our discoveries and wonderings – we entrust our hidden truths to God's tender
> care.

Silence.

Recollection and music:

Please take your 'Gathering the gifts' worksheet – make any changes you want to
over the next five minutes and then, when the background music starts, share as
much or as little as you wish with another person for about ten minutes.

After 15 minutes, fade the music to indicate a return to the group.

Listening:

Read *Colossians 3.12–17 – The New Life in Christ. Allow time for reflection.*

Sharing symbols:

Invite each retreatant to offer a symbol of the retreat. They may choose to speak
about it briefly or they can 'pass' – it is an opportunity for leaders to share too.

Singing:

Sing together one of the Taizé chants or one of the hymns used during this retreat.

Silence:

A period of silence long enough to allow you to set up quietly for the Eucharist if
you haven't done it earlier.

Eucharist:

This may be offered if appropriate for your tradition and that of the retreatants.

Thanksgiving:

Invite each retreatant to offer a word or short phrase of thanksgiving – then continue:

**For these and all your gifts, received and yet to come, we give you thanks,
O generous God, giver of all good things.**

Encouraging:

Be gentle with yourselves as you move from the slower pace of this retreat to the
faster pace of life all around you.
By daily prayer and praise, and immersion in the Scriptures, guard the
space within your heart where you and God meet, spirit to Spirit.
Take time to be still so that, in the midst of the fullness of life,
God can surprise and bless you.

Closing prayer:

Please stand – when you are ready please come forward and take your candle, lit
at the start of the retreat. At the end, as we blow out our candles we'll say together
– 'Light of Christ, shine on in us'.

*When everyone is standing with their lit candles in a semi-circle, continue with the
blessing:*

**O God, Creator of twinkling starlight, and the brilliance of diamonds,
companion us in all the seasons of our lives; help us shine for you
wherever we are, whatever we are doing, so that others may be drawn
to Christ – the Light of the World.**

Light of Christ – shine on in us. Amen.

*Have available details of any contemplative services or Quiet Days/Snack retreats,
etc. – give them out before people leave or email/post them out within the week.*

Do not be afraid – weekend retreat

Preparation and resources

Note: In this retreat 'Do not be afraid' we are *not* talking about serious and debilitating anxiety disorders or other mental illness characterized by obsessive thoughts and fears.

For *anyone* beset by crippling mental pain of this kind, specialized help from a trained therapist or psychologist may well be part of the healing process. Rather, this retreat is more for 'worriers' who may be missing out on some of the joys and opportunities of life, but who still manage to go about their daily routines.

Focus:

Spread a large, dark-coloured cloth on the floor and place on it cut-out foil hearts to represent each retreatant and the leaders present; place a lit, white candle at one side, and a 6–8-inch-high simple cross in the centre.

Music:

Choose from Taizé; Margaret Rizza chants, such as *Chants 1*, Kevin Mayhew Ltd, CD 1490102, 2002, Track 7 'Keep watch with me'; or Bernadette Farrell, *Restless Is the Heart*, OCP Publications, CD 10827, 2000, Track 7, 'Do not be afraid'; or Libera (contemporary boys' voices), such as *Libera*, Robert Prizeman, Erato disques (Warner) 3984 290532, 1999; or *Luminosa*, Warner, 0927 401172, 2001.

Resources:

A scallop shell for use in opening prayer.
Copies of Joshua 1.1–9, relevant L&F resource sheets and reflection sheets, etc. for all retreatants.
A supply of good quality tea-light candles, enough for each retreatant.
Details of social justice agencies associated with the Church or local communities; and some examples of people who have 'made a difference' in some small or large way in your community or nation – helps if the retreatants can also add their ideas/ people.
Appendix 8 – 'Using guided meditation on a retreat'.

Nuts and bolts:

Any housekeeping issues, etc. (see earlier retreats).

Extension:

Again, this material could be offered in a series of Quiet Days or adapted for a Lenten retreat, in which case the focus Scripture would be the Garden of Gethsemane experience of Jesus – Matthew 26.36–46.

Friday evening

Gathering:

See earlier overnight retreats for details.

Opening prayer:

You may want to sing a hymn of praise or songs of thanksgiving, according to your, and the retreatants' custom.

We light this candle to remember Jesus, Light of the world, who, by his life, shows us how to live abundantly; who, by his death, overcomes our fear of death; who, by his resurrection, gives us hope, now and in eternity. Amen.

Silence, and then the leader picks up a scallop shell and continues:

The scallop shell has been a symbol of the Christian journey, a symbol of pilgrimage for hundreds of years, long before it became the logo for a global oil company. As we hold this shell and take turns to introduce ourselves, may we be reminded of those who have gone before us, that cloud of witnesses, the communion of saints who, like us, have longed to come closer to God, who have sought the Lord, sometimes on *an actual physical journey*, but perhaps more often on *a journey inwards*.

As they did, we acknowledge our need of God and of God's love.

Once every retreatant and the leader/s have briefly spoken, the scallop shell is placed alongside the candle. The leader says:

Through the ages countless Christians have experienced the wonder-full mystery of journeying towards Christ while at the same time being accompanied by Christ, for God in Christ is just a thought away ...

In turn let us light our candles from the central candle and place them around the cross. As we do, we acknowledge that God is indeed Emmanuel, God with us, God who will never leave us or forsake us.

Scripture reading:

'As I was with Moses, so I will be with you; I will not fail you or forsake you. Be strong and courageous; for you shall put this people in possession of the land that I swore to their ancestors to give them. Only be strong and very courageous, being careful to act in accordance with all the law that my servant Moses commanded you; do not turn from it to the right or the left, so that you may be successful wherever you go. This book of the law shall not depart out of your mouth; you shall meditate on it day and night, so that you shall be careful to act in accordance with all that is written in it ... I hereby command you: Be strong and courageous; do not be frightened or dismayed, for the LORD your God is with you wherever you go.' (Joshua 1.5b–8a, 9)

Loving God, you know our hopes and our needs.
Be with us during this retreat time as we confront
our fears, little or large.
May your Holy Spirit aid our reflection;
may the courage and strength of your Son help us go deeper –
in our relationship with you, in our compassion towards
ourselves and in our love for others and for the world.
Amen.

Leader's address 1:

We know that some people seem to be born 'worriers', while others seem to take each day and even each setback with equanimity, apparently untouched by anxiety or the 'what ifs' of life. Being afraid and being Christian at the same time seems a contradiction. After all, Scripture clearly says, 'Do not worry about anything, but in everything by prayer and supplication with thanksgiving let your requests be made known to God' (Philippians 4.6). In this verse, however, Paul was reminding us of the *ideal* way to respond to life's uncertainties, but many of us find that, whether because of upbringing, experience, personality traits or habit, our response to the 'downs' of life is often to worry.

🕯 Take a few minutes to think about your own 'worry' or 'anxiety' profile, rating yourself on the continuum on your reflection sheet. This is a private exercise so no one's going to see it; it is just an opportunity to begin to consider this part of your life and the effect it may be having on your well-being, your relationship with God and your capacity to respond to God's call to service and mission.

Open up for brief discussion if you want to.

Fear of course is a natural response to any perceived threat – it alerts us, triggering the 'fight or flight' stress response to help us avoid literal danger. So it is right to be wary of those things which could cause us, or our loved ones, physical or emotional harm. However, we limit our responsiveness to God and all that life holds if we are bound by fear for ourselves or our loved ones, or by greater fears for our global community.

There is an idea abroad that the words 'Do not be afraid', or its variations, appear 365 times in the Bible, one for every day of the year! Whether this is literally true or not, in reading Scripture, we can't help but notice how often God reassures, calms, encourages or even tells people firmly, that there is no need to fear. All through Scripture weave the words 'Do not be afraid', and they apply to us now as clearly as they applied to the Hebrew people then.

Discuss a few examples: 'Do not be alarmed', Mark 16.5–8 (angel after Jesus' resurrection); 'Do not be afraid', Luke 1.30 (the annunciation to Mary); or others which the retreatants raise from their familiarity with Scripture.

For many of us, worries focus on the well-being of our families and close friends, people who are God's gifts to us, as we learn how to love and be loved – and how to let go. A personal example will highlight this:

Because we live in a small regional city without a university, once our children reach the end of secondary school, they must go elsewhere to further their education. While our son, an only child, was excitedly getting ready for this adventure, I was agonizing over what might go wrong, what trouble he might get into, who his friends might be and so on. I even wrote a poem about it, part of which included parents' 'worst nightmare' scenarios:

What if this is the final letting go
  – into the drunk driver's car
  – into the drug-dealer's snare
  – into the terrorist's bomb
  – into the tidal wave's rush …?

You can see the state I was in. Anyway, a week after we'd delivered him to the university hall of residence, I was praying, pouring out all the fears that were festering in my mind and destroying my peace. Once I'd stopped talking to God and was still enough to listen, I heard the quiet words, 'All shall be well.' I knew these words – they were from the writings of Mother Julian of Norwich, a woman who, in the Middle Ages, listened daily to the cares of those who passed by her window and who was convinced of the profound love and grace of God.

These particular words were like balm to my spirit. I let them wrap around my anxious mother's heart and felt at peace. Was it just 'coincidence' then, that my son's text message a few days later began, uncharacteristically, with the words, 'All is well …'? I don't think so. I think it was God's way of assuring me that my son was in good hands – God's hands. And so my trust in God was nurtured, and I began to let go a little more.

Invite other examples if you want to provide another short time of discussion for the retreatants.

Jesus recognized how hard it is for human beings to live fully without fear or anxiety. He addressed this common struggle in Matthew 6:

'… can any of you by worrying add a single hour to your span of life?
… do not worry, saying, "What will we eat?" or "What will we drink?" or "What will we wear?" For it is the Gentiles who strive for all these things; and indeed your heavenly Father knows that you need all these things. But strive first for the kingdom of God and his righteousness, and all these things will be given to you as well.'

Instead of *dwelling* on all the difficulties of life – Jesus clearly tells us that we are to 'strive for the kingdom of God' (Luke 12.31), and live as he would live:
• knowing he was beloved of God and
• sharing that love with those he met,

- bringing hope and healing,
- challenging injustice,
- speaking against life-denying religion.

If we do this, then all our needs and those of our families will be addressed in the best way possible – God's way. We will be assured of God's faithful presence in the hard things of life and will begin to let go the weight of our worries.

In this first period of silent reflection there is the opportunity to think prayerfully about the place of fear and worrying in your own life, to consider how these concerns are taken to prayer and to pray with the passage from Matthew 6 referred to earlier.

Hand out, and if necessary briefly go over, the relevant L&F resource sheets, 2.2, 2.4 and 2.9, emphasizing honest prayer, learning to recognize God in the present, and using journalling. For praying with Scripture see L&F sheets 2.16, 2.17.
Remind retreatants when and where you will gather for Night Prayer.

Night Prayer (otherwise known as Compline)

For tonight and Saturday night either use a form of Night Prayer from the Church of England Common Worship resources – the text is available on:

www.cofe.anglican.org/worship/liturgy/commonworship/texts/daily/night/compline.html

OR

For a simpler form of evening prayer, use a resource such as that offered in the Northumbria Community: *Celtic Daily Prayer: A Northumbrian Office*, compiled by Andy Raine and John T. Skinner, Marshall Pickering, 1994, pp. 19–24.

Choose readings and chants on the 'Do not be afraid' theme, reflecting the particular needs of the group of retreatants and the leading of the Holy Spirit.

Morning Prayer (on both Saturday and Sunday)

As for Night Prayer, choose the Morning Prayer from the Church of England Common Worship Resources or from the Northumbrian Community resources or similar contemporary liturgies.

Again, be guided by the Holy Spirit and the needs of retreatants, in choosing readings and chants on the 'Do not be afraid' theme.

'Do not be afraid!' – reflection sheet 1

What's your 'worry' or 'anxiety' profile? Put a ✓ and a brief description where you think you fit into the continuum, and then make a few notes about the things you worry about most.

1 Don't really worry at all	2	3	4	5	6	7	8	9	10 Worry all the time; it affects my health and relationships

I worry mostly about/I am afraid of:

....
....
....
....

✠

In the silence, ask the Holy Spirit to bring to mind something you are *currently* worrying about. How are you praying about this issue?

....
....
....
....

How long do you take to bring your worrying thoughts and feelings to God in heart-to-heart prayer?

....
....
....
....

✠

Pray with the following Scripture using either *lectio divina* or *imaginative prayer*.

'Therefore I tell you, do not worry about your life, what you will eat or what you will drink, or about your body, what you will wear ...
Look at the birds of the air; they neither sow nor reap nor gather into barns, and yet your heavenly Father feeds them. Are you not of more value than they?
And can any of you by worrying add a single hour to your span of life?'
Matthew 6.25a, 26–27

Reproduced by permission   © Sue Pickering 2010

Saturday morning

Leader's address 2:

One of the most wonderful aspects of being a Christian is to know the truth of the old, beautiful verse: 'The eternal God is your refuge, and underneath are the ever-lasting arms' (Deuteronomy 33.27, NIV). This verse paints a picture of a God who is *always* there to hold us, to catch us if we are falling, a God who is neither fickle nor absent, but eternally, lovingly, present.

Part of the work of unpicking our fear-full patterns of behaviour and thinking, is to re-examine who we think God is. This is vital because our image of God can either help or hinder our spiritual growth. If, for example, we think of God as unpredictable, punishing, emotionally distant, and physically remote, it's no wonder we would hesitate to put our trust in such a God. However, if we think of the God who is made visible in Jesus – and Scripture tells us that Christ *is* 'the image of the invisible God' (Colossians 1.15) then, instead of viewing God as a faceless, ruthless judge, we see someone who is loving, committed to bringing wholeness and healing, welcoming of sinners, wanting our good, full of grace and mercy, willing to risk everything for humanity. This God in Jesus is a someone whom we can approach, who is trustworthy, whose right hand holds us fast no matter where we are, whatever we are doing. Looking to Christ helps us gain the trust we need to become less anxious and more able to expand our experience and understanding of God.

Why does Scripture tell us so often to stop worrying?

Gather ideas before continuing ...

One reason is that worrying is actually a way of avoiding intimacy with God because it focuses on *self*. Worrying is so often about 'me' – what I fear – what might or might not happen – it's a way of being tied to an imagined gloomy future of our own making, rather than being free to engage with the present moment where God meets us, where we can dwell until the Spirit reveals the next step on our journey.

Constant worrying knocks us off balance, and undermines our sense of God's goodness and provision. God wants us to enjoy 'the glorious freedom of the children of God' (Romans 8.21b NIV), and the good news is that one of the consequences of following Jesus, of allowing God into our deepest centre with all its fears and foibles, is that, as our trust grows, our worries begin to diminish; gradually we relinquish to Christ their power to hold centre-stage in our lives.

How does our ability to trust God grow? It grows as our relationship with God deepens, as we study and learn more about God's character and faithfulness, and as we come to know for ourselves that we are precious in God's sight. It grows, too, as we practise letting go of our need to control our environment, to 'micro-manage' events and people around us as a way of coping with our anxiety.

This movement from worry to trust is often seen in the stories of Scripture, when *relationship promotes reassurance and builds confidence*:

- 'Take heart, it is I; do not be afraid' (Mark 6.50). Jesus walks on the water and calms his terrified disciples – his *presence* brings relief from fear and expands their vision of God's power.

- 'Do not fear. Only believe, and she will be saved.' (Luke 8.50) Jairus' desperate plea to Jesus is interrupted by a woman needing healing. Jesus does not overlook the leader of the Synagogue's plight and, when he has healed the woman, he *travels home* with Jairus and restores his daughter to life.

Add other favourites if you wish.
Make sure all have the L&F resource sheet 2.8 regarding the image of God, and reflection sheet 2.

We are going to do a guided meditation now – remembering that God has made our imagination and sanctifies it as we make it available for the Spirit to help us know the truth of our relationship with God – that God made us for love and we are fulfilled in God's love alone.

Guided meditation based on the story of Zacchaeus, Luke 19.1–10

I am going to read the story through so you can refresh your memories before we begin the guided meditation. Remember that this exercise is not compulsory: you can participate if you wish, and at any time during the meditation you can tune out if you want to. Don't try to make anything happen, just be open to the movement of the Holy Spirit and be alert for ongoing revelation in the days ahead.

I will finish the meditation at the point where Jesus says, '… (your name) … hurry and come down; for I must stay at your house today'. Let the rest of the story unfold in your own context – take as long as you need. Once you are ready to leave, please do so quietly. We reconvene at 5 pm for our Eucharist.

Leader Let us pray:
All   God our Creator, we lift our imaginations to you today, that through them
        we may become more aware of your welcoming love and your victory over
        fear.
        May your Spirit guide us and protect us as we enter this story and wait
        upon you.
        Amen.

Let's begin by sitting comfortably, no books or papers on our knees, eyes closed, letting our breathing settle into a gentle unforced rhythm … *(Pause.)*

Spend a few minutes mentally checking your body for tension, releasing each muscle group in turn, and deepening your breathing … *(Pause.)*

Read Luke 19.1–10.

Now in as much detail as you like, imagine that you are in the same position as Zacchaeus – socially isolated because of your job, but wealthy enough to live in luxury. Let the interior of your home come to mind – its beauty and opulence – those who are there to serve you – those whom you love.

Pause

As you are looking around, you remember that someone told you Jesus was coming to town. You are intrigued enough to want to see him for yourself because you've heard the stories of healings. You know that you need healing too – think for a moment of the areas in which you need the healing touch of Jesus – it may be for your body, or for your mind, or it may be in your relationships or your sense of purpose … let the Spirit bring to mind what you need …

232

Now you leave your home and walk to the street – people are already gathering, two and three deep in places, ready to try to reach Jesus, to touch him. There's no way you are even going to catch sight of this man whom others are calling the blessèd One of God.

Pause

You look ahead and see a tree that overhangs the street – and suddenly you know what you must do … you climb the tree and sit on a strong limb, holding the trunk tightly until you get your balance.

Pause

There is a buzz of excitement below you and you catch bits of conversation – the name of Jesus keeps floating up to you like a fragrance and you find yourself beginning to get anxious.
    What if you still can't see him?
    What if you fall off the tree and make a fool of yourself?
    What if someone sees you and starts to laugh at you?
    What if Jesus sees you?
But that's not likely – after all, people rarely look up as they walk along. Your inner turmoil increases as the shouts and cheers get louder. You can see the back of Jesus' head as he turns to touch someone behind him. And then he turns back – you see his face for the first time.

Pause

Suddenly it is as if all the sounds fade into silence as he raises his glance and looks at you. There is such love and acceptance in his eyes … such love … *(Pause.)*

Pause

You hear him call your name and then say, with a smile:
'Hurry and come down; for I must stay at your house today.'

Repeat gently and then quietly leave the room so the retreatants can finish in their own time.

233

'Do not be afraid!' – reflection sheet 2

Use the L&F resource sheet '2.8 Exploring our image of God' exercises to get you started, before considering the following.

Consider the following list of ways of seeing God in Scripture. Choose one that appeals and one that repels, and take these to prayer:

Woman in labour	Isaiah 42.14
Potter	Jeremiah 18
Midwife	Psalm 22.9–10
Door or gate	John 10.7
Shepherd	Luke 15.4–7
Mother bear	Hosea 13.8
Fire	Malachi 3.2
Mother eagle	Deuteronomy 32.10–12
Husband	Isaiah 54.5
Light	John 8.12
Lover	Song of Solomon

Talk to God or write or draw your response, and then spend some time in silence, open and receptive to the voice of the Spirit.

Make a diagram or collage to help you explore how your image of God has developed over the years.

You may like to include Scripture, music, or any other resource or experience that has shaped your way of seeing God.

Include those times of struggle or doubt and any questions …

Pray with what emerges.

A matter of trust

Trust in the LORD with all your heart, and do not rely on your own insight.
In all your ways acknowledge him, and he will make straight your paths.
Proverbs 3.5–6

Spend some time considering how trusting of God you currently are.
For example do you trust God with your family, money, health, career … ?
In what do you place your security?

How good are you at 'letting go' – stepping back from organizing, micro-managing or making things happen for those around you?

Talk to God about what you discover, and then spend some time listening, alert for the prompt and guidance of the Holy Spirit.

Saturday evening

Leader's address 3:

When we are anxious we often 'tighten up' – we might become less flexible in our decision-making, reduce our social contacts, increase our demands on those around us, and we may worry a lot more about those whom we love, and our various roles and responsibilities. However, as Christians, we are called to live life to the full. Jesus says in Matthew 11.30, 'Keep company with me and you'll learn to live *freely and lightly*.' (The Message, *my italics*)

How do we learn to live in this way?

In essence it is straightforward – the closer we get to God, the more we begin to trust God.

The more we begin to trust God, the more we let God into our lives and let go of our need to control.

The more we let go, the more God is able to work in our lives and effect change and bring healing.

The more we seek the kingdom of God, the more God can change our interior landscape, conforming us to the mind of Christ and ripening the fruits of God's Spirit within us.

How do we get closer to that attitude of heart which sees the wonder and grace of God brought to life in the midst of our daily existence? God will do the work within us if we are willing, open and attentive. God helps us to *become aware* of our need to let go *in the ordinary ups and downs of our lives*, as this example illustrates. *(Use your own examples here and below if you prefer)*:

> Fifteen years ago, when I was on retreat before being ordained, God revealed that I needed to give up my habit of worrying about trying to make my mother happy. Her life had been difficult, her emotional needs high, her responses not always helpful to those around her, and for years I had been anxiously shaping my life according to what would please her. Now I was about to become, willingly, a priest in the Anglican Church, and God knew that, in order to do this freely, I had to *let go* of my unhealthy preoccupation with my mother's well-being. I had to let God fill her need instead of trying to do that myself.
>
> In the year that followed my ordination, I saw my mother being ministered to by her Brethren neighbour and, through the love of a network of friends, coming to some peace within herself before she died. I had let go, got out of God's way and God had worked wonders in her life.

If we do have a habit of worrying, God helps us break this habit by reminding us not to 'entertain' our worrying thoughts – not to *dwell* on them or give them room to take root in our minds or infiltrate our soul's well-being – but instead to 'take every thought captive to obey Christ' (2 Corinthians 10.5b). If we listen to what's going on inside us and to the Spirit as we think about a situation, if we pay attention to our experience and recognize our fears, we can bring our fears and anxious thoughts to Christ *as soon as they occur* and ask for the grace we need to cope. Instead of giving these thoughts time to fester, we take a time of silence and solitude, and name before God what we are afraid of – no matter how small or silly, embarrassing or overwhelming. Another example to consider:

> I had arranged to go to Jerusalem to study, and was praying about my fear of flying. I soon realized that my fear was not just about terrorism or crashing. As I waited on God in the silence, my deeper fear surfaced: I was afraid that in the panic of an emergency I would lose sight of God. As a priest, I was afraid of letting God down, and of not being able to support others in their last moments. In the silence, after I had *honestly faced this fear*, there was no condemnation, only an inner assurance that God would hold me, even if I 'lost it'.

None of us is immune to feelings of doubt, worry or fear. All of us can come to the One who wants to free us from all that stops us experiencing the joy and peace of God even in the midst of hardship.

We are simply called, day by day, faithfully, to let go of the little things that cause us worry or anxiety, and so to build up our trust in our God, who will not let us down and *will not let us go*.

'Do not be afraid!' – reflection sheet 3

Onset of worrying thoughts or feeling unsettled, fearful, anxious.	Bringing anxious thoughts and associated feelings to God in heart-to-heart prayer

| ← | **TIME** | → |

Thinking back over the past few months, how long do you usually take to bring your worrying thoughts and feelings to God in heart-to-heart prayer?

....
....
....

In the silence, ask the Holy Spirit to bring to mind something you are currently worrying about.
Name it as honestly as you can, taking time to wait with God for insights and clarity.

....
....
....

How have you been praying about this issue?
What would you like to say to God about it now?

....
....
....

| Using a diagram or mind-map, reflect on your own circle of relationships, those which you can celebrate and those which cause you anxiety.

Bring both to prayer, particularly asking God to give you the grace to step back, to let go, and trust that God is more than capable of meeting the needs of those you care about and your needs too. | Pray with one of these Scriptures:

Cast all your anxiety on God, because he cares for you.
1 Peter 5.7

There is no fear in love, but perfect love casts out fear; for fear has to do with punishment, and whoever fears has not reached perfection in love.
1 John 4.18

'Do not let your hearts be troubled. Believe in God, believe also in me.'
John 14.1 |

Sunday morning

Leader's address 4:

Summarize what has been the focus of the last three sessions – dealing with fears on a personal and family/collegial level.

We do not live our lives solely in nuclear or blended families, in office workgroups or communities of faith. We live in a wider community of national and global interests and influences. Through the availability of the media and the worldwide web, we witness significant events all over the world and can access information on a scale never before possible. Our retreat theme is about 'not being afraid'; so what about our fears for the world we are bequeathing to our children and grandchildren? What are we to do with our worries about people stressed by poverty, family breakdown and unemployment, whose frustration spills over into street violence, random vandalism, or antisocial behaviour?

Christians have always responded to God's call to serve, motivated by a concern for justice and a passion for sharing, in deeds or in words, the good news of God's love for everyone. As Frederick Buechner writes: 'The place God calls you to is the place where your deep gladness and the world's deep hunger meet.[32] This is where we can exercise our vocation, express our uniqueness and make a difference, for each of us has the chance to meet a part of the world's deep hunger. Richard Foster describes one such person:

> In 1955, Rosa Parkes, sometimes called the mother of the modern civil rights movement, refused to follow the convention of segregated bus riding. Blacks were expected to pay their fare at the front door of the bus and then exit, entering again through the rear to find a seat. Rosa Parks entered, paid her fare, and then sat down in the front; and she refused to give her seat up to a white man when asked to by the driver. Her action against injustice in Montgomery, Alabama (USA), spurred people of conscience to protest (against) the denial of rights to African-Americans, and it continues to be an example of how one person can inspire positive, lasting change. [33]

We are called, not to complain from the sidelines of life, but to become involved, informed and courageous participants in the affairs of our nation and even of our 'global village'. Robert Kennedy is quoted as saying: 'Each time a man (or woman) stands up for an idea, or acts to improve the lot of others, or strikes out against

---

32 Frederick Buechner, *Wishful Thinking: A Theological ABC*, HarperCollins: NY, 1973, p. 95, quoted in Alistair Mackenzie, Wayne Kirkland and Annette Dunham, *SoulPurpose – Making a Difference in Life and Work*, NavPress: Christchurch, 2004, p. 111.

33 Richard Foster, *Streams of Living Water*, HarperCollins: London, 1998, p. 352.

injustice, s/he sends forth a tiny ripple of hope ...'[34] Think about William Wilberforce and the drive to abolish slavery; think about the disciples going out, two by two, with no means of support, empowered by Jesus and ready to respond to whatever they found (Luke 9.1–6). Think about others known to you who have changed something for the better simply by being fully alive in the place where God places them.

Make some time for discussion here.

Even thinking about taking some sort of public action, even on a small scale, will inevitably raise our anxiety levels but, if we are listening to God, if we are discerning about where and how we become agents of change, if we face our fears and bring them to God as honestly as we can, if we trust God for our words and actions, then God knows what differences we can make.

Invite further discussion around the process of beginning to engage in action for justice, etc. before finishing with this quote:

> For this reason I remind you to rekindle the gift of God that is within you through the laying on of my hands; for God did not give us a spirit of cowardice, but rather a spirit of power and of love and of self-discipline. (2 Timothy 1.6–7)

---

34 Quoted by Deborah Myerson in *Tempered Radicals: How People Use Difference to Inspire Change at Work*, Harvard School Press: Boston, 2001.

'Do not be afraid' – reflection sheet 4

Where and when do you feel what Buechner describes as your 'deep gladness' – the sense of joy which comes from being in the right place at the right time, with just the right mix of skills, experience, attitudes and flexibility?

If you are not sure, take some time in the silence to be with God and wait to see what comes to mind as you pray, journal, walk and wonder ...

Talk to God about any longing which surfaces.

Ask for God's guidance.

Draw a road that represents your life of faith so far. Consider the colours you want to use, the shapes and the landscapes through which it runs.

On this road put the initials of those people who have made a difference in your life (such as those you know personally or who have influenced you even though you've never met them – writers, singers, artists, etc.).

Give thanks to God for them and their part in your spiritual journey.

Pray with this Scripture:

For this reason I remind you to rekindle the gift of God that is within you through the laying on of my hands; for God did not give us a spirit of cowardice, but rather a spirit of power and of love and of self-discipline.
2 Timothy 1.6–7

Spend some time journalling and listening to God.

Ask God for what you need to be able to 'make a difference' – somewhere, somehow.

Do not be afraid – closing liturgy

The focus is the same as at the start, but with retreatants' individual candles already lit and put in an easily accessible place so participants can pick them up at the end. Have copies of 'Gathering the gifts' available (see Appendix 7)

Leader:	From places of anxiety and the worries of our lives, we have moved to a new awareness of God's love which holds us in our comings and goings. We come together now to listen, to share symbols and words of thanksgiving, and to honour the work of God's Spirit among and within us.
Silence.	We hold silence as we gather the gifts of this weekend, and reflect on our hopes, any unmet expectations, our wonderings – we entrust our hidden truths to God's tender care.
Recollection and Music:	We name out loud or in our hearts some of our discoveries. We listen together to 'Do not be afraid' (Bernadette Farrell).

Listening:

Read Psalm 34.1–10. Allow time for reflection.

Sharing symbols:

Invite each retreatant to offer a symbol of the retreat; they may choose to speak about it briefly or they can 'pass'; it is an opportunity for leaders to share too.

Singing:

Sing together 'Jesus casts no shadow' (see next page for melody and words) – or another suitable hymn or chant.

Silence.	A period of silence long enough to allow you to set up quietly for the Eucharist if you haven't done it earlier.

Eucharist:

This may be offered if appropriate for your tradition and that of the retreatants, incorporating thanksgiving and anointing.

Jesus Casts No Shadow

Sue Pickering, setting by Harry Brown

Women *mf*

Je-sus casts no shad-ow, as he walks a-long side you. For Christ is liv-ing light with

tread as soft as dew. There is no need to wor-ry, to run a-way or hide, For

mf rall Men

Je-sus walks in splen-dour, shin-ing by your side. When

mf

earth-ly cares are press-ing, and all seems dark and grim. Re-

mp *mf*

mem-ber Christ your bro-ther and put your trust in Him. Let

f

Him bring hope and heal-ing, in to your world of strife. For

mf rall

God des-ires your free-dom, and prom-is-es new life.

Women *mf*

Nine bar organ and flute interlude

Je-sus walks be-side you,

shad-ow less and bright. The road un-folds be-fore you, e - merg-ing from the night.

mp *decresc.* *cresc.*

There is no need for an - guish, or fears of things un - known, For

(slower) *mp* *a tempo*

your com-pan-ion Christ, your Sav-iour friend and home.

242

Thanksgiving:

Invite each retreatant to offer a word or short phrase of thanksgiving – then continue:

For these and all your gifts, received and yet to come, we give you thanks, O generous God, giver of all good things.

Anointing:

Each person in turn anoints his/her neighbour around the circle – this can be done in silence or with a few words of blessing spoken.

Closing:

Please stand – when you are ready please come forward and take your candle, lit at the start of the retreat. At the end, as we blow out our candles we say together – *(have this written on a whiteboard):*

In Christ we need not fear. Christ's peace lights hearts and homes.

When everyone is standing with their lit candles in a semicircle, continue:

Closing prayer:

God of hope, you dispel our fears; God of peace, you calm our anxiety;
God of mercy, you hold us lovingly; God of grace, you are all we need.
In Christ we need not fear, Christ's peace lights hearts and homes.
Be with us, now as we go from this place, and all our days. Amen.

Have available details of any contemplative services or Quiet Days/Snack retreats, etc. – give them out before people leave or email/post them out within the week.

Appendices

Scripture verses for retreatants

'Take my yoke upon you,
and learn from me;
for I am gentle and humble in heart,
and you will find rest for your soul.'
Matthew 11.29

'Be still and know that I am God!'
Psalm 46.10

'I have called you by name, you are mine.'
Isaiah 43.1b

'You are precious in my sight ... and
I love you.'
Isaiah 43.4

'Before I formed you in the womb
I knew you.'
Jeremiah 1.5a

'I have come that [you] might have life,
and have it abundantly.'
John 10.10b

'Cast all your anxieties on me,
Because I care for you.'
1 Peter 5.7 (NRSV personalized)

'Be strong and courageous; do not be
frightened or dismayed,
for the Lord your God is with you
wherever you go.'
Joshua 1.9

'My grace is sufficient for you,
for my power is made perfect in
weakness.'
2 Corinthians 12.9

... absolutely nothing can get between us
and God's love because of the way that
Jesus our Master has embraced us.
Romans 8.39 (The Message)

'As the Father has loved me, so I have
loved you; abide in my love.'

John 15.9

'Remember, I am with you always,
to the end of the age.'

Matthew 28.20b

Create in me a clean heart, O God,
and put a new and steadfast spirit
within me.

Psalm 51.10

When you pass through the waters,
I will be with you; and through the rivers,
they shall not overwhelm you.

Isaiah 43.2a

'What do you want me to do for you?'

Luke 18.41

Welcome to this short retreat – may it be a time of blessing for you.

Some hints to help you enjoy this time apart with God:

1 Be prepared for God to 'speak' to you through any aspect of the retreat, not just through Scripture and creation.

2 If you are new to taking time in silence, or you are an extrovert who loves to talk, ask the Holy Spirit to give you the grace you need to 'fast from talking' when silence is offered during the retreat.

3 As you work with the material the retreat offers, be as honest as you can with God, particularly about anything that still puzzles you or causes you pain or grief.

4 Don't be anxious about trying to make something 'spiritual' happen. Remember the Holy Spirit is already at work in you or you wouldn't be here to read this! Trust that God will communicate with you in some way during this retreat time, or in the days/weeks ahead if you are turning your heart and mind towards God in attentive expectation and love.

Where to from here?

Now that you have sampled a short time of silent prayer and reflection, you may want to find out a little more about contemplative spirituality and how it can help you to deepen your relationship with God.

There are a number of ways of doing this, for example:

- Attend another short retreat (give details).

- Attend a Quiet Day (6 hours) (insert date and details of any Quiet Days you or others are running in the next few months).

- Join a group to practise *lectio divina* together (find out what is available/offer one yourself).

- Begin to work with a spiritual director on a regular basis (have names of local spiritual directors and retreat houses available).

249

Quiet Day
'[Theme]'

[Date]

[Venue]

Leader/s: [name/s]

Some hints to help you enjoy this 'set-apart' time with God

It can take a little while for your mind and body to settle into the slower pace of a Quiet Day, so don't expect to sink into the deepest of silences within five minutes! Give yourself time to get used to being in God's company and away from the busyness.

Similarly, take your time to look through the options on the reflection sheets – ask the Holy Spirit to help you choose the prayer passage or activity which is best for you at this point – even if it is the very one that you really *don't* want to do!

Try something new! God is always singing a new song in our hearts if we are open to hearing it – or joining in!

In between intense times of attentiveness to God it can be helpful to go for a walk outside, to stop and look with love at a tree or flower, to listen and enjoy the song of a blackbird, or to wonder at the ability of an architect as you consider a building or bridge … wandering with God can be a wonder!

A Quiet Day is designed to give you space to listen deeply to God and to yourself, to pay attention to what the Spirit may be 'saying' to you, to open up your heart to the heart of God, and to let yourself be loved.

May this be a time of blessing for you.

(Insert title of Quiet Day – sample timetable)

Please feel free to take or leave any part of the day if you and God have an agenda that runs to a different schedule!

9.30 am   Gather – cup of tea, coffee, etc.

           Welcome, outline of the day
           Opening worship and short input
           Personal reflection – listening and responding to God

12.00 noon Midday prayer (optional)

12.15 pm   Time for lunch – quiet music will be playing in the lunch area

1.00 pm   Gather for the second short input, followed by time for further personal silent reflection

2.15 pm   Gathering for closing ritual or Eucharist

3.00 pm   Home-going

If you want to talk to one of the leaders on your own – please tick a suitable time slot and go to .... [give DETAILS]

[Insert Scripture, song or poem relevant to the theme], for example:

The fruit of silence is prayer

The fruit of prayer is faith

The fruit of faith is love

The fruit of love is service

The fruit of service is peace

Mother Teresa of Calcutta

[SAMPLE]

Weekend Retreat

FOUR SEASONS IN ONE LIFE

[Insert suitable illustration and details of date, venue and retreat leaders' names]

[Date]

[Venue]

Leader/s: [name/s]

[Insert quote relevant to theme], for example:

We labour in the fields for six years, and we dedicate the seventh as a sabbatical year unto the Lord … During our productive years we build our careers and raise our families.

Now, during a well-earned Sabbath period, we can catch our breath and listen meditatively to where our inner promptings are leading us.

Zalman Schachter-Shalomi,
Age-ing to Sage-ing, A Profound New Vision of Growing Older, New York: Grand Central Publishing, 1995, pp. 24–5

252

Friday evening

5.00 pm	Gather and settle in
6.00 pm	Dinner
7.00 pm	Introduction to the retreat and silence
	Opening prayer
	First address 'Winter'
	Time for reflection
8.30 pm	Night prayer

Saturday

Breakfast at a time to suit	
8.45 am	Morning prayer
9.00 am	Second address: 'Spring and Summer' followed by silent reflection
12 noon	Midday prayer (optional)
12.30 pm	Lunch followed by rest and re-creation with space for individual spiritual direction if available
5.00 pm	Contemplative Eucharist
6.00 pm	Dinner
7.00 pm	Third address: 'Autumn'
	Time for reflection
8.30 pm	Night prayer

Sunday

Breakfast at a time to suit	
8.45 am	Morning prayer
9.00 am	Fourth address: Life review followed by silent reflection and individual spiritual direction if offered
12 noon	Midday prayer (optional)
12.30 pm	Lunch
1.30 pm	Closing ritual and thanksgiving.
2.30 pm	Home-going

253

The Eucharist – a contemplative celebration

We gather while reflective instrumental music is playing.

We stand in preparation.

    The candles are lit as a reminder of
    the presence among us of Christ, our Light.

We sit, becoming still before God.

    We allow the concerns of our minds to be held
    in the love of God.

Confession:

    We take a stone from the basket and take time to feel the pain
    of our roughness, our hardness of heart, our struggles and the
    fears, which get in the way of our relationship with God, with
    others and with ourselves.

When we are ready we place that stone at the foot of the cross.

Forgiveness:

    As we, in turn, blow the bubbles up and away,
    we acknowledge our cleansing from sin.
    As children of God we rejoice in the
    new start that God gives to us.

We listen to a Taizé chant.

We read the psalm of the day by alternate verses.

We stand for the Gospel and, once read, we spend 5–10 minutes
in silent reflection.

We sit for the Intercessions:

In silence we place before God our prayers for the Church
    (a Bible)
    for the mission of God in the world (an atlas)
    for those whom we love (sprigs of rosemary)
    for ourselves (a personal symbol)

We stand to share Christ's peace:

    We share the peace, remaining silent,
    as we greet one another.

The Eucharist:

    Jesus took the bread and wine
        Jesus gave thanks
        Jesus broke the bread
        Jesus raised the cup.

We communicate the sacrament to each other.

We reflect on the gift of the Eucharist.

We join hands to pray aloud the Lord's Prayer.

We say together:

**The grace of Our Lord Jesus Christ and the Love of God
and the Fellowship of the Holy Spirit be with us all,
    now and always. Amen.**

Go in peace to love and serve the Lord.
    Amen. We go in the name of Christ.

Unforgettable Moments

Gathering the gifts of this retreat

Using guided meditation on a retreat or Quiet Day

Guided meditation can provide a context for imaginative engagement with Scripture or with a stage on one's life journey. Generally speaking, I would use guided meditation only when there is ample time for the retreatants to process what did or did not happen; usually this would be on a Quiet day or on a longer retreat, where there would be an opportunity for each person to talk the experience through if they wished.

🕯 Take a few moments to consider your own experience of guided meditation,
  a) as a participant and/or b) as a facilitator?
  What was helpful/unhelpful?
  What would you want to do differently/the same?

The following points are important:

- If you have not offered a guided meditation before then it is wise to discuss this element with your supervisor before proceeding.
- Do not use this with anyone who has trouble distinguishing between reality and fantasy, such as someone with a serious mental health issue.
- Choose a Scripture passage in which someone has a one-to-one meeting with Christ.
- *Do not leave* participants in a risky or scary place, for example on a cliff, in the sea, alone in a forest. *Always* leave them with Jesus present in the imagined scenario.
- Preface this exercise with a clear explanation:
  - not everyone finds this type of exercise straightforward, so don't strive or worry
  - participation is *voluntary*
  - God made our imagination and we can invite God to use it for our growth
  - if anything occurs which makes the retreatants feel unsettled, they can talk to you about it
  - remind retreatants that they may be an observer or a key character in the story
  - you will stop once the passage reaches the point where Jesus and the individual meet
  - the retreatants are then free to let the scene continue to unfold, or to return to whatever appeals to them from other available material
  - it helps to do some reflection after the exercise.

General process:

- pray before you begin, asking for God's grace, guidance and protection

- read aloud the portion of Scripture first, so people can get a sense of the story and context
- read again slowly, inviting retreatants to be part of the scene and elaborating where appropriate
- when you reach the meeting point with Christ, invite the retreatants to be open to what Jesus might say or do
- remind them that whether or not they experienced anything profound, the Holy Spirit is at work in them and the benefit of the exercise may become clearer later.

Further reading

Adam, David, *The Edge of Glory*, London: SPCK/Triangle, 1985

Bourgeault, Cynthia, *Centering Prayer and Inner Awakening*, Cambridge, Massachusetts: Cowley, 2004

Bradbury, Paul, *Sowing in Tears: How to Lament in a Church of Praise*, Cambridge: Grove, 2007

Brueggemann, Walter, *The Message of the Psalms*, Minneapolis: Augsberg, 1984

Buechner, Frederick, *Wishful Thinking: A Theological ABC*, HarperCollins: NY, 1973

Carlson, Carole E., *Corrie ten Boom: Her Life, Her Faith*, Eastbourne, UK: Kingsway, 1983

de Mello, Anthony, *Awareness*, London: Fount, 1990 (still in print and readily available)

Ferder, Fran, *Words Made Flesh*, Notre Dame, Indiana: Ave Maria Press, 1986

Foster, Richard, *Prayer: Finding the Heart's True Home*, London: Hodder & Stoughton, 1992

Foster, Richard, *Streams of Living Water: Celebrating the Great Traditions of Christian Faith*, London: HarperCollins, 1999

Frankl, Viktor E., *Man's Search for Meaning*, first translated in 1959. Still in print and available.

Goodall, Jane with Berman, Phillip, *Reason for Hope – A Spiritual Journey*, Melbourne: Warner Books, 1999

Harris, Peter, *Kingfisher's Fire – A Story of Hope for God's Earth*, Oxford, UK: Monarch, 2008

The Iona Community Worship Book, Glasgow: Wild Goose Publications

Keating, Thomas, *Open Mind, Open Heart*, 1986; *The Mystery of Christ*, 1987, and *Invitation to Love*, 1992. All published by St Benedict's Monastery, Snowmass, Colorado

Brother Lawrence, *Practising the Presence of God* (trans. John J. Delaney) New York: Doubleday, 1977

Lonsdale, David, *Listening to the Music of the Spirit*, Indiana: Ave Maria Press, 1993

Linn, Matthew, Linn, Sheila Fabricant and Linn, Dennis, *Sleeping with Bread, Holding What Gives you Life*, New York: Paulist Press, 1995

McBeth, Sybil, *Praying in Color*, Orleans, MA: Paraclete Press, 2007

Mackenzie, Alistair, Kirkland, Wayne and Dunham, Annette, *SoulPurpose – Making a Difference in Life and Work*, Christchurch: NavPress, 2004

Mother Teresa, Brian Kolodiejchuk (ed.), *Come, Be My Light*, New York: Doubleday, 2007

Mother Teresa of Calcutta, *A Gift for God*, London: Collins, 1975

Nouwen, Henri, *The Return of the Prodigal*, New York: Doubleday, 1994

Peterson, Eugene, *The Message: The New Testament in Contemporary Language*, Colorado Springs, CO: NavPress, 1993.

Peterson, Eugene, Johnson, Jan, Briggs, J. R. and Peckham, Katie, *The Message//REMIX Solo: An Uncommon Devotional*, Colorado Springs, CO: Navpress, 2007

Pickering, Sue, *Spiritual Direction – A Practical Introduction*, Norwich: Canterbury Press, 2008

Pope John XXIII, *Journal of a Soul*, New York: Image Books, 1980

Raine, Andy and Skinner, John T. (compiled by) *Celtic Daily Prayer: A Northumbrian Office*, London: Marshall Pickering, 1994

Rupp, Joyce, *Praying our Goodbyes* (revd edn) Indiana: Ave Maria Press, 2009

Savary, Louis M., Berne, Patricia H., and Williams, Strephon Kaplan, *Dreams and Spiritual*

Growth: A Judeo-Christian Approach to Dreamwork, New York: Paulist Press, 1984

Schachter-Shalomi, Zalman and Miller, Robert S., *From Age-ing to Sage-ing, A Profound New Vision of Growing Older*, New York: Grand Central Publishing, 1995

Shakespeare, William, *As You Like It*. Widely available in a range of editions.

Silf, Margaret, *Landmarks: An Ignatian Journey*, London: Darton, Longman & Todd, 1998.

Simpson, Ray, *Exploring Celtic Spirituality*, Suffolk: Kevin Mayhew, 2004

Vennard, Jane E., *Be Still: Designing and Leading Contemplative Retreats*, Herndon VA: The Alban Institute, 2000

Yancey, Philip, *What's So Amazing about Grace?*, Strand Publishing: Sydney, 1999

Websites to explore

Anthony de Mello
www.youtube.com/watch?v=4Y3Q7H2urto (accessed 14.08.09)

Art and Spirituality
The National Gallery, London:
www.nationalgallery.org.uk

Sr Wendy Beckett in conversation with Bill Moyers – especially part 5:
www.youtube.com/watch?v=cjFVRXjrjAE (accessed 19.09.09)

Care of creation
A Rocha (the rock) network of Christians in Conservation:
www.arocha.org/int-en/index.html

Website for *Springwatch* BBC United Kingdom:
www.bbc.co.uk/springwatch/

Christian hope, sermon by Revd Rob Yule:
www.stalbans.org.nz/teachings/rob_yule/power_of_hope/power_of_hope_.htm
(accessed 20.10.09)

Dancing and music
www.scottishdance.net/ceilidh/dances.html#GayGordons (accessed 5.10.09)
www.wheelchairdance sportusa.org (accessed 6.10.09)

Chris Rice singing 'Great is thy Faithfulness':
www.youtube.com/watch?v=ok1WhFtVpoo

Growth
Eriksen's tasks of psychospiritual growth:
psychology.about.com/library/bl_psychosocial_summary.htm (accessed 21.11.09)

Labyrinth
Ten ways to walk the Jubilee labyrinth at Norwich Cathedral, UK:
www.cathedral.org.uk/visitorinfo/the-labyrinth--the-labyrinth.aspx
(accessed 17.10.09)

Liturgy
For alternative resources for evening prayer etc.:
www.scm-canterburypress.co.uk
www.cofe.anglican.org/worship/liturgy/commonworship/texts/daily/night/
compline.html
(Night prayer text accessed 5.12.09)

For information about Wild Goose Publications and resources:
www.iona.org.uk (accessed 5.12.09)

Pilgrimage
Lindisfarne Easter pilgrimages:
www.northerncross.co.uk

Pilgrim's route to the burial place of St James in northern Spain:
www.santiago-compostela.net (accessed 16/10/09)

Prayer
Kiefer, James E., *Teresa of Avila*:
www.justus.anglican.org/resources/bio/268.html

Centring Prayer and Christian Meditation:
www.centeringprayer.com

Details of how to make and use prayer beads:
www.kingofpeace.org/prayerbeads.htm

On Practicing the Jesus Prayer by St Ignaty Brianchaninov (Orthodox Christian
Information Centre):
www.orthodoxinfo.com/praxis/ignaty_jesus.aspx (accessed 14.08.09)

UK Jesuit daily guided-prayer site suitable for MP3 or iPod download:
www.pray-as-you-go.org

Irish Jesuit prayer site suitable for use during a break at work, etc.:
http://sacredspace.ie

Reconciliation and forgiveness
Details of services of reconciliation for local use:
www.cofe.anglican.org/worship/downloads/pdf/cirecon.pdf (accessed 26.11.09)